OPERATIONS AND THE WORKING ENVIRONMENT

Nursing Administration Quarterly Series

Barbara J. Brown, RN, EdD, FAAN

Editor, Nursing Administration Quarterly

AN ASPEN PUBLICATION®
Aspen Publishers, Inc.
Gaithersburg, Maryland
1994

Library of Congress Cataloging-in-Publication Data

Operations and the Working Environment / [edited by] Barbara J. Brown.
p.   cm. — (Nursing administration quarterly series)
Includes bibliographical references and index.
ISBN 0-8342-0508-4. — ISBN 0-8342-0386-3 (series)
1. Nursing services—Administration.   I. Brown, Barbara J.
II. Series.
[DNLM: 1. Nursing—organization & administration—collected works.
2. Personnel Management—methods—collected work. 3. Nursing
Staff, Hospital—organization & administration—collected works.
WY 105 061   1994]
RT89.063   1994
362.1'73'068—dc20
DNLM/DLC
for Library of Congress
93-11493
CIP

Editorial Resources: Ruth Bloom

Library of Congress Catalog Card Number: 93-11493
ISBN: 0-8342-0508-4
Series ISBN: 0-8342-0386-3

Printed in the United States of America

1 2 3 4 5

Table of Contents

Series preface

*E*IGHTEEN YEARS AGO *Nursing Administration Quarterly* was launched—a journal in which each issue concentrates on a single topic in nursing administration, examined from different viewpoints by prominent practitioners. At the time, nursing administration was looked at as a less than acceptable specialty of practice. Only clinical domains were deemed to be prestigious and sufficiently imbued with a body of knowledge requiring advanced preparation. There were only a few graduate programs in the field and even some of those were only "pathways" in administration.

I was teaching the pathway in administration at Marquette University College of Nursing, Milwaukee, Wisconsin, while practicing as Administrator, Patient Care Services at Family Hospital and Nursing Home, and found insufficient literature for graduate students and practicing Directors of Nursing. I had also written and been awarded a research and development grant from the National Institute of Health to establish The Greater Milwaukee Area Sexual Assault Treatment Center. There was no forum for nursing administrators to share their successes and accomplishments with colleagues in a way that was useful and applicable to others in like settings.

So *Nursing Administration Quarterly* was conceived as a permanent library collection, topically focused, addressing the most timely and pertinent issues for nursing administrators to use as a resource which could be referred to in order to solve problems, create new approaches, and learn how others accomplish the ever challenging endeavor of *leading* the practice of nursing.

Leadership in nursing administration is many things to many people, depending on what task is being performed at a given moment; but it is probably best described as the positive and proactive handling of professional interaction, such as between nursing and the medical staff, the hospital administration, the patient, and the nursing staff. Leadership is a learned activity based on knowledge, skill, experience, attitudes, responsibility, accountability, and autonomy. It requires creativity and innovation, courage of one's convictions, and concern for all people, whether they be the patients and families we serve, our professional colleagues, or our personal friends and families. The nurse leader must have a high level of aspiration toward goals which nurses are seeking and should demonstrate actual success or high potential for success for attaining these goals.

Nurse executives must be knowledgeable about societal forces and constraints, political processes, and the effect on the health care systems and subsequent work accomplishments. Role theories, human relations, finance and budget, business strategies, front-line management of human resources, wage and labor standards (including collective bargaining, sexual discrimination, and harassment), continuous quality improvement according to agreed upon standards, the latest innovations in clinical practice, information systems, technology and research developments, population based care systems, empowerment, and transformational leadership are but a small representation of topics from *Nursing Administration Quarterly* throughout the years. A nurse executive today needs to be encyclopedic in order to keep abreast of all the information needed to succeed in an administrative position.

The editorial board of *NAQ* decided that it was time to cull out the best or "classics" from past issues of *Nursing Administration Quarterly* and provide a series of volumes that give this encyclopedic resource to nurse executives as well as to graduate students. The editorial board has been selected with great care to ensure readers a representation from academic settings as well as expertise in all areas of administration, with geographic distribution, different care settings, and as comprehensive a coverage of subject matter as possible. These *NAQ* editorial board members therefore have diligently sorted, reviewed, and selected the most representative articles over time, and study questions were developed for each section so that the reader can develop a thorough understanding with applicability to the future. As editor of *NAQ* for all these years, it is a special privilege to bring these volumes to the present and future generations of nurse executives.

BARBARA J. BROWN
Editor
Nursing Administration Quarterly

Preface

Spiraling hospital costs are one of the most complex problems facing the health care industry. Because each hospital and each health care system is charged with delivering efficient, high-quality health care, it must accurately define cost factors in order to maximize the effects of necessary expenditures. When carefully conceived, properly developed, and wisely administered, financial management in nursing is a tremendous administrative asset to any health care system management efforts. The budgeting process is a management tool in meeting this financial responsibility.

When understood, the budget provides a nursing administrator with the ability to define in detail the many cost factors involved in delivering the best possible patient care at the lowest possible price. A cost-benefit ratio is established to indicate accurately the level of nursing care and its cost to all patient populations. The budget is a plan that states in dollars and cents anticipated results. It is the financial translation of that part of the health care system's goals which apply to nursing services, and it serves as a guide for the fiscal year for which the budget is prepared. The primary purpose of the budget is to prevent expenditures in excess of reasonable need, and is a means of check-ing progress made in keeping expenses and cost in compliance with an organization's financial plan.

Nursing administrators are challenged to generate plans and proposals that reflect responsiveness to payment systems for patient care needs. Most important is the preparation of nursing staff for the changes in the payment system that will affect patient care practices. If nursing staff are used efficiently through a variety of alternative assignment systems, there will be a positive impact on the cost of nursing. The implementation of employees' ideas for innovative proposals that are intended to create cost savings without sacrificing quality can be rewarded and will serve as an incentive for nurses to participate in the effort to hold down costs in each care setting. The staff nurse is the most challenging role in all of professional nursing.

Patients and families experience a continuous barrage of emotional and psychosocial stress as they confront crises in their lives resulting from the need for medical intervention. Dealing with this stress places demands on the staff nurse to continuously give of herself or himself in a way that very few, or perhaps, no other employees do. The inappropriate allocation of nurses as resources leads to diminishing resources and increased nurse dissatisfaction. Nurses have long been known for "doing everything when there is no one else there to do it"; but allowing this practice to continue is a blatant misuse of nurses. Nursing is the raison d'être for patient admission to hospitals as well as for home health care.

Home care, extended care, acute care, psychiatric care, and all other care settings should allow individuals to have access to nurses as providers, with third party reimbursement acknowledging the client's choice of provider. Access to nursing care in the home or in a nursing home or skilled nursing facility should not have to be gained through a physician's order. Nurses should be able to admit patients to health care systems to receive nursing care when needed and deemed appropriate.

Consumers should not pay for services they do not use. If nursing administrators consider cost effectiveness as it relates to direct patient care need through a fee-for-service reimbursement, we must ensure that we will have financial support for variables that are not related to direct patient care. Such variables include quality improvement programs, peer review, continuing education, research in nursing, administrative costs, and staff development. Automated health care information systems that include comprehensive financial management for nursing will allow nurse managers to focus their attention on the clinical essence of nursing.

Nursing shares with other health professions responsibility for the development and continuation of desirable health practices among individuals and for the general health environment in the community. Nursing has met this responsibility directly by presenting health as a priority goal and by educating the community in those measures that have proved effective in promoting and maintaining good health. To maximize the leadership role of clinically advanced nurses, it is essential that management skills are developed beyond, and in addition to, the specialized clinical knowledge base expected. This volume of the *Nursing Administration Quarterly Series: Operations and the Working Environment* assists all nurses in developing management skills.

These skills include planning, organizing, staffing, directing, controlling, reviewing, and evaluating the budgetary process. In addition, being in a management position requires accountability for the budgetary process. The leadership role demands that nurses become change agent role models. Without knowledge in organizational behavior theories, it is next to impossible to represent the collaborative role model in the nurse/physician negotiation game. Establishing standard-setting for patient care and convincing others of nursing care standards are of utmost importance. The development of patient education and counseling and resource development requires interdisciplinary collaboration.

The strongest power base that nursing has to offer is advanced clinical knowledge. The utilization of this knowledge is dependent upon strong knowledge in management. Health care systems cannot afford to hire expert nurses who cannot be accountable through the management process for the quality of patient care. Nursing practice is the responsibility and prerogative of the professional nurse and the nursing system of a health care organization. We need to ensure that nurses who have special preparation for advanced practice in nursing are credentialed and granted privileges just as the medical staff has monitored its profession.

Let us not allow functions to be strictly defined; rather, let us create systems for flexibility in utilization of nurses. We have not begun to exercise our minds in creating health care systems that are innovative in matching the health care needs of the public utilizing the unique and distinctive roles that the nursing educational systems are preparing. It is our responsibility to create and shape the future through creating and shaping the environment for nurses to practice the full role of professional nursing.

BARBARA J. BROWN

Part I
Financial management

Katherine W. Vestal, R.N., Ph.D.,
   F.A.A.N.
National Director of Work Transformation
   Services
Hay Management Consultants
Dallas, Texas

The magnitude of change that has occurred in the financial management of
healthcare over the past decade is clearly
chronicled in a review of *NAQ* articles on
financial issues. Over the years, superb articles were published that kept readers up to
date on changes in reimbursement, resource
allocation, productivity, and cost effective
approaches to care. At this time, as the
political picture is changing, the pressure to
reduce costs and the need to manage care in
a more cost effective manner continues to
put tremendous stress on nurse executives.

The articles that have proven to be classics, have stood the test of the changes in
financing, and are generally related to basic approaches to cost management. That
has *not* changed with each new generation
of reimbursement skills. In 1978, Prescott

and Sorensen published their article on
evaluating the cost effectiveness of nursing programs. Their advice—to be able to
prove that resources allocation for programs results in effective outcomes—is a
critical issue today. Covaleski and
Dirsmith, in 1984, wrote a practical and
lucid article on the advocacy role of the
nurse manager in preparing and managing a budget. In many ways, with the
constant pressure to reduce costs, the
nurse manager faces high expectations to
manage the impact of the budget on the
department and inpatient care. This article addresses the often forgotten aspects
of budgeting—managing the "budgetees."

By 1988, the focus on resource allocation
was reflected in Dowd's article on participative decision making in managing resources. The premise of this article—that
both qualitative and quantitative issues
must enter into setting resource allocation
priorities—recognizes that the "bottom line"
must be achieved without compromising
quality. This message is critical today, as
resources are scarcer and decisions must be
made with the involvement of many con-
stituencies.

Closely associated with resource allocation is the continuing need to be able to determine the resource needs by patient activity. Jennings et al., (1989) provided an overview of the issues related to selecting, implementing, and evaluating patient classification systems. Because PCS systems are still a fundamental tool for productivity management and budgetary monitoring, this article provides an excellent overview of the basic issues related to patient classification systems. Likewise, the article by Johnson provides an overview of the perspectives on costing nursing services. The issues around costing out nursing services continue to be of interest as health care organizations try to improve cost structures to be competitive in a managed care environment. This article provides a global discussion that can support more detailed institutional debates.

In 1990, Hesterly and Robinson published an excellent article on alternative caregivers. This approach, of leveraging work to less costly providers while utilizing RNs to their maximum professional capacity, is being operationalized in most institutions today. The concepts of developing roles for different level providers is not new, but continues to present challenges to nurse executives.

The financial management component of the nurse manager's role has increased dramatically in recent years. Undoubtedly, this focus on fiscal responsibility will continue to gain importance as the nurse manager's jobs grow and change. These classic articles provide a variety of issues for thought and can serve as a foundation for managers as they seek resources for development of financial knowledge.

Cost-effectiveness analysis: An approach to evaluating nursing programs

Patricia A. Prescott, R.N., Ph.D.
Associate Professor
School of Nursing
University of Colorado
Denver, Colorado

James E. Sorensen, C.P.A., Ph.D.
Professor
School of Accountancy
University of Denver
Denver, Colorado

AS THE COSTS of health care continue to increase at an alarming rate, health care funders are concerned that programs be both effective in achieving desired results and efficient in using resources to obtain those results.[1] Program evaluators can no longer simply limit their studies to program outcomes. Now evaluation must relate program outcomes to program costs. This type of analysis, called cost-outcome and cost-effectiveness analysis, answers evaluation questions such as "What resources were consumed to produce the results of Program A?" or "Is Program A more effective relative to resources consumed than Program B?"

Cost effectiveness is defined ". . . as the comparison of cost outcomes to identify the most beneficial outcomes to cost of programs, modalities, or treatment programs."[2] The method of comparing outcomes relative to costs of programs emerges as the last of the sequential steps outlined in Figure 1.

The evaluation of outcomes relative to costs is certainly not a new idea. Methods such as cost-benefit analysis which relate monetary inputs to monetary outputs have been used in governmental and profit organizations for some time.[3] Such techniques have slowly been adopted for use in nonprofit human service organizations. The application and modification of business techniques for use in nonprofit service organizations such as schools and health care facilities have been slow, especially because of the unique character of human service organizations.

Nurs Admin Q, 1978, 3(1), 17–40
©1978 Aspen Publishers, Inc.

Time Frame	Tasks to be Performed
One	Identifying the objective or treatment goals to be achieved (e.g., increased mobility of patients, decreased length of hospital stay). Specifying treatment programs to be used (e.g., primary versus team nursing).
Two	Determining the costs of each program cost per unit of service, and amounts of service rendered (e.g., use of accounting methods, operating statistics, cost-finding and rate-setting).
Three	Assessing the effect or outcome of the program intervention on the target group (e.g., preintervention mobility versus post-intervention mobility). Combining cost and outcome information to present cost-outcome and cost-effectiveness analyses (e.g., use of cost outcome matrices and statistical analyses to determine if program differences are greater than would be expected on the basis of chance).

Source: Sorenson, J.G. and Grove, H.D., "Cost-Outcome and Cost-Effectiveness Analysis: Emerging Non-Profit Performance Evaluation Techniques." *Accounting Review* Lii: 3 (July 1977) p. 658–675.

Figure 1. Sequential Steps in Cost-Outcome Cost-Effectiveness Analysis

UNIQUE CHARACTERISTICS OF HUMAN SERVICE ORGANIZATIONS

Human service organizations have a number of characteristics which make them different from profit business organizations. These characteristics not only distinguish nonprofit service organizations, they also make direct application of profit cost-benefit systems either impossible or meaningless.

For example, human service organizations in general, and health care organizations in particular, are characterized by qualitative and quantitative outcomes as contrasted with quantitative outcomes of business organizations. Qualitative, nonmonetary outcomes such as lives saved or sicknesses cured are neither easily nor objectively expressed in quantitative monetary terms as required by the cost-benefit form of analysis. Further, human service organizations rarely operate with the precise technology needed to be able to express the number of units of output produced for a given number of units of input. In general, an evaluator may have difficulty in using the analogy of processing raw materials into a finished product when considering the objectives of a mental health program designed to increase "positive life-styles." If a program has vaguely specified outcomes, such as positive life-styles, and also has no standardized set of procedures for how that output is to be produced, it is exceedingly difficult to make the causal inferences basic to cost-benefit analysis.

To further complicate the issue, most human service organizations have large numbers of professional employees who frequently resist efforts to standardize treatments or to document staff time and effort, arguing that such practices ignore individual human needs and threaten to replace quality of care with quantity of care. Historically, there also has been a reluctance to adopt the practices of business, such as management information systems with detailed statistical and financial reports. Many human service organizations do not have management information systems or do not have systems with sufficient sophistication to generate the financial data needed to answer crucial cost questions about services and programs.

COST-EFFECTIVENESS ANALYSIS

Cost-effectiveness analysis differs from cost-benefit analysis in that monetary inputs (costs) are linked to nonmonetary outcomes to analyze the benefits relative to costs produced by a particular program. Cost-effectiveness analysis may be, therefore, considered a variant of cost-benefit analysis. As such it is not a new method of evaluation. Cost-effectiveness analysis is a method which combines evaluation research methods with cost-accounting methods to produce a system able to express outcomes of programs relative to cost of programs.

Figure 2 distinguishes among the financial or accounting tasks, the statistical tasks and the research or program evaluation tasks associated with cost-effectiveness analysis.

Cost-effectiveness analysis is a method which combines evaluation research methods with cost-accounting methods to produce a system able to express outcomes of programs relative to cost of programs.

The Research Tasks

Specification of Objectives

The first research task outlined in Figure 2 is specification of the objectives or treatment goals to be achieved by a program. As discussed elsewhere, this task, while essential, is not always easily accomplished.[4] Treatment goals for a group of patients must potentially be measurable in an empirically reliable and valid manner before programs can be meaningfully evaluated.

For example, a nurse administrator might wish to compare the cost effectiveness of two systems of staffing—primary versus team. The presumed or intended influences of these staffing methods on nurses, patients, and other interested parties need enumeration before their impact can be measured. Another nurse administrator might be interested in comparing the cost effectiveness of a nursing program that feeds newborn infants based on their cycles of activity (sleepfulness-wakefulness) as compared with the usual nursery program of feeding infants every four hours. In this example, the desired outcomes for nurses, infants, and presumably their parents would be of interest. Objectives of such a program might be that infants consume more food, lose less weight after birth, go home from the hospital earlier, sleep for longer periods, and indicate less irritability. (This example of program objectives is derived from a study currently being conducted by Mary Lepley and Sylvia Winchester, University of Colorado School of Nursing.) Each of these objectives is suitable for inclusion in a cost-effectiveness analysis as they are specific, potentially measurable in a reliable and valid manner, and achievement of these objectives is likely to occur as a result of the program under study.

While clearly measurable objectives are highly desirable in program evaluation,

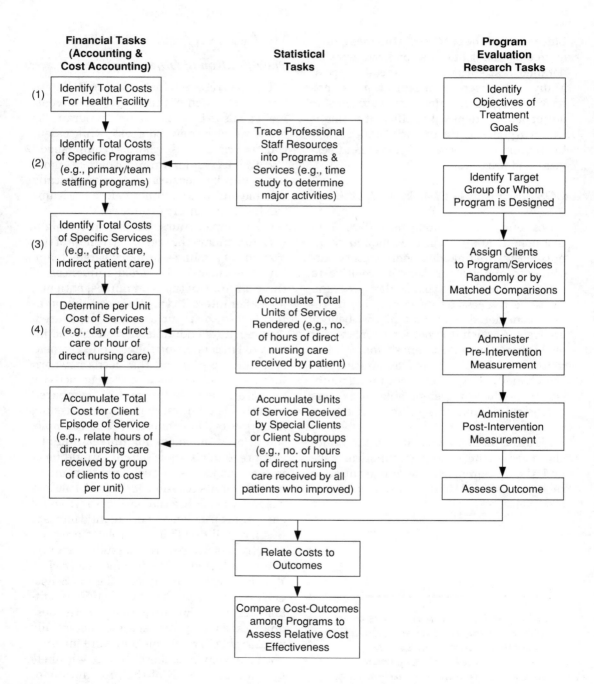

Figure 2. Financial, statistical, and program evaluation tasks associated with cost-effectiveness analysis. *Source:* C. Attkisson, et al., *Evaluation of Human Service Programs* (New York: Academic Press, Inc., 1977).

they frequently are difficult to specify. This is especially true when neither the "ends," i.e., improved patient status, nor the "means," i.e., individualized nursing care, is clearly defined. The selection of clearly measurable objectives is further confounded in complex programs where it is difficult or impossible to control unwanted influences and alternative explanations, where potential outcomes are time delayed, and where treatment effects are conditional.

Under these real and difficult conditions of evaluation research, there is an understandable tendency to select the most easily measurable objectives for study. The impact of a well-conducted cost-effectiveness analysis, however, depends at least in part on what dimension of effectiveness is analyzed. Although patient or staff satisfaction may be easily measured dimensions of program effectiveness, for example, they may not be as powerful as health status indicators in demonstrating cost effectiveness of a program to critical audiences such as program funders. While the objectives chosen for cost-effectiveness analysis must be measurable in the usual research sense, they must also reflect important dimensions of the program being evaluated.

Development of Measures

After selecting suitable treatment objectives, the research task is to develop reliable and valid operational measures of these objectives. The process of instrumentation from both a political and methodological point of view is critical to the cost-effectiveness analysis. Issues related to instrumentation are discussed in "Research Issues in Program Evaluation" by P.A. Prescott, *Nursing Administration Quarterly*, Summer 1978. Besides the general problems associated with instrumentation in evaluation research settings, there are several issues of particular concern when the intent is to evaluate programs by expressing client outcomes relative to program costs. For example, the amount of pre- and post-treatment change for a group of clients is expressed relative to the amount of program resources consumed by those clients. The purpose of outcome measurement in cost-effectiveness analysis is to compare homogeneous groups of clients along some common dimensions rather than to determine the unique outcomes of varied individual clients.

The type of outcome measure frequently used in cost-effectiveness analysis is global in nature.[5,6] An example of this type of measure taken from the field of mental health is the social functioning scale seen in Table 1.

While this type of outcome measure is appropriate for comparing a group of clients, global scales are frequently so general that they do not have the sensitivity needed to detect specific client changes. A client, for example, might improve in some areas of social functioning but regress or get worse in other areas. The clinician rating the client on a global scale has no means to express these specific changes. Thus the client who improves in some areas but gets worse in others is likely to receive the same rating after treatment as he did before treatment. Averaging of patient improvement and regression decreases the sensitivity and results in "no change" scores when pre-treatment scores are compared with post-treatment scores.

The ability to detect pre- to post-treatment changes is essential to obtaining meaningful estimates of program outcomes. Figure 3 illustrates how pre- and post-treatment scores on a global scale such as that in Table 1 are used to determine treatment outcomes.

A client scoring a 3 on the pre-treatment social functioning scale and a 6 on the same scale after treatment would be placed in the

Table 1. Sample global outcome measure: Nine-point scale for rating by level of functioning

---

Definitions of the Nine-Scale Levels of Functioning

With regard to the balance of the four criteria (personal self-care, social, vocational/educational, and emotional symptoms/stress tolerance), the person's ability to function autonomously in the community is at "Level X," where "X" can assume one of the following nine levels.

Level I: Dysfunctional in all four areas and is almost totally dependent upon others to provide a supportive protective environment.

Level II: Not working; ordinary social unit cannot or will not tolerate the person; can perform minimal self-care functions but cannot assume most responsibilities or tolerate social encounters beyond restrictive settings (e.g., in group, play, or occupational therapy).

Level III: Not working; probably living in ordinary social unit but not without considerable strain on the person and/or on others in the household. Symptoms are such that movement in the community should be restricted or supervised.

Level IV: Probably not working, although may be capable of working in a very protective setting; able to live in ordinary social unit and contribute to the daily routine of the household; can assume responsibility for all personal self-care matters; stressful social encounters ought to be avoided or carefully supervised.

Levels 5 through 8 describe persons who are usually functioning satisfactorily in the community, but for whom problems in one or more of the criteria areas force some degree of dependency on a form of therapeutic intervention.

Level V: Emotional stability and stress tolerance is sufficiently low that successful functioning in the social and/or vocational educational realms is marginal. The person is barely able to hold on to either job or social unit, or both, without direct therapeutic intervention and a diminution of conflicts in either or both realms.

Level VI: The person's vocational and/or social areas of functioning are stabilized, but only because of direct therapeutic intervention. Symptom presence and severity is probably sufficient to be both noticeable and somewhat disconcerting to the client and/or to those around the client in daily contact.

Level VII: The person is functioning and coping well socially and vocationally (educationally); however, symptom reoccurrences are sufficiently frequent to maintain a reliance on some sort of regular therapeutic intervention.

Level VIII: Functioning well in all areas with little evidence of distress present. However, a history of symptom reoccurrence suggests periodic correspondence with the center; e.g., a client may receive a medication check from a family physician who then contacts the center monthly, or the client returns for bimonthly social activities.

Level IX: The person is functioning well in all areas and no contact with the mental health center is recommended.

Source: D. Carter, and F. Newman, *A Client Oriented System of Mental Health Service Delivery and Program Management: A Workbook and Guide* (Philadelphia: Department of Public Welfare, Commonwealth of Pennsylvania 1975).

Global Level of Functioning
after Treatment

		Dysfunctional					Functional					
		1	2	3	4	5	6	7	8	9		Total
Dysfunctional	1	NC										
	2		NC									
	3			NC			"I"					
	4				NC							
	5					NC						
Functional	6						NC					
	7							NC				
	8	"R"							NC			
	9									NC		
	Total											

Global Level of Functioning before Treatment

Where NC = **No change;** clients scoring 1 on the pre-treatment social functioning scale also score 1 on the post-treatment measure. All cells in the diagonal of this matrix represent a no-change position.

I = **Improved;** in the cell marked "I" the client scored 3 prior to treatment and a 6 after treatment; all cells above the NC diagonal are indicative of improvement.

R = **Regression;** in the cell marked "R" the client scored 8 before treatment and a 2 after treatment; all cells below the NC diagonal are indicative of regression.

Figure 3. Sample outcome matrix for global outcome measure

cell of the matrix marked with an "I" indicating improvement. The costs associated with the program resources consumed by this group of clients would be identified, and "improved" client outcomes would be expressed relative to the cost of resources consumed to effect the change. Similarly, the cell marked "R" indicating regression represents those clients scoring 8 on the social functioning scale before treatment and 2 on the same scale after treatment. Program costs associated with the clients in the "regressed" cell would be identified, and client outcomes would be expressed

relative to costs just as in the case of "improved" clients.

If the instrument used has inadequate sensitivity or specificity to detect client change, then the majority of clients will fall along the diagonal of the matrix indicated by the cells marked "NC" for no change in Figure 3. If this happens, one might falsely conclude that the treatment program had no effect on clients when actually the lack of variability was related to measurement error rather than to a lack of program impact.

In addition, internal consistency reliability is in part dependent upon a continuous range of scores on an instrument. The attenuation of range which results from inadequate sensitivity of measures creates threats to both potential reliability and validity. In summary, global measures of program outcome can be used to assess program impact on groups of clients. Comparisons across clients are appropriate as all clients are compared using the same scales. However, global measures frequently have sensitivity problems which threaten their effectiveness as indicators of program outcome.

Generally, measures that are client specific avoid the insensitivity problems of global measures but raise questions about the meaning of comparisons across clients. For example, "goal attainment scaling"[7] is a measurement approach which identifies scales and behavioral guidelines for the scales specific to each individual client. An example of the scales and descriptions for a sample patient may be seen in Figure 4.

The goal attainment approach to measuring client outcomes sets specific goals for each client. However, the goals are different for each client, making it difficult to compare one client's goal attainment with another's. While it is possible to obtain average goal attainment scores and compare these averages across a group of clients, the individual scales are of differing importance. See for example Scale 1 dealing with education and Scale 2 dealing with suicide in Figure 4. Most people would agree that a patient obtaining a −2 for "most unfavorable outcome" on Scale 2, Suicide, would be very different from obtaining a −2 score on Scale 1, Education, indicating a failure to enroll in school.

The goal attainment method of measuring client outcomes avoids the sensitivity problem frequently encountered with global measures by tailoring the measurement scales and criteria to the individual patient or client. The specificity of the goal attainment method thus has some advantages; however, it also has the disadvantage of creating client-specific measures which, while useful in judging the progress of an individual patient, are problematic for comparing clients for purposes of program evaluation.

In general, outcome measures that compare subjects on a common set of scales are more desirable than client-specific measures for evaluating the impact of a treatment program. When using global outcome measures the researcher should be alert to the problem of insensitivity in global measures and take steps such as pilot testing the instrument to insure adequate sensitivity prior to use in a cost-effectiveness study.

Assessment of Program Outcomes

Joining the issues in the measurement of outcomes are research design and sampling issues involved in adequate assessment of program outcomes. First assuming that client outcomes are a result of a program of treatment rather than a result of other factors, we must be able to assume that the clients exposed to different programs of treatment were equivalent prior to treatment. Second, if we wish to generalize about the effectiveness of a program of treatment, the treated clients must be representative of the population about which we wish to generalize. Finally, assuming equivalent pretreatment groups which are representative of the population of interest, we need to establish an experimental situation in which we have control over extraneous fac-

The goal attainment method of measuring client outcomes avoids the sensitivity problem frequently encountered with global measures by tailoring the measurement scales and criteria to the individual patient.

Check whether or not the scale has been mutually negotiated between patient and CIC interviewer.	SCALE HEADINGS AND SCALE WEIGHTS				
	Yes_X_ No___	Yes___ No_X_	Yes___ No_X_	Yes_X_ No___	Yes_X_ No___
SCALE ATTAINMENT LEVELS	SCALE 1: Education ($w_1 = 20$)	SCALE 2: Suicide ($w_2 = 30$)	SCALE 3: Manipulation ($w_3 = 25$)	SCALE 4: Drug Abuse ($w_4 = 30$)	SCALE 5: Dependency on CIC ($w_5 = 10$)
a. Most unfavorable treatment outcome thought likely (−2)	Patient has made no attempt to enroll in high school.	Patient has committed suicide.	Patient makes rounds of community service agencies demanding medication and refuses other forms of treatment.	Patient reports addiction to "hard narcotics" (heroin, morphine).	Patient has contacted CIC by telephone or in person at least seven times since his first visit.
b. Less than expected success with treatment (−1)	Patient has enrolled in high school, but at time of follow-up has dropped out.	Patient has acted on at least one suicidal impulse since first contact with the CIC, but has not succeeded.	Patient no longer visits CIC with demands for medication but continues with other community agencies and still refuses other forms of treatment.	Patient has used "hard narcotics," but is not addicted, and/ or uses hallucinogens (LSD, Pot) more than four times a month.	Patient has contacted CIC 5–6 times since intake.
c. Expected level of treatment success (0)	Patient has enrolled and is in school at follow-up, but is attending class sporadically (misses an average of more than a third of her classes during a week).	Patient reports she has had at least four suicidal impulses since her first contact with the CIC but has not acted on any of them.	Patient no longer attempts to manipulate for drugs at community service agencies, but will not accept another form of treatment.	Patient has not used "hard narcotics" during follow-up period, and uses hallucinogens between 1–4 times a month. *	Patient has contacted CIC 3–4 times since intake.
d. More than expected success with treatment (−1)	Patient has enrolled, is in school at follow-up, and is attending classes consistently, but has no vocational goals. *		Patient accepts nonmedication treatment at some community agency. *	Patient uses hallucinogens less than once a month.	
e. Best anticipated success with treatment (−2)	Patient has enrolled, is in school at follow-up, is attending classes consistently, and has some vocational goal.	Patient reports she has had no suicidal impulses since her first contact with the CIC.	Patient accepts nonmedication treatment, and by own report shows signs of improve-ment.	At time of follow-up, patient is not using any illegal drugs.	Patient has not contacted CIC since intake. *

Level at Intake
* Level at Follow-up

Level at Intake:	29.4
Goal Attainment Score (Level at Follow-up):	62.2
Goal Attainment Change Score:	+32.3

Figure 4. Sample clinical guide: Crisis Intervention Center (CIC) (Program Evaluation Project, Goal Attainment Follow-up Guide) Source: National Institutes of Mental Health. *A Working Manual of Simple Program Evaluation Techniques for Community Mental Health Centers* DHEW Pub. No. (ADM) 76-404 (Washington, D.C.: Government Printing Office 1976): 224.

tors that could alter the intended effect of the treatment program.

Cost-effectiveness analysis assumes that the changes in clients between pre- and post-treatment scores can be attributed to the impact or effect of the treatment program. This assumption of a causal relationship between treatment programs and client outcomes is best examined within the context of experimental research designs. Without the control afforded by experimental designs, the assumptions about the causal relationship between programs and client outcomes would be seriously jeopardized.[8,9]

In summary, the research issues involved in conducting a cost-effectiveness analysis are the same issues involved in conducting any research-oriented program evaluation. These issues involve the reliability and validity of measures, the equivalence of pre-treatment groups, the representativeness of the study sample, and the adequacy of the research design to support the assumption of causality.

Financial and Statistical Tasks

In addition to concern with research issues, cost-effectiveness analysis involves a number of cost accounting and statistical tasks. As seen from the outline of financial tasks in Figure 2, the ability to conduct the cost part of a cost-effectiveness analysis is based on the ability of an organization or program to identify costs associated with the program as a whole, costs of specific services within a program, and also the costs associated with a particular unit of service within a program.

Identification of Program Costs

To identify total program costs, costs associated with the following major categories must be identified:

1. direct salary and donated time;
2. other direct and traceable costs, e.g., equipment, travel;

3. administrative costs; and
4. indirect costs, e.g., depreciation, overhead.

Next, the above cost categories are broken down by the major services offered within a program or the major categories of activity within a program. As an illustration, the total costs associated with a program for providing primary nursing may be broken down into services such as direct patient contact activities, coordination activities with other nursing staff, referral and coordination activities with other allied services, and record keeping and other maintenance activities. There are numerous ways to conceptualize the services of a program and the unit of service to be used in any particular cost-effectiveness analysis. While choice of program services or unit of service is somewhat arbitrary, the services chosen and the unit of service used should be related to objectives being evaluated. If, for example, the major difference between two programs is thought to be the amount of time spent in direct patient care, then the activities comprising direct patient care should be grouped together and defined as a program service for costing purposes.

Similarly, the choice of a unit of service should be made considering clinical factors such as the time frame within which services are usually delivered and the objectives of the analysis. For example, a unit for the direct patient care service might be a day of care, an hour of care, or five minutes of direct patient care. While any of these units of service might be used for determining the unit costs of direct patient care, there is little sense in using five minutes as the unit cost if cost per day of direct care is an acceptable unit for the objectives of the cost-effectiveness analysis.

After selecting an appropriate unit of service, operating statistics are used to identify the number of units of service consumed by patients with various outcomes. The cost

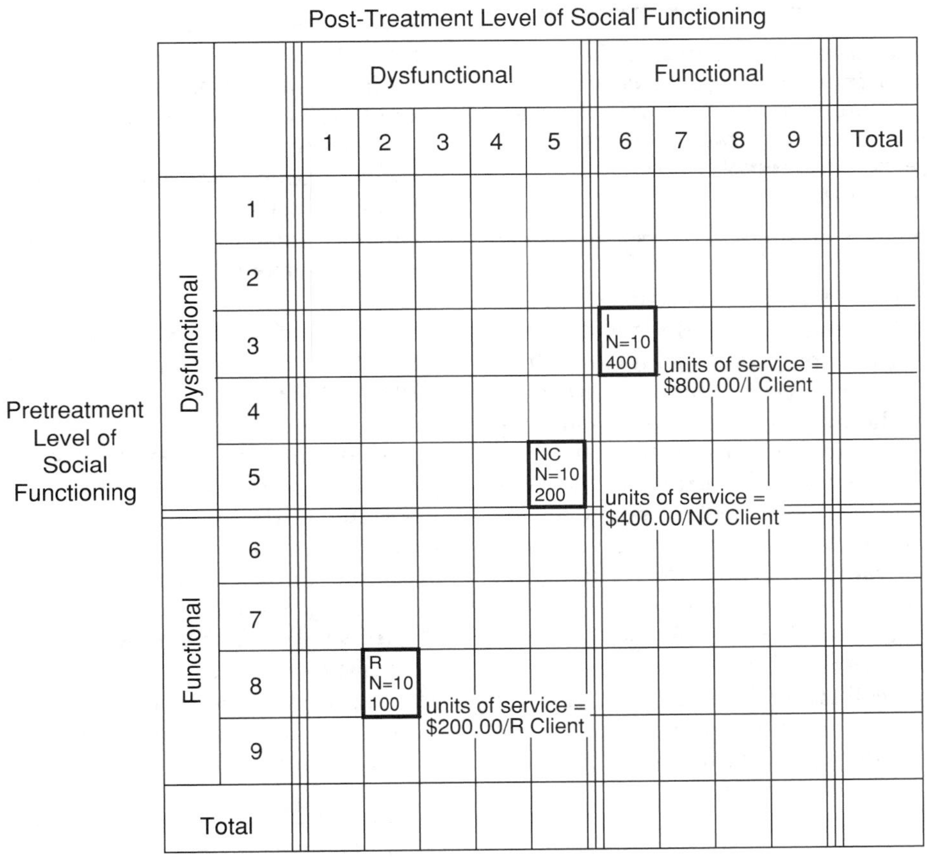
Post-Treatment Level of Social Functioning
Dysfunctional
Functional
1
2
3
4
5
6
7
8
9
Total
Pretreatment Level of Social Functioning
Dysfunctional
Functional
I
N=10
400
units of service =
$800.00/I Client
NC
N=10
200
units of service =
$400.00/NC Client
R
N=10
100
units of service =
$200.00/R Client

Figure 5. Cost-outcome matrix (hypothetical)

and outcomes for clients in each program are identified. Figure 5 illustrates a cost-outcome matrix.

As seen from the hypothetical numbers in Figure 5, the costs associated with any given client outcome may be determined by multiplying the unit cost by the number of units of service consumed and dividing by the number of patients with a particular outcome. For example, the ten "regressed" clients consumed 100 units of service at a unit cost of $20.00 for an average cost of $200.00 per regressed client. On the other hand, the ten "improved" clients consumed 400 units of service at a unit cost of $20.00, yielding an average cost of $800.00 per improved client.

Comparison of Program Costs

Cost-outcome matrices for two different programs can be compared using a cost-effectiveness matrix such as that illustrated in Figure 6. Programs can be compared in terms of their average outcomes and average costs across all clients or they can be compared in terms of any particular cost-outcome combination, such as those represented by each cell in the matrix of Figure 5. Decisions about which of two

---

Programs can be compared in terms of their average outcomes and average costs across all clients or they can by compared in terms of any particular cost-outcome combination.

---

programs is more cost effective are generally made using statistical tests of significance such as analysis of variance or analysis of covariance.[10] These techniques provide the evaluator with decision rules with determinable error rates. Once the cost effectiveness of Program A relative to Program B is established, the decision matrix illustrated in Figure 6 can be used. If two nursing programs were equally effective but Program A was less expensive than Program B, Program A would be more cost effective than Program B, and as indicated in cell 21 of Figure 6, Program A would be chosen over Program B. On the other hand, if the two programs were

equally effective but A was more costly than B, the conditions in cell 23 of Figure 6 would arise and Program B would be more cost effective than Program A.

The choice of Program A or Program B is clearly identified in seven of the nine cells of Figure 6. In cells 11 and 33 the decision is not clear and must be based on factors other than cost-outcome comparison.

EXAMPLE: COMPARISON OF COST EFFECTIVENESS OF TWO NURSING PROGRAMS

Perhaps an example will help to illustrate some of the accounting and statistical tasks associated with a cost-effectiveness analysis. Suppose that a director of nursing wished to compare the cost effectiveness of primary nursing and team nursing staffing methods. The director would begin by identifying the total costs associated with these programs within the categories outlined in Table 2.

Next the total program costs would be broken down according to the major services

		Cost of Program A Relative to Program B		
		A is less costly	A is as costly	A is more costly
Effectiveness of Program A Relative to Program B	A is less effective	11 ?	12 choose B	13 choose B
	A is as effective	21 choose A	22 no difference	23 choose B
	A is more effective	31 choose A	32 choose A	33 ?

Figure 6. Cost-effectiveness matrix. *Source:* Fishman, D. *Development and Testing of a Cost-Effectiveness Methodology for CMHCs.* NTIS Evaluation Study Reports Accession Nos. PB 246-676 (Vol. 1), PB 246-677 (Vol. II) (Springfield, Va. 1975).

Table 2. Total yearly nursing program costs (hypothetical)

Type of Cost	Cost	
	Primary	Team
Direct Costs		
Personnel salaries and fringe benefits (including donated time)*	$400,000	350,000
Other direct and traceable costs (e.g., travel, equipment)	40,000	40,000
Indirect Costs (including allocations of general administration, depreciation, and other indirect costs)	60,000	60,000
Total	$500,000	$450,000

*These hypothetical costs were estimated for a 35-bed inpatient unit, with approximately one staff member to every seven patients plus a head nurse; all patients needed approximately the same hours of nursing care. We assumed a staff distribution of 32 RN positions at $12,000 for the primary unit and 16 RNs; 10 LPNs at $8,500, and six nursing aides at $6,500/year for the team unit. The salary figures are approximate and rounded to ease computation and simplify the illustration.

within the programs. The definition of relevant program services is based on how program staff spend their time. Frequently a time study of staff activities is necessary to generate this information. Table 3 represents a hypothetical distribution of staff time in a primary and team nursing program. In this example, primary nursing

Table 3. Distribution of professional staff time by type of staffing system (hypothetical)

Program Service	Percent of time by Staffing System				Difference (Primary over Team)	
	Primary		Team			
	Hours per Year	%	Hours	%	Hours	%
Direct patient care (e.g., giving medications; treatments; patient teaching)	35,040	40	26,280	30	+8,760	+10
Indirect patient care (e.g., team conferences about patients; coordinating patient care with others)	35,040	40	43,800	50	−8,760	−10
System maintenance (e.g., record keeping, ordering supplies, attending conferences on operation of staffing system)	17,520	20	17,520	20	—	—
Total	87,600	100	87,600	100		

staff spent ten percent more time in direct patient care activities, ten percent less time in indirect patient care activities, and the same amount of time in system maintenance activities as did team nursing staff. A number of operating statistics relevant to the example are given in Table 4. These operating statistics are needed to identify the number of patients served and the number of units of service consumed by these patients.

Each unit had the same number of beds and the same occupancy rate yielding the same number of patient days per year. The number of individual patients cared for varied, however, because of the shorter length of stay in the primary unit.

Table 5 combined the financial data with the operating statistics and the distribution of staff time to yield the sought-after figures of cost per hour of direct patient care and average cost of direct care per episode of patient illness.

After establishing the desired cost per unit of service, the cost data are ready for combination with outcome data. Figure 7 illustrates two hypothetical outcome matri-ces. The outcome measure used in this example is a mobility rating score where a low score of 1 indicates the patient is immobile and a high score of 5 indicates the patient is mobile. From the percentage distribution of patients on the left of each scale, we can see that the team and primary unit patients were exactly equivalent in mobility prior to treatment. However, the distribution of patients' mobility scores after treatment is dramatically different. Reading below the diagonal of each matrix we can see that two percent of primary and two percent of team patients lost mobility or regressed on the outcome measure. Reading within the diagonal of each we see that 16 percent of primary patients (4% + 3% + 6% +3%) and 30.5 percent of team patients (7.5% + 8% + 11% + 4%) were maintained at their pre-treatment level of mobility. Finally, reading above the diagonal, we see that 82 percent of primary patients and 67.5 percent of team patients improved their mobility rating. Thus the outcome matrices suggest that the primary program is more effective, that is, produces better mobility outcomes than does the team program.

Table 4. Yearly operating statistics by type of staffing system (hypothetical)

	Staffing System	
Statistic	Primary	Team
Number of beds	35	35
Number of patient days (per year)	8,000	8,000
Percent of occupancy $\dfrac{\text{no. of actual patient days}}{365 \times 35}$	.6262	.6262
Number of patients (separate episodes)	1,600	1,333
Length of stay	5 days	6.0015 days

Table 5. Costs of nursing care in primary and team (hypothetical)

Variable	Staffing System	
	Primary	**Team**
Total cost of program	$500,000	$450,000
Total hours of direct nursing care provided	35,040	26,280
Cost per hour of direct nursing care	$14.27	$17.12
Total days of care provided	8,000	8,000
Cost per day of care	$62.50	$56.25
Average length of stay	5 days	6.0015 days
Standard deviation of length of stay	2.0	2.2
Total average cost per episode of care	$312.50	$337.58

We do not yet know if the primary program is more cost effective than the team program. To determine cost-effectiveness we need to express program costs relative to program outcomes. Figure 8 combines the hypothetical cost and outcome data for the two staffing programs. From this matrix, the cost associated with any particular program outcome can be identified. For example, 200 primary unit patients had a pretreatment mobility score of 2 and a post-treatment score of 5. It costs $62,500 to improve these 200 patients three scale points (see outlined cell). To determine whether the primary or team program is more cost effective in increasing patient mobility, we average the amount of change across all patients and use a statistical test of significance to determine if the change in one group of patients is significantly greater than in the other group. Table 6 illustrates the statistical test of the hypothetical outcomes and costs of primary and team nursing programs. From Table 6 we conclude that there is no significant difference in the costs of the primary and team programs. However, there is a difference in their effectiveness with the primary program producing significantly greater mobility gains than the team program. This cost-outcome represents the cell 31 in Figure 6 where Program A is as costly but more effective than the team program.

In summary, cost-effectiveness analysis is an evaluation technique that compares costs and nonmonetary outcomes for two or more programs. The meaningfulness of this comparison is dependent on three critical factors:

• the reliability and validity of the client outcome measure and the costing procedures;

• the experimental research design which rules out the possibility that the observed cost and outcome differences were caused by nonprogram factors occurring concurrently with the treatment program; and

• the random assignment of subjects to treatment programs to assure that comparisons were made between equivalent groups of patients.

To the degree that the evaluator can meaningfully measure client outcome under experimentally controlled conditions, and to the degree that program costs can be

Primary
Post-Treatment Mobility Scores*

Pretreatment Mobility Scores*		1	2	3	4	5
N = 300 19%	1	N = 60 4%	N = 40 2.5%	N = 200 12.5%		
N = 500 31%	2		N = 50 3%	N = 110 7%	N = 140 9%	N = 200 12%
N = 600 37%	3			N = 100 6%	N = 150 9%	N = 350 22%
N = 200 13%	4			N = 30 2%	N = 50 3%	N = 120 8%
N = 0 0%	5					
Total N = 1,600 100%		N = 60 3.75%	N = 90 5.63%	N = 440 27.50%	N = 340 21.25%	N = 670 41.87%

Team
Post-Treatment Mobility Scores*

Pretreatment Mobility Scores*		1	2	3	4	5
N = 250 19%	1	N = 100 7.5%	N = 100 7.5%	N = 50 4%		
N = 416 31%	2		N = 110 8%	N = 215 16%	N = 91 7%	
N = 500 37%	3			N = 150 11%	N = 200 15%	N = 150 11%
N = 167 13%	4			N = 30 2%	N = 50 4%	N = 87 7%
N = 0 0%	5					
Total N = 1,333 100%		N = 100 7.5%	N = 210 15.75%	N = 445 33.3%	N = 341 25.5%	N = 237 17.7%

Percentage Distribution of Patients by Mobility Level

Level of Mobility	Pretreatment			Post-Treatment		
	Primary	Team	Diff.	Primary	Team	Diff.
1	18.25	18.25		3.75	7.50	3.75
2	31.25	31.25		5.63	15.75	10.12
3	37.51	37.51		27.50	33.38	5.88
4	12.50	12.50		21.25	25.58	4.33
5	00.00	00.00		41.87	17.78	24.09

*Mobility Scale (Hypothetical)
1 Bed rest
2 Ambulate to chair
3 Ambulate in home with help
4 Limited ambulation outside
  of house with help
5 Ambulate ad lib without aid

Figure 7. Hypothetical outcomes of primary and team nursing

Primary
Post-Treatment Mobility Scores*

Pretreatment Mobility Scores*		1	2	3	4	5
$93,750 N = 300	1	$18,750 N = 60	$12,500 N = 40	$62,500 N = 200		
$156,250 N = 500	2		$15,625 N = 50	$34,375 N = 110	$43,750 N = 140	$62,500 N = 200
$187,500 N = 600	3			$31,250 N = 100	$46,875 N = 150	$109,375 N = 350
$62,500 N = 200	4			$9,375 N = 30	$15,625 N = 50	$37,500 N = 20
$0 N = 0	5					
Total $500,000		$18,750	$28,125	$137,500	$106,250	$209,375

Team
Post-Treatment Mobility Scores*

Pretreatment Mobility Scores*		1	2	3	4	5
$84,396 N = 250	1	$33,758 N = 100	$33,759 N = 100	$16,879 N = 50		
$140,435 N = 416	2		$37,134 N = 110	$72,581 N = 215	$30,720 N = 91	
$168,792 N = 500	3			$50,638 N = 150	$67,516 N = 200	$50,638 N = 150
$56,577 N = 167	4			$10,127 N = 30	$16,880 N = 50	$29,370 N = 87
$0 N = 0	5					
Total $450,000		$33,758	$70,893	$150,225	$115,116	$80,008

*Mobility Scale (Hypothetical)
1 Bed rest
2 Ambulate to chair
3 Ambulate in house with help
4 Limited ambulation outside
  of house with help
5 Ambulate ad lib without aid

Figure 8. Hypothetical cost-outcome matrices for primary and team nursing

tracked using sound accounting methods to accomplish the financial and statistical tasks, cost-effectiveness methodology can provide a powerful basis for programmatic decision making.

COST-EFFECTIVENESS STUDIES IN NURSING

Nursing administrators have long recognized the importance of identifying costs of nursing care programs as distinct from other related costs such as those associated with equipment, housekeeping and patient transportation services. Nonnursing costs such as housekeeping are frequently included in nursing service budgets. These costs inflate the direct costs of nursing programs. Despite the acknowledgment of and concern over these practices, very few evaluations of nursing programs have included any attempt to (1) systematically identify costs related to a specific program of nursing care, or (2) systematically relate reliable and accurate program costs to program outcome.

The few pioneering efforts to include costs in program evaluations have not completed the full range of financial, statistical and research tasks outlined in Figure 2. At best these studies represent early preliminary efforts in a previously undeveloped area, and at worst they provide program administrators with unreliable, incomplete or invalid data.

Very few evaluations of nursing programs have included any attempt to systematically identify costs related to a specific program of nursing care, or systematically relate reliable and accurate program costs to program outcomes.

The Loeb Center Study

A recent evaluation study of Loeb Center was sensitive to the importance of identifying and comparing costs of Loeb Center care with general hospital care.[11] The research tasks outlined in Figure 2 were well executed and costs per day of care were associated with the two groups of patients. Cost data were derived from the accounting and statistical procedures in place in the general hospital selected for comparison with the Loeb Center. No mention of the comparability of the existing cost data was made. Nor were the accounting and statistical methods described in sufficient detail to allow reader assessment of how costs were determined. Further study is required in order to determine the impact of Loeb Center care on patients. However, ". . . the data support the premise that Loeb patients may indeed have fared better and at less overall cost."[12] Careful attention to the financial and statistical tasks outlined in Figure 2 is necessary to obtain believable and comparable cost figures for this kind of study.

The Marram Study

The Marram et al. study of cost effectiveness of primary and team nursing has been widely quoted as documentation that primary nursing is cost effective relative to team nursing. This is unfortunate, as the study does not complete the accounting, statistical or research tasks which constitute an adequate cost-effectiveness analysis. Costs were based on salaries; other salary-dependent variables such as overtime, sick time, vacation time; operating costs associated with supplies; and inservice education cost.[13] The costs were totaled and divided by the number of beds on each unit to yield a cost-per-bed figure. The cost-per-bed figures represent ". . . a

Table 6. T-tests between average mobility and costs of primary and team nursing (hypothetical)

Comparison	Primary		Team		Level of Significance	
	$\overline{x}$	sd	$\overline{x}$	sd	(mean)	(sd)
Mobility scores						
Pre-treatment	2.43	1.13	2.48	1.21	NS*	NS
Post-treatment	3.95	1.13	3.30	1.21	p < .05	NS
Cost per episode of treatments	$312.50		$337.58		NS	NS

Sample N = 30 which represents a random sample from larger population.
*NS = not significant.

significant difference and cannot be overlooked in establishing the cost-effectiveness of the two units."[14]

To the extent that this conclusion is related to cost effectiveness, it is unwarranted for several reasons. First, the cost data used were limited to salary and equipment costs. Total program costs associated with major cost categories such as:

- personnel and donated time;
- other direct and traceable costs, e.g., travel, equipment;
- indirect depreciation, overhead, etc.; and
- administration

were not identified or related to program services. Further, the observed difference in salaries were due to differences in staff longevity and staff vacancies, a fact acknowledged by Marram et al.[15] The financial data used in this analysis were partially complete and reported at the second level (total program costs) identified in the financial tasks of Figure 2. Financial data in the form of a unit of service (e.g., day of nursing care or hour of direct care) were not identified or combined with operating statistics (e.g., number of hours of nursing care consumed by a patient) to yield a cost per unit of nursing care (e.g., cost per day of nursing).

Without a cost per unit of service it is not possible to associate programmatic costs with the outcomes of nursing care. The cost-per-bed figure used by the authors is better treated as cost of capacity or of an ability to provide treatment rather than a cost associated with treatment outcomes. To relate the cost per bed to treatment outcomes it would be necessary to identify and hold constant variables such as occupancy rate, and also to assume that all patients in all beds required and received the same amount and type of nursing care and had the same outcome as a result of treatment. The differences in capacity (24 versus 27 beds) allow the opportunity for more service as well as spreading the fixed costs differently since the per-bed share of fixed costs decreases as the number of beds increases. The cost per bed is an inappropriate figure to express the relationship between nursing program costs and client outcomes. A comparison of the cost per unit of nursing service, such as cost per day of direct nursing care, relative to the outcomes for clients across the two programs would provide the desired data.

The equivalency of patients on the two units was questionable, as neither random assignment nor other equivalency techniques such as use of covariates or matching of subjects was used. Even though the two units involved were both medical-surgical units with the same average length of stay, it is entirely possible that one unit has more seriously ill patients with poor prognoses, requiring more nursing time and larger numbers of supplies than the other. The inability to insure pre-treatment equivalency is a serious threat to internal validity of any study.[16] In addition to concerns about patient equivalence, there is reason to question the equivalence of the care provided by nurses on each unit. No mention was made of how the authors controlled the administration of the independent variable (primary or team nursing). Finally, the outcome measures used in this study were primarily attitudinal measures of patient and staff satisfaction. While satisfaction with care is certainly one dimension of program effectiveness, other outcomes associated with patients' health status would have been useful.

In summary, the study does not satisfy the criteria of a cost-effectiveness analysis in that (1) costs reported in this study were not accumulated using acceptable cost accounting procedures, (2) costs were linked to beds rather than to units of service and client outcomes, and (3) outcomes are of questionable reliability and validity due to design problems.

The Komaroff Study

Another study addressing the costs and effectiveness of two systems of providing care to diabetic and hypertensive patients has some of the same difficulties from a cost effectiveness perspective as does the Marram et al. study.[17] The Komaroff et al.

study addresses some of the financial, statistical and research tasks outlined in Figure 2. They accumulated man-power and laboratory costs associated with two systems of providing care for diabetic and hypertensive patients. Manpower costs were based on total time spent with clients and the salaries of the care givers for an average clinic session. While not producing a unit of service measure, Komaroff et al. did trace personnel costs to total time spent with clients; and this linkage of costs to program activities, frequently time spent, is an important part of cost-effectiveness analysis. Unfortunately, they did not develop this linkage further to use cost per unit of service idea.

This study used only the selected aspects of manpower and cost of laboratory tests to reflect program costs. Additionally, while both quantitative and qualitative outcome measures were available, they were not directly linked to programmatic resources; and finally, the assignment of patients to treatment groups was not clearly discussed, leaving doubts about pretreatment equivalency of patients.

Other Studies

The studies by Seigal, Jensen, and Coffee[18] and Yankauer[19] focused on establishing total costs of a nurse practitioner program. They determined total practice costs associated with salaries, other direct and traceable costs, indirect costs, and administrative costs, which are all the major cost categories used in cost-effectiveness analysis. The apparent absence of control over the variability in cost accounting methods and the exclusion of donated facilities or services make questionable the comparability of the cost data from the three practice sites in the Seigal, Jensen, and Coffee study. Further, this study uses cost data to conduct a "break-even analysis" which indicates the volume of patients necessary for a practice to break even rather than the effectiveness of a practice in providing care at a specified cost.

The Yankauer et al. study established nurse practitioner training program costs using the major cost categories for the financial tasks of cost-effectiveness analysis. A faculty time survey was conducted, but costs were not broken down into the major categories of service identified in the time sample. A cost per graduate was obtained by computing educational costs and production losses associated with the nurse assuming a student role. This study demonstrates a thorough identification of direct and indirect program costs. It is not a cost-effectiveness analysis, however, nor did the authors make this claim. To do this, they would have had to relate the costs systematically to the effectiveness of the training program. The Hall et al. study used acceptable research methods and had some operating statistics but was weak in the area of the financial tasks. The Seigal, Jensen and Coffee, and Yankauer et al. studies used a complete range of cost categories, but did not systematically link costs to outcomes. The Marram et al. and Komaroff et al. studies were weak in all three areas.

Cost effectiveness is a recent and newly emerging approach in nursing evaluation studies. It is important that some authors such as those cited above have recognized the need to identify and incorporate cost data as part of a comprehensive program evaluation. It is equally understandable that these efforts are beginning ones.

FUTURE COST-EFFECTIVENESS ANALYSES

Future cost-effectiveness analyses should include completion of all three types of tasks outlined in Figure 2. No administrator wants to support programs that are not cost effective. However, few administrators have the skill or the time to devote to a careful analysis of how the data are obtained. Thus evaluators employing cost-effectiveness methods must take care that the data produced are complete, reliable and valid.

With the continually growing cost of health care programs and the steadily increasing demand for accountability from funders and consumers, nurse administrators are recognizing the need for carefully conducted studies to serve as the basis for evaluation of nursing programs. Cost-effectiveness analysis is a potentially powerful evaluation method to aid decision makers in the choice of programs that are both effective in meeting their objectives and efficient in their utilization of resources. In responding to the need for cost-effectiveness studies, care must be taken to conduct the studies in a sound and defensible way if they are to be useful to nurse administrators.

REFERENCES

1. Controller General of the United States, U.S. General Accounting Office. *Standards for Audit of Governmental Organization, Program Activities, and Functions* (1972).
2. Sorensen, J. and Grove, H. "Cost-Outcome and Cost Effectiveness Analysis: Emerging Nonprofit Performance Evaluation Techniques." *Accounting Review* Lii:3 (July 1977) p. 658–675.
3. Lewin, H. "Cost Effectiveness Analysis in Evaluation Research" in Guttentag, M. and Struening E. *Handbook of Evaluation Research* II (Beverly Hills, Calif.: Sage Publications 1975).
4. Prescott, P.A. "Evaluation Research: Issues in Evaluation of Nursing Programs." *Nursing Administration Quarterly* 2:4 (Summer 1978) p. 63–80.

5. Fishman, D. *Development and Testing of a Cost Effectiveness Methodology for CMHC's.* NTIS Evaluation Study Reports Accession Nos. PB 246–676 (Vol. I), PB 246–677 (Vol. II) (Springfield, Va.: NTIS 1975).

6. Carter, D. and Newman, F. *A Client-Oriented System of Mental Health Service Delivery and Program Management: A Workbook and Guide* (Philadelphia, Pa.: Department of Public Welfare, Commonwealth of Pennsylvania 1975).

7. Kiresuk, T. and Lund, S. "Process and Outcome Measurement Using Goal Attainment Scaling" in Zusman, J. and Wurster, C.R., eds. *Program Evaluation: Alcohol, Drug Abuse, and Mental Health Services* (Lexington, Mass.: Lexington Books 1975).

8. Prescott. "Evaluation Research: Issues in Evaluation of Nursing Programs."

9. Sorensen, J. and Grove, H. "Using Cost-Outcome and Cost-Effectiveness Analysis for Improved Program Management and Accountability" in Attkisson, C., Hargreaves, W. and Horowitz, M. eds. *Evaluation of Human Service Programs* (New York: Academic Press, Inc. 1977).

10. Ibid.

11. Hall, L. et al. *Final Report. Longitudinal Effects of an Experimental Nursing Process* HEW, PHS Division of Nursing Grant NU-00308 (Washington, D.C.: August 1975) p. 1–97.

12. Ibid.

13. Marram, G. et al. *Cost Effectiveness of Team and Primary Nursing* (Wakefield, Mass.: Contemporary Publishing, Inc. 1976) p. 79–83.

14. Ibid. p. 84.

15. Ibid. p. 81.

16. Campbell, D. and Stanley, J. *Experimental and Quasi-Experimental Designs for Research* (Chicago, Ill.: Rand McNally 1963).

17. Komaroff, A. et al. "Quality, Efficiency, and Cost of Physician-Assistant-Protocol System for Management of Diabetes and Hypertension." *Diabetes* 25:4 (April 1976) p. 297–306.

18. Seigal, B., Jensen, D. and Coffee, E. "Cost-Effectiveness of FNP versus MD-Staffed Rural Practice" in Bliss, A. and Cohen, E., eds. *The New Health Professionals* (Germantown, Md.: Aspen Systems Corporation 1977).

19. Yankauer, A. et al. "The Costs of Training and Income Generative Potential of Pediatric Nurse Practitioners." *Pediatrics* 49:6 (June 1972) p. 878–887.

Building tents for nursing services through budgeting negotiation skills

Mark A. Covaleski, Ph.D.
Assistant Professor
Programs in Health Care Fiscal
Management and Health Services
Administration
University of Wisconsin-Madison
Graduate School of Business
Madison, Wisconsin

Mark W. Dirsmith, Ph.D.
Associate Professor of Accounting and
Management Information Systems
Price Waterhouse Auditing Professor
Pennsylvania State University
University Park, Pennsylvania

NURSE MANAGERS are becoming increasingly concerned about the level and nature of their involvement in the hospital's budget system. This concern is often expressed as their need and desire to use the budget as a management control tool for establishing and assessing the accountability of nursing units and for guiding and reinforcing the behavior of nurses regarding the use of hospital resources.[1,2] This management-control-oriented or inwardly directed aspect of budgeting deals with the impact the budgeter (the nurse manager) has on the behavior of budgetees (the nursing staff).

It may be argued, however, that one, if not the essential, factor that has led to an increased awareness of the importance of budgetary involvement on the part of nurse managers is the use of budgeting information in communicating with and influencing the behavior of those outside of the nursing department, such as hospital administration, who supply resources necessary to its functioning. This use of budgeting information largely involves politically advocating "the cause" of the department.

This process of communication is, in turn, directed at legitimizing the nursing services area so that it can maintain some degree of bureaucratic autonomy and flexibility. In effect, this outwardly directed use of budgeting information emphasizes the impact the budgetee (the nursing ser-

The authors wish to thank Henry Mintzberg and Barbara Stevens for their help in better understanding their work.

Nurs Admin Q, 1984, 8(2), 1–11
©1984 Aspen Publishers, Inc.

vices area as represented by the nurse manager) has on the behavior of the budgeter (the hospital administration). It is important for nurse managers to consider this dual use of budgets—as a management control device and as a political advocacy device—and to find ways of using budgets as political advocacy devices.

ORGANIZATIONAL CONTROL— SOME THEORETICAL FOUNDATIONS

The purpose of management control is to ensure that resources are obtained and used effectively and efficiently in accomplishing organizational objectives.[3] Budgeting has been traditionally viewed as one specific form of management control that is directed at planning, coordinating, and controlling activities performed in different parts of the organization.[4]

Ostensibly, such management control techniques are designed to serve the managerial level, within which two necessary, qualitatively different functions are performed.[5,6] First, individual managers must coordinate and control the behavior of subunit members to achieve the objectives of the subunit effectively and efficiently. The information flow (i.e., objectives, operating procedures, etc.) involved in performing this first type of activity is essentially downward.

The objectives of the subunit are more or less accepted from a larger organization and are, in turn, passed on to subunit members, whose activities are monitored and directed by the subunit manager. But subunits do not act in isolation. Not only must the subunits accomplish their missions, but subunit managers must convince others in the organization that their subunits' missions are being accomplished, which is the second function of managers.

In performing this second function, individual managers must act as a buffer or mediator between the subunit and a larger social context, particularly the rest of the organization. Subunit managers must appropriately act as advocates of their subunits in order to procure needed resources. This advocacy function involves communicating with others outside of the subunit concerning its past and current performance, as well as its future resource needs.

This process of communication is largely dependent on performance information, and the information flow involved is directed essentially upward. Thus, when budgeting is designed to serve the managerial level, its meaning, use, and direction in the performance of the control function may differ significantly from its meaning, use, and direction in the performance of the advocacy function.

Control and environmental context

Recent accounting literature suggests that budgeting systems should be shaped by the nature of the environment in which the organization operates: In stable environments, budgeting systems should be more formally structured; in dynamic environments, they should be more flexible in nature.[7] At a general level, this reasoning is consistent with discussions that appear in the contingency theory literature.[8–10]

Hedberg et al., for example, discussed how the environment should broadly shape an organization's control philosophy; they argued that organizations that have constant or benevolent surroundings can afford to have a structure much like that of a palace—intricate, rigid, and refined.[11] Because the environment is constant, the organization has time to develop formal guidelines for addressing the problems it faces.

The organization can routinize decision making and assess the performance of subunits using means that compare operating results with prespecified standards of performance (e.g., "actual with budget"). In such settings, the means used for coordinating and controlling subunits and subunit members may be centrally orchestrated.

In contrast, organizations that face a turbulent, changing environment require a structure much like that of a tent—flexible, creative, and immediate. The methods employed in gauging performance and controlling the behavior of organizational members should be flexible enough to reflect changes in the environment so as to encourage appropriately responsive actions on the part of the individuals being evaluated. Emphasis is placed on adapting to the environment rather than adhering to rules and regulations.

Organizations that face a turbulent, changing environment require a structure much like that of a tent—flexible, creative, and immediate.

Basically, the tent-living life style should involve extensive delegation of decision-making discretion to subunit managers who are most sensitive and responsive to the problems the subunit faces. Consequently, upper-level management must divest itself of exercising control so that appropriate control strategies are developed and administered at the local or subunit level. The information system should be designed to funnel information up from the subunit concerning the problems it faces rather than to transmit information down to the subunit, whose purpose is to effect control.[12–14]

Although he agreed with the reasoning of Hedberg et al., Den Hertog suggested that it is difficult, if not impossible, to achieve a coalignment between an organization's environment and its control system.[15] He argued that there is a strong tendency for control systems to move the organization in the direction of further bureaucratization by evoking centralization, specialization, standardization, and formalization—a pathogenic condition that renders the organization insensitive to its environment. Furthermore, he argued that this movement can be especially detrimental to an organization functioning in a turbulent environment, where flexibility and autonomy are required for organizational survival.

In combination, the authors cited the need for organizations that face rapidly changing environments, such as hospitals and nursing services within hospitals, to keep the complexity and comprehensiveness of their control mechanisms to a bare minimum. Hospitals and nursing services should gear themselves to impermanency and gauge plans as if the underlying decisions being evaluated were necessarily temporary and imperfect.

It appears that in hospitals the emphasis on a downward flow of information and the exercise of centralized control over nursing services should be displaced by (1) an upward flow of information from nursing services to hospital administrators and (2) control functions being performed locally by nursing services managers. The effectiveness of nurse managers can be improved by training them in bargaining and negotiating skills, enabling them to control their subunit activities more effectively.[16] It is now possible to examine how control is achieved in organizations.

Behavioral control versus output control

Ouchi[17] and Ouchi and Maguire[18] have provided empirical support for their contention that there are only two phenomena that can be observed, monitored and counted in achieving control: (1) behavior and (2) outputs that result from behavior. Approaches used to effect control involving these phenomena are thus termed *behavioral control* and *output control*. Essentially, these two forms of control are not interchangeable and serve different purposes; they are also useful in all organizations, though to varying degrees.

Behavioral control

Behavioral control can be applied if the controller and controllee at least agree on the processes by which resources are converted to desired outcomes by the subunit. Thus if the controller-controllee relationship takes place on a fairly frequent, day-to-day basis, and if the controller has adequate technical training concerning the tasks performed by the controllee (e.g., the controller is a nurse manager, and the controllee is a nurse), judgment and evaluations can be more subtle, flexible, substantive, and subjective regarding duties and the accomplishment of duties. Contextual factors can be incorporated into assessments of performance and feedback provided to subunit members.

In the nursing services area, behavioral control may involve the direct, personal observation of the behavior of the nursing staff by a trained, informed, and experienced controller—the nurse manager. In making their assessments, nurse managers are able to incorporate their professional experience and raw, firsthand knowledge of the all-important nurse–patient relationship into the performance of controller functions. Guidance and reinforcement activities may involve considerably more intuition and less performance appraisal and decision making "by the numbers" than will output control.

An inherent disadvantage of behavioral control, however, is its subjectivity. If subunit representatives must actively compete with one another for scarce resources (e.g., nursing services may compete with other departments for a share of scarce hospital resources), qualitative information will tend to be poorly transmitted throughout the organization. This poor transmission arises because rivals will usually dispute the "soft" information being used to advocate the needs of competing subunits. Thus this qualitative information does not serve well the negotiating and bargaining skills needed by nurse management.

Output control

When the controller-controllee relationship expands and becomes less frequent and more impersonal (e.g., the relationship between hospital administration and nursing function), behavioral control becomes severely limited and tends to be supplanted by output control for at least two reasons. First, the process by which resources are transformed into desired subunit outcomes may not be readily understood by the uninitiated (e.g., where subunit tasks are complex, technical, or take place over a long period of time). Thus behavioral control (where hospital administrators rather than nurse managers are acting as controllers) cannot be relied on in communicating how effectively the nursing services area is performing its mission because hospital administrators may not have the technical training necessary to understand what was being observed. Does administration understand (or has it the time to understand) how "quality of patient care," as indicated by patient contact, medical expertise, and so forth, contributes to patient recovery?

Second, even if the process by which resources are converted to desired outcomes is understood, the administrator-controller has to compare many subunits with one another in allocating resources and rewarding performance. In effect, hospital administrators must be able to calculate what nursing services has accomplished in relation to other departments, a feat difficult to achieve in a multipurpose hospital.

With the use of qualitative, subjective information such as that attendant with behavioral forms of control, comparisons among subunits are not readily performed, for often the relevant dimensions along which behavior is monitored within each unit are dissimilar. In contrast, with output control, which quantitatively depicts the performance of a subunit in terms of outputs achieved (often relative to some desired, prespecified level of output), comparisons among subunits are more easily made by higher level administrators. What counts is literally just that—what counts.

This need for output control information by higher level administrators for purposes of comparing subunits is not unilateral, however. Because such information is typically expressed in quantitative terms and has the appearance of being objective in the sense that prescriptions usually exist for the reports generated, subunit managers tend to be more successful in communicating the results of operations to higher levels.

This political success arises largely because quantitative information is more defensible in meeting the challenges of other subunit managers who question the validity of competitors' reports. Thus subunit managers employ output control information as a means for advocating the cause of the subunit; so quantitative output information is used primarily as a tactic for self-legitimization rather than for control, guidance, and reinforcement.

Ouchi and Maguire concluded, however, that a paradox exists in the use of output control.[19] Because of the inherent complexity of performing nursing tasks (i.e., the process by which resources are converted to desired subunit outputs is not readily un-derstood by the uninitiated), and consequently because higher level administrators may not possess the expertise or time necessary for understanding the tasks being performed, the nurse manager must resort to using output control information in advocating the cause of nursing services and negotiating for needed resources.

Because of this same inherent task complexity, however, the behavior of nurses that is observed is not readily reducible to numbers; that is, the quantitatively based output control information does not capture the essence of nursing care. This may be true, for example, in the use of patient classification systems. Thus output-oriented forms of control are used most when least appropriate—in the face of behavioral complexity. Consequently such forms of information may be ill-suited to satisfy nurse managers' needs for evaluating the performance of nursing staff.

The organization, however, has reached a compromise. The hospital's need for quantitative, organizationally transferable, defendable information has been satisfied at the cost of not providing nurse managers with information sufficient to their purposes of achieving control within nursing services. It may be due to this compromise that Den Hertog suggested that control systems tend to move organizations toward bureaucratization by evoking standardization and formalization, which, in turn, become adopted for purposes of control within the subunit by the subunit managers.[20]

Tent living

A three-pronged depiction of control has been presented. First, when management control devices are designed to serve the managerial level, they should both accommodate the guidance and reinforcement function directed at achieving subunit objectives effectively and efficiently and promote the subunit advocacy function directed at influencing the behavior of higher level administrators.

Second, the control philosophy adopted by an organization should broadly reflect its environment. In a stable environment, a standardized, regimented or palacelike approach should be taken; in a shifting environment, a flexible, immediate or tentlike approach should be taken.

Third, there are available to organizations two basic control techniques that are not interchangeable and serve different purposes. In situations where the controller (e.g., a nursing manager) has day-to-day contact with the controllee and has the technical expertise and time necessary to understand the behavior of the controllee (e.g., the "quality" of nursing care), behavioral control (e.g., direct, personal observation of the nursing staff) may be used to monitor, guide and reinforce the behavior of the controllee. In situations where a controller (e.g., a hospital administrator) has infrequent contact with the controllee and does not have the technical expertise or time necessary to understand the behavior of the controllee, output control (e.g., the number of patient days or the cost per patient day) may be used by subunit managers to legitimize the activities of the subunit.

Consistent with the contingency theory literature, it appears that in turbulent environments control systems should be made more flexible. But the true flexibility that should be embraced in adapting to a tent-living life style concerns recognizing the dual, partitioned use of control information rather than merely making the control system more flexible.[21,22]

The flexibility that results from a tent-living life style in which the dual, partitioned use of budgets is recognized differs in several respects from "flexible" or "partici-

pative" budgeting systems. First, tent living suggests that the subunit should have discretion to adopt its own means of monitoring, guiding, and reinforcing its members' performance. Second, it suggests that output "control" information transmitted to higher organizational levels is really not control information at all, but a separate means of conveying influence attempts.

In effect, quantitative information found in hospital classified budgets or patient classification systems should be used for negotiation and bargaining, but not necessarily used as control information within nursing services. If these dual uses of control information are not adequately partitioned, Den Hertog's[23] warning of inappropriate bureaucratization may haunt the host organization.

BUDGETS AND NURSING AS AN EMERGING PROFESSION

Nurse managers are not learning anything new in the conclusions that the importance of budgeting lies in its use as a political and communicative tool useful for advocating the needs of the nursing services area (as opposed to a guidance and reinforcement tool), and that their needs related to this use are left unmet by hospital administrators and the budgeting literature. What is meaningful is that this political use of budgeting information is legitimate and necessary to the emergence of nursing as an autonomous profession. Like most implications that derive from conceptual development, these

The political use of budgeting information is legitimate and necessary to the emergence of nursing as an autonomous profession.

more specific recommendations can be divided into those for practitioners and those for researchers.

Implications for practitioners

A nurses' association in a mid-Atlantic region invited the authors to conduct an inquiry concerning the current and potential uses of budgeting systems in the nursing services area. Some of the facts the nurses presented the authors with were (1) budgeting systems were being increasingly imposed on them by hospital administrators, (2) the nurses could understand the emphasis placed on such information because of the cost control ethos that pervades the industry and (3) the nurses could see the necessity for better understanding the language of budgeting if they were to have some control over their future.

In retrospect, the nurses' ability to articulate their needs and the authors' ability to comprehend what they were requesting were quite limited. Now it is understood that these limitations are reflective of an administrative and control environment that is unresponsive to the needs of these middle management practitioners. In addition, it is reasonable to question substantial portions of the budgeting literature that stress the use of budgets as control mechanisms and that, where the advocacy use is recognized, criticize this use as bordering on contemptible. It can also be concluded that the budgeting literature is unresponsive to the needs of practitioners, at least at the subunit level.

It appears that nurse managers stand pretty much alone on the frontier of recognizing the appropriateness of using budgeting systems as political advocacy devices. These nurses are not in an enviable position. Nurse managers sometimes get tired of being involved in budgeting; they perceive

budget systems as being merely "shell games." But is their involvement worthwhile? Yes, it is.

At this point, the question of how the nurse manager can develop budget negotiation and bargaining skills becomes important. Based on the authors' conceptual analysis and numerous discussions with nursing services representatives, the following recommendations can be made.

Nurse managers should recognize that there are two control functions relevant to serving as a nurse manager: (1) providing guidance and reinforcement to subordinates and (2) advocating the cause of the nursing services area. It appears that behavioral control is appropriate in serving the first function, and output control is appropriate in serving the second. The functions and uses of information should be partitioned, however, because behavioral control information is not sufficiently robust to withstand the challenge of competitors. However, the complex behavior of nursing staff is not readily reducible to numbers, so output control should be used for purposes of providing guidance and reinforcement. But nurse managers should not reveal to higher level administrators that these activities and related information uses have been partitioned.

After the final budget has been approved, nurse managers should send a memorandum to the appropriate hospital administrators indicating what suggestions they had made concerning the original budget and how the budget has been modified as a consequence. Nurse managers should accentuate the contribution they made to the budget and, *explicitly,* how they had exercised some discretion.

Nurse managers should initiate contact with the financial staff in preparing the nursing services area budget. They should acknowledge their cooperation and support in memorandums sent to them and to appropriate administrative staff charged with approval of the budget. Nurse managers should accentuate the effort that went into making the budget as sophisticated and comprehensive as possible. The implicit message conveyed is that the nursing services area is behaving responsibly in an administrative sense.

Nurse managers should send a memorandum to the appropriate administrators indicating that they understood the budget as approved and that every effort will be made to stay within its boundaries. The implicit message conveyed is one of informally approving the budget.

After completion of the budget period, and after comparisons of actual with budget have been made, nurse managers should provide documented, quantitatively substantiated analyses of why variances occurred and what unfavorable variances were unquestionably caused by factors outside of their control. The message conveyed is one of showing the burden of addressing the cost-control ethic environment that hospitals currently enforce.

Nurse managers should not expect any positive effects or recognition within one, two, or even three budget periods. The effects are more long term than that. Eventually, when the voluntary reports and memorandums are tardy, and hospital administrators question their absence, it will be known that some progress is being made in effectively using budgets as political advocacy devices.

Although it was not discussed previously in this article, the authors have found in their continuing research in this area that nurse managers tend to be chosen more for their clinical skills than for their administrative skills. Given the general attitude of seasoned managers that budgetary participation is a shell game and that they have a tendency to become "tired," it is important for nurse managers to actively participate in the selection of qualified successors. Every attempt should be made as soon as possible to isolate from among the staff of nurses under the nurse manager's supervision a candidate who possesses good administrative and political skills. Before retirement, the nurse manager should involve the successor in drafting the formal and informal influence-directed reports and memorandums. In the performance of this activity, the emphasis placed on the dual, partitioned functions of exercising control and advocating the cause of the nursing services area should be passed on to the successor.

Implications of researchers

This article is directed at exploring the advocacy role that must be performed at the managerial level in all organizations. The negotiating and bargaining skills related to this advocacy role are particularly appropriate for managers of professional workers who perform intensive, skilled tasks such as nurses.

Unfortunately, this role has received little attention in the academic literature. As a consequence, the very real advocacy needs of middle managers have been left unmet. If the adjective "advocacy" can be appropriately applied, the advocacy function as a meaningful and necessary area of research should be supported. This assertion represents *the* implication for future researchers.

REFERENCES

1. Donovan, H. *Nursing Service Administration: Managing the Enterprise*. St. Louis: C.V. Mosby, 1975.
2. Stevens, B.J. *The Nurse as Executive*. Wakefield, Mass.: Contemporary Publishing, 1980.
3. Anthony, R.N. *Planning and Control Systems: A Framework for Analysis*. Boston: Harvard University Press, 1965.
4. Vatter, W.J. *Operating Budgets*. Belmont, N.Y.: Wadsworth, 1969.
5. Parsons, T. *Structure and Process in Modern Societies*. New York: Free Press of Glencoe, 1960.
6. Thompson, J.K. *Organizations in Action*. New York: McGraw-Hill, 1967.
7. Bruns, W.J., Jr., and Waterhouse, J.H. "Budget Control and Organization Structure." *Journal of Accounting Research* 13 (Autumn 1975): 177–203.
8. Duncan, R. "Characteristics of Organizational Environments and Perceived Environmental Uncertainty." *Administrative Science Quarterly* 17 (June 1972): 313–27.
9. Hedberg, B.L.T., Nystrom, P.C. and Starbuch, W. "Camping on Seesaws: Prescriptions for a Self-Designing Organization." *Administrative Science Quarterly* 21 (March 1976): 41–65.
10. Lawrence, P.R., and Lorsch, J.W. *Organizations and Environment*. Homewood, Ill.: Irwin, 1967.
11. Hedberg et al., "Camping on Seesaws," 43–44.
12. Covaleski, M.A., and Dirsmith, M.W. "Budgeting in the Nursing Services Area: Management Control, Political and Witchcraft Uses." *Health Care Management Review* 6 (Summer 1981): 17–24.
13. Hedberg, B.L.T., and Jonsson, S. "Designing Semi-Confusing Information Systems for Organizations in Changing Environments." *Accounting, Organizations and Society* 3, no. 1 (1978): 47–64.
14. Weick, K.F. "Educational Organizations as Loosely Coupled Systems." *Administrative Science Quarterly* 21 (March 1976): 1–19.
15. Den Hertog, J.F. "The Role of Information and Control Systems in the Process of Organization Renewal: Roadblocks or Road Bridge." *Accounting, Organizations and Society* 3, no. 1 (1978): 29–45.
16. Stevens, B.J. "Power and Politics for the Nurse Executive." *Nursing and Health Care* (November 1977): 208–12.
17. Ouchi, W.G. "The Relationship Between Organizational Structure and Organizational Control." *Administrative Science Quarterly* 22 (March 1977): 95–113.
18. Ouchi, W.G., and Maguire, M.A. "Organizational Control: Five Functions." *Administrative Science Quarterly* 20 (December 1975): 559–69.
19. Ibid., 565.
20. Den Hertog, "The Role of Information and Control Systems," 32.
21. Burns and Waterhouse, "Budget Control and Organization Structures," 185.
22. Swieringa, R.J., and Moncur, R.H. *Some Effects of Participative Budgeting on Managerial Behavior*. New York: National Association of Accountants, 1975.
23. Den Hertog, "The Role of Information and Control Systems," 32.

Participative decision making in strategic management of resources

Ronald P. Dowd, Dr.P.H.
President and CEO
R & R Dowd, Inc.
Long Beach, California

COMPETITION IN THE health care marketplace, continued regulation, and prospective product-based reimbursement approaches have placed severe constraints on the availability of resources and have forced a redirection of management effort. "Alternative modes of services delivery," "productivity analysis," "marginal costs," "strategic business unit portfolio analysis," and "return on investment" are buzzwords being tossed around in health care management circles. Nurse executives somehow must deal with financial management concepts and practices in their planning, decision making, and priority setting. However, not all decision making in health care is predicated on the bottom line dollar value. Community needs, patient care, and quality of service are still important issues in the field, and these issues must be addressed in decisions related to resource allocation. It is, therefore, important that decision makers be capable of recognizing the distinction between a quantitative approach and a qualitative approach to priority setting. Both approaches are valid and appropriate.

PRIORITY-SETTING CRITERIA

All decisions are made on the basis of human values. When a resource is not allocated because "it's too expensive," someone is saying that the purpose to which the resource will be applied is not worth the dollars it would require. Unless there is absolutely no hope of acquiring the dollars, and all concerned agree, the decision is purely a value judgment. If this were not the case, why would an institution order staff reductions at the same time a massive building program was under way? The answer is simple. Someone has concluded that the building program has value and that continued staffing at existing levels has less value. Although many such decisions are temporal in nature, the fact remains that a value judgment has been rendered.

Nurs Admin Q, 1988, 13(1), 11–18
©1988 Aspen Publishers, Inc.

Resource allocation in a health care setting must take into account the range of values held by those involved in decision making and priority setting. This task requires, at the outset, that participants come to agreement on the criteria to be used. These criteria are particularly important in nursing today because it is a field undergoing transition, and the supply of nurses is not keeping pace with demand.[1,2] It is useful practice in planning and budgeting to develop consensus on highly significant factors that should be included in the decision-making process. These factors would then be used as "directing criteria" and would serve the purpose of guiding priority setting throughout all levels of the organization. Criteria may be financially oriented or not, depending on the circumstances.

The author recently had the opportunity to develop a strategic plan for a medical school. It was interesting that words such as "profit," "return on investment," and "marginal cost" did not appear in the set of directing criteria formulated for the planning effort. Financial feasibility, of course, is always a practical constraint and must enter the equation somewhere along the line. The point is that health services organizations have an obligation to the community, as well as a responsibility to remain financially solvent. Therefore, it is reasonable and appropriate for such organizations to formulate directing criteria that strike a balance between financial and other considerations.

Nurse executives are being asked to participate in planning and budgeting decisions that require the exercise of judgment based on their unique perspective of patient care needs in combination with their views on resource requirements.[3] This is a difficult balancing act. Management effectiveness requires a blend of skills that preserves the rights of patients to expect excellence in service and, at the same time, protects the institution from financial ill health.

This balance can be ensured through application of directing criteria that adequately address issues of quality service, patient satisfaction, community obligation, and profitability. A useful set of directing criteria would include the following elements.

Compatibility with purpose addresses the issues of consistency with the mission and major goals of an organization. A resource commitment to an activity or program that correlates strongly with the purpose of an organization should be high on the priority list compared to one that seems to be at odds with the purpose.

Community service is another important element. The contribution of an activity or program to an institution's sense of community obligation must always be considered. Health care organizations have a social responsibility that cannot be ignored.

Profitability is essential. Like it or not, only the federal government can print money to cover its deficit. Everyone else must figure out how to generate sufficient revenue to cover costs. It follows that an activity or program that contributes to profit (or surplus in voluntary institutions) will more likely be rated higher on the priority list than those that show a negative bottom line.

Feasibility covers a multitude of considerations. Certainly, financial ability to carry out a program is important; but beyond that, organizational skills, staff availability and knowledge, technology, and physical space are additional constraints to take into account.

Quality is an attribute that is expressed in terms of degree of goodness or excellence. This criterion is the most complicated of them all because quality is subject to a high level of relativity. To a certain extent, quality of service (or product) can be measured in terms of structural or process attributes. Typically, health care quality is graded according to training and skill levels of staff, staff-to-patient ratios, and the like. On the other hand, consumer satisfaction is also a measure of quality. Patients view things from a different perspective, and somehow that perspective must be brought into the priority-setting exercise.

WEIGHTING AND RATING

A consensus on directing criteria may differentiate among the various factors in terms of their relative importance. A simple methodology is presented in Figure 1, where all participants are asked to rate each criterion according to their placement on a scale of values from one (totally unimportant) to ten points (extremely impor-

PURPOSE: To involve staff leadership in determining the relative importance of critical factors in providing guidance in the setting of resource allocation priorities.

INSTRUCTIONS: Assign a numerical rating to each and every factor by placing a check mark (✓) on the point along the scale that most closely expresses your opinion of the importance of the factor.

CRITICAL FACTOR | RATING

CRITICAL FACTOR	Totally Unimportant							Extremely Important		
	1	2	3	4	5	6	7	8	9	10
1. COMPATIBILITY WITH PURPOSE The extent to which an activity or program is consistent with the mission and major goals of the institution.								✓		
2. COMMUNITY SERVICE The contribution of an activity or program to the institution's community obligation.						✓				
3. PROFITABILITY The contribution to profit or return on investment of an activity or program.					✓					
4. FEASIBILITY The ability of the institution to secure adequate resources to successfully implement a plan of action.										✓
5. QUALITY OF SERVICE The extent to which an activity or program adds to the overall prestige and image of the institution.										✓

Figure 1. Rating directing criteria.

tant). The hypothetical example shows a ranking of criteria based on average responses from participants.

Once agreement is reached on the list of directing criteria and their relative importance, the priority-setting exercise is extended throughout every level of the organization, addressing all objectives, activities, and resource requirements being considered. This exercise typically occurs during a strategic planning or budgeting cycle involving every facet of an organization's operations. The focus of the exercise is to formulate plans and budgets that have institutional support from key participants.[4]

In a typical hospital, if there were such a thing, it is not difficult to envision hundreds of activity proposals, each requiring a distinct resource commitment. How could these be prioritized so as to maximize participation by key staff and optimize the blend of criteria applied to decision making? Each proposal must be examined and assigned a rating by participants. A rating system linked to directing criteria is presented in Figure 2. It should be noted that a total score for each proposal can be computed by multiplying the rating score by the criterion weight (importance rating). Admittedly, this calculation requires a great deal of time and energy, but the exercise is

PURPOSE: To develop consensus priorities by rating activity and program proposals in terms of critical factors.

INSTRUCTIONS: Assign a rating to each and every proposed activity or program by placing a check mark (✓) in the box which most closely expresses your opinion of the value of the proposal for each critical factor.

Proposal	Compatibility with Purpose			Community Service			Profitability			Feasibility			Quality of Service		
	Low	Mod	High	Low	Mod	High	Low	Mod	High	Low	Mod	High	Low	Mod	High
1															
2															
3															
4															
5															
6															
7															
8															
9															

Figure 2. Rating proposals using directing criteria.

well worth the effort if it produces decisions that have the support of all concerned.

The priority-setting exercise can be lightened by establishing organizational priority-setting levels that address corresponding fewer proposals as review progresses through the institutional hierarchy. For instance, the initial set of proposals generated at the section or unit level could be subject to priority screening at the departmental level. Those proposals passing departmental priority screening could be further screened at the divisional level. Those surviving divisional screening would be candidates for executive review. As a matter of course it would be good practice to allow each succeeding level to see all proposals, regardless of rating scores. Cutoff points for screening proposals should be arbitrarily set according to the judgment of participants at each level. It is far better to commit errors of commission than to omit a proposal that has participant sentiment, because of a few points here and there.

QUANTITATIVE FACTORS

All proposals requiring a commitment of resources must include activity descriptions, cost estimates, and specific resource needs expressed in terms of human capital and support requirements. Once assembled, these become "decision packages" that can be evaluated on the basis of their respective costs and benefits.[5] The cost side of the equation is relatively easy to quantify, especially if cost is limited in definition to dollar cost. Financial experts and accountants have developed standards and pro forma approaches to deal with money questions. Benefits, if expressed in terms of revenue, profit, or return on investment can also be easily quantified. At the risk of oversimplification, a limited number of financial concepts will be explained here to assist in basic understanding of quantitative factors in decision making.

Pro forma projections

Essentially, pro forma projections amount to a standardized format consisting of a set of revenue and expense projections over a specified period of time (usually five years). The bottom line is the mathematical difference between the two variables. Obviously, when revenues exceed expenses the bottom line is positive (good). When expenses exceed revenue the bottom line is negative (bad). These can be tricky, however, and questions should be asked about each category of revenue and expense. For example, it is wise to question the workload volume assumptions made in preparing revenue projections. If anticipated volume (e.g., hospital admissions) seems to be out of line with the hospital's experience, then the revenue linked to that volume may be seriously off the mark. It is also wise to ask whether reserve funds are included in the pro forma. A financial cushion is comforting. If there is no reserve, should trouble develop down the line, the enterprise could be headed for disaster. Finally, changes in the bottom line over time need to be observed. Positive growth in profit or surplus should be noted. However, it is not unusual to see negative bottom lines on new services or programs for the initial years.

Return on investment and payback

These terms, commonly used in financial analysis, need to be understood. Return on investment addresses the question, "What's in it for me?" If an organization spends a dollar, it expects that dollar to produce income in excess of one dollar. The return is expressed as a percentage of the original dollar investment, and is computed for each year of the life of the investment. For example, if a dollar is invested and produces $1.10 per year in income, the return is 10 percent per year on the investment.

Payback refers to the amount of time required to realize a positive bottom line. Should a dollar be invested in a new program, and the bottom line is negative over a three-year period but shows a profit in the fourth year, the payback period is four years.

QUALITATIVE FACTORS

Many (if not most) resource allocation decisions in health care are not based purely on financial considerations. As was mentioned previously, directing criteria would typically include concepts such as community service, compatibility with purpose, and quality of service, a concept that seems to defy quantification. It is possible, however to assign numerical values to judgments about these factors. Commonly used approaches to priority setting employ a variety of scaling techniques to derive scoring and ranking measures.[6,7] Participants in the decision-making process would be asked to render judgments relative to each criterion with respect to each proposal being evaluated. Qualitative factors and quantitative factors are used in combination to produce overall judgments in many cases. For example, a favorable rating on profitability may be based on evidence of high return on

Table 1. Mid-size hospital department budget requests

Department	Activity/Service	Cost ($)
Medicine	Add 5 full-time equivalent (FTE) nurse practitioners to Geriatric Clinic	150,000
	Purchase new overhead lighting system for Cardiology Service	180,000
Pediatrics	Renovate Newborn Nursery Unit B	375,000
	Purchase word processing system for Nursing Administration	5,000
	Add program in pediatric intensive care nursing research	50,000
Surgery	Purchase new sterilizers for ambulatory surgery	15,000
	Add 2 FTE nurse anesthetists	70,000
Obstetrics	Convert Room 19 in 5 West Unit to A-B-C	25,000
	Purchase new nurse call system for 5 East Unit	60,000
	Install Anesthesia column in Delivery Room 3	25,000
Critical Care Unit/Intensive Care Unit (CCU/ICU)	Develop guest relations program in critical care	180,000
	Replace patient monitoring units in ICU Room 2	250,000
Total requests		1,385,000

Table 2. Results of resource allocation priority setting in patient services division of mid-size hospital

Proposal	Cost ($)	Compatibility with purpose			Community service			Profitability			Feasibility			Quality of service			Total* score	Rank	Priority group
		Rate†	Wt	Score‡	Rate	Wt	Score	Rate	Wt	Score	Rate	Wt	Score	Rate	Wt	Score			
Staffing																			
Geriatric clinic	150,000	H	8	24	H	6	18	L	5	5	M	10	20	M	10	20	87	5	B
Nurse anesthetists	70,000	M	8	16	L	6	6	M	5	10	H	10	30	H	10	30	92	4	B
Capital projects																			
Lighting system	180,000	M	8	16	L	6	6	L	5	5	H	10	30	M	10	20	77	7	C
Newborn nursery	375,000	H	8	24	H	6	18	M	5	10	H	10	30	H	10	30	112	2	A
Sterilizers	15,000	L	8	8	L	6	6	L	5	5	H	10	30	M	10	20	69	9	C
A-B-C room	25,000	H	8	24	H	6	18	H	5	15	H	10	30	H	10	30	117	1	A
Nurse call	60,000	M	8	16	M	6	12	L	5	5	M	10	20	M	10	20	83	6	C
Anesthesia column	25,000	M	8	16	L	6	6	L	5	5	H	10	30	H	10	30	87	5	B
Patient monitoring	250,000	H	8	24	M	6	12	M	5	10	H	10	30	H	10	30	106	3	B
Programs																			
Word processing	5,000	M	8	16	L	6	6	L	5	5	H	10	30	L	10	10	67	10	C
Pediatric research	50,000	M	8	16	M	6	12	L	5	5	M	10	20	M	10	20	73	8	C
Guest relations	180,000	H	8	24	H	6	18	M	5	10	H	10	30	H	10	30	112	2	A
Totals	1,385,000			224			138			90			340			290	1,082		
Averages	115,417			19			12			8			28			24	90		

*Total score = sum of scores across all critical factors
†Rate: H = high (3 points), M = moderate (2 points), L = low (1 point)
‡Score = rate point value × weight point value

investment, short payback period, and a generalized "gut feeling" that the service question is a winner.

FORMULATING THE PRIORITY LIST

The bottom line in any priority-setting exercise is to produce a list of services or activities that are ranked in order of preference. Resources are then allocated to those highest on the list, in descending order until all resources are exhausted. Suppose, for the sake of illustration, that a vice-president of patient services for a moderately sized acute care hospital is faced with developing a budget proposal based on the department output shown in Table 1.

The vice-president agrees that all proposals are worthy and needed and that they should be approved by the hospital executive council. Unfortunately, financial guidelines issued by the president clearly show that new discretionary dollars for patient services will be in the neighborhood of $500,000, if anything. The vice-president is a staff-oriented executive and wishes to set priorities in a consultative fashion. Employing the participative approach, and using the directing criteria suggested earlier, the vice-president invites key staff to a one-day retreat to consider alternatives and develop

a priority list. During the retreat, each department has an opportunity to present its proposals in sufficient detail to allow an appreciation by all in attendance. The group is then organized into three focus groups: staffing, capital projects, and programs. Each proposal is classified into one of the three groups, further discussed, and rated during the focus group sessions. Every retreat attendee rotates through each focus group to ensure that every proposal is rated by all involved. The results are presented in Table 2. Those proposals in priority group A will be included in the vice-president's budget request to the hospital executive council. Priority B proposals will be submitted in the event additional resources become available. Finally, priority C proposals will be deferred to a future budget cycle.

STRATEGIC MANAGEMENT

The participative decision-making process described in this article is the capstone of strategic management practice. Tapping into the knowledge and aspirations of participants will optimize the validity of decisions made, while at the same time bonding people to a commitment of support for priorities selected. This approach can only strengthen the overall program and add credibility to its leaders and sponsors.

REFERENCES

1. Mattaz, C. "Work Satisfaction Among Hospital Nurses." *Journal of the Association of Health Services Administration* 33, no. 1 (1988): 57–74.
2. Palmer, P.N. "Dealing with the Nurse Shortage Again." *Journal of the Association of Operating Room Nurses* 46, no. 1 (1987): 13–14.
3. Nash, M., and Opperwall, B. "Strategic Planning: The Practical Vision." *The Journal of Nursing Administration* 18, no. 4 (1988): 12–16.
4. Nutt, P.C. *Planning Methods for Health and Related Organizations,* New York: Wiley, 1984.
5. Berman, H.J., and Weeks, L.E. *The Financial Management of Hospitals.* Ann Arbor, Mich.: Health Administration Press, 1982.
6. Warner, M., Holloway, D., and Grazier, K. *Decision Making and Control for Health Administration.* Ann Arbor, Mich.: Health Administration Press, 1984.
7. Spiegel, A., and Hyman, H. *Basic Health Planning Methods.* Rockville Md.: Aspen Publishers, 1978.

Selecting, implementing, and evaluating patient classification systems: A measure of productivity

Bonnie Mowinski Jennings, R.N., D.N.Sc., L.T.C., A.N.
Researcher, Health Care Studies Division

Ruth E. Rea, R.N., Ph.D., C.E.N., L.T.C., A.N.
Researcher, Health Care Studies Division

Beverly B. Antopol, R.N., M.S., L.T.C., A.N.
Researcher, Health Care Studies Division

John L. Carty, R.N., M.S., L.T.C., A.N.
Researcher, Health Care Studies Division
U.S. Army Health Services Command
Fort Sam Houston, Texas

AS PROSPECTIVE payment and other economic issues served as catalysts for change in health care delivery during the early 1980s, health care facilities became more attuned to business strategies. Consequently, the need to address productivity became apparent. Productivity, the ratio of input to output, is not a straightforward issue in the health care arena because output is defined in services rather than as objects produced or income. Nevertheless, nursing resources are the input that meets patient needs. Greater patient needs, often expressed as greater acuity, generally consume more nursing resources. Patient classification systems (PCSs) are one way to identify patient needs, or acuity, and thus delineate staffing requirements.[1-4]

If a PCS is used to reflect patient needs and thus to drive nursing requirements, it is then essential to select the PCS in a thoughtful manner. The decision to implement a PCS must also take into account marketing strategies that will "sell" the system to users on all levels—staff nurses, head nurses, nurse executives, physicians, and nonnurse administrative personnel. In addition, it is important to plan an ongoing evaluation of the chosen PCS: The dynamic nature of health care clearly mandates that the sys-

The opinions or assertions in this article are the private views of the authors and are not to be construed as official or representing the views of the Department of the Army or the Department of Defense.

The authors thank Yolanda Miller for reviewing a draft of this article.

Nurs Admin Q, 1989, 14(1), 24–35
©1989 Aspen Publishers, Inc.

tem be reassessed routinely, according to a proactive plan, to assure that it accurately classifies patients.

A GENERIC OVERVIEW OF PCSs: MEASUREMENT AND PRACTICE

It is not surprising that nurse administrators turned to PCSs as a way to quantify the input of a productivity ratio. Nevertheless, several individuals have echoed King's comments concerning the difficulty of measuring the domain of nursing due to the inherent complexity of nursing practice.[5–9] While the complexity of nursing cannot be ignored, the more encouraging view is that individuals who pioneered the development of PCSs made a valid effort to tackle the very difficult task of measuring nursing care and classifying patients according to their consumption of resources.

Although King[9] articulates the belief that industrial engineering techniques are too reductionistic and mechanistic to depict the total domain of nursing, they were nevertheless an integral part of the development of the early PCSs. The industrial engineering approaches such as work sampling, operational audit, or time and motion studies, applied to existing methodologies, albeit not service-industry focused, that had a higher degree of consistency and accuracy than systems based on self-report and expert opinion. Furthermore, the industrial engineering approaches were based on objective, quantifiable data.[10] Thus, regardless of the possible limitations, most PCSs currently in use are based on various modifications of industrial engineering methodology.

Prototype versus factor systems

Prototype and factor systems are the two most common frameworks for PCSs. As stated by Giovannetti and reiterated by Gallagher, the primary difference in these two systems is their design.[1,11] Prototype systems described characteristics typical of patients in each category, whereas factor systems categorize patients based on the total value derived from rating patients on critical indicators. Prototype systems are often credited with incorporating, at least in part, various professional standards of care.

This move to reflect professional standards may represent an attempt to stretch beyond some of the constraints imposed by adopting industrial engineering techniques to measure health care. Nevertheless, while a certain degree of subjectivity is inherent in any classification system, prototype systems are regarded as more subjective than factor systems. PCSs derived from more objective data are regarded more favorably than those with a more subjective slant.

Direct and indirect care

Perhaps as a consequence of subscribing to the industrial engineering model, it has become common to designate care as direct or indirect. Direct care is commonly defined as those activities that occur in the presence of the patient, and indirect care refers to those activities performed away from the patient.[12,13] For example, giving a bed bath is direct care, and patient-based communication, such as exchanges during a patient care conference, is indirect care. In the strictest sense, this nomenclature is predominantly concerned with nursing interventions or tasks. However, a broader interpretation allows other components of the nursing process such as assessing and planning to come into play. The nomenclature seems less important than attempting to measure the full scope of nursing practice. The cognitive elements so critical to nursing care are clearly the most difficult to capture.

Nursing intensity

Because of the complexity and scope of nursing practice, investigators are trying to advance PCSs to better reflect the full range and depth of nursing. As Reitz states, "Nursing practice is not a simple sum of discrete tasks with specific points of beginning and end."[7(p.22)] Nursing intensity is one approach to reflect the complexity of care through a PCS, thereby moving beyond the limits imposed by systems that capture information that primarily concerns intervention. Prescott and Phillips and Reitz attempt to bridge the gap between existing PCSs and the full domain and complexity of nursing by measuring nursing intensity.[6–8]

Actual practice versus ideal practice

Measurement and practice issues also raise a question as to whether the PCS is a reflection of nursing care rendered or patient needs met. Perhaps this element raises the issue of measuring nursing as actually practiced or "what is" rather than ideal practice or "what should be." In other words, is the goal of the PCS to measure nursing care that is provided, which may be constrained by limited resources, or is the goal to measure patient needs, which then reflect the full spectrum of patient requirements?

Although it is evident that PCSs must become more sophisticated in order to reflect the complex spectrum of nursing practice, existing systems are being used as a guide to staffing and measures of productivity. For this reason, it is important that

The cognitive elements so critical to nursing care are clearly the most difficult to capture.

administrators consider various issues when selecting a PCS for use in a health care facility.

SELECTING A PCS

Realizing that acuity information derived from PCSs can be translated into information on nursing resource consumption and, hence, productivity, nurse administrators have the option to either develop their own patient classification system or use an existing system. While developing a new PCS might optimize the match between the system and the facility where it will be used, this option is costly in terms of both financial and human resources. Developing a PCS requires the same rigor associated with developing any new research instrument. Giovannetti and Mayer include those who emphasize that a PCS must have documented validity and reliability if the data generated by it are to be used confidently.[2]

In many cases, hospitals do not have either personnel with sufficient research knowledge or the time necessary to devote to constructing their own PCS. Consequently, a pragmatic alternative to developing a PCS is to obtain an existing system, either through purchasing one developed by a corporation or through borrowing a system used at another hospital. In either case, nurse administrators must critically examine the PCS prior to implementing it within their facility. The following questions/criteria can guide nurse administrators in assessing an existing PCS for use in a particular facility.

Does the patient classification system reflect nursing care as practiced in the facility?

The patient classification tool should reflect the full range of nursing as practiced in the facility where it will be used. Nurse administrators should first review the nursing activities listed on the patient classification tool to identify activities commonly practiced in the particular facility that are missing from the PCS. For example, are practices related to patient teaching and emotional support included? If items are missing, the PCS developers should be questioned as to whether these activities were originally included in the task listing. If items were eliminated, the basis for deciding to exclude the activities—such as evidence from statistical analysis—must be considered. If commonly practiced activities are not measured by the classification tool, nursing practice may be underrepresented.

The operational definitions of the nursing activities used in the PCS should also be reviewed. Although, as previously stated, many PCSs focus on activities representing nursing interventions, the operational definitions should reflect time needed to assess patients, to teach patients about procedures and their health, and to assemble and remove any equipment used in providing care. In this manner, a broader scope of nursing practice is represented than that displayed by merely considering interventions.

The indirect nursing care activities captured by the PCS need to be evaluated. Activities within the indirect arena include tasks related to unit management and personal activities as well as activities done in support of patient care but accomplished away from the patient. Many of these indirect activities reflect professional nursing actions within the planning and evaluating components of the nursing process.

Finally, the direct and indirect activities should be evaluated as a unit to ensure that activities that affect the total spectrum of nursing practice are not missing. For example, if the time to attend patient care conferences or inservice classes has not been accounted for in either direct or indirect care, the PCS will not reflect sufficient staffing to provide patient care as well as attend these meetings without increasing the number of hours each staff member is required to work.

Can the patient classification system be modified to reflect the unique aspects of care as provided in the specific facility?

The patient classification tool should allow the addition of new activities if these proposed activities consume a substantial amount of staff time. For example, care for critically burned patients in a specific facility may involve a large number of postoperative dressing changes that are appreciably more complicated than major dressing changes otherwise reflected by the PCS. If the borrowed patient classification tool does not capture this workload, required nursing care and, hence, resource consumption may be significantly underrepresented.

In a similar manner, timings should be adjusted if the operational definitions are changed as compared with the original patient classification tool. For example, if vital signs are obtained electronically in the specific hospital, the original patient classification tool should be modified if it is based on timings for manually obtained vital signs. In this example, care requirements and, thus, staffing will be overrepresented to the extent that vital signs taken electronically are done more quickly than vital signs taken manually. In either of the preceding examples, the psychometric attributes of the tool, namely reliability and validity, will be adversely affected by the mismatch between original task timings and actual task time requirements.

The borrowed patient classification tool's staffing recommendations also need to be evaluated. Some PCSs recommend exact professional-to-paraprofessional staffing mixes. These recommendations need to be reviewed for congruence with the specific facility's goals. If there is an incongruence between PCS staffing guidelines and the institution's ideal staffing plan, the tool's recommendations need to be altered prior to its implementation.

Does the instrument demonstrate acceptable psychometric properties?

Although volumes can be written regarding the importance of psychometric parameters, the nurse administrator should, minimally, evaluate the reliability and validity of the patient classification tool. Reliability refers to the reproducibility of the results from patient classifications derived by different raters. Depending upon the exact type of reliability, comparing a reliability statistic with a known standard allows nurse administrators to know if the borrowed patient classification tool consistently measures patient acuity.

Validity refers to how accurately the PCS reflects actual nursing care requirements; it is considerably more difficult to evaluate than reliability. As a minimum, the nurse administrator should ascertain if the content of the PCS reflects the scope of nursing practiced in the specific institution and the degree of congruence between the nursing time, as reflected by the tool and some outside standard, such as actual clock time.

IMPLEMENTING THE PCS

In order to maximize the value of any PCS, it is essential to garner support for and commitment to the system from the individuals who will be involved with it; to create a sense of ownership and acceptance of the PCS by users at all levels. In fact, in a nationwide survey, Giovannetti and Mayer identified inadequate implementation as a major problem with PCSs.[2]

The thrust of implementation must, therefore, be to generate acceptance of the PCS among all users. By creating a climate of enthusiasm and anticipation, nurse administrators may find the PCS will be received more positively. Prior to the arrival of the new PCS, the nurse administrator should provide the staff with specific examples of how it will benefit them. It is essential for nurse administrators to have a well-articulated plan for implementing their PCS; it should be a plan that establishes policies and procedures and educates all individuals who will put information into the system or use information from it.

Policies and procedures

To enhance acceptance and compliance with the PCS, it is essential that individuals representing users of the system at all levels actively participate in developing procedures and policies that will govern the system. Many questions should be addressed in these guidelines: Exactly who will classify patients? What preparation must they have? What level of expertise in classifying must they demonstrate? Will float, agency, or student nurses be expected to classify patients? How often will patients be classified? What automation support will be needed? What types of reports will be generated? What mechanisms will be used to ensure continued reliability of the system?

Once consensus is reached regarding these policies and procedures, a detailed implementation plan should be developed to facilitate a smooth transition to the new acuity system. It is important to consider not only the obvious issues such as procuring computer software and hardware, but also less tangible but equally vital concerns such as marketing and educational strategies. Timelines and responsible individuals need to be identified for each step of the implementation plan.

Education

A comprehensive education program must precede the actual implementation of the system. All personnel who may affect or be affected by the new PCS should participate in the education program. This includes not only staff nurses and nurse and hospital administrators, but physicians and data processing personnel as well. The program should be individualized to the needs of each particular group. Whereas training for staff nurses should emphasize how to use the system to classify patients, nurse and hospital administrators need to know what data will be available to them and how they can use that data.

Staff nurses

Some form of experimental learning should be incorporated into the education program for staff nurses, as they will classify patients. One method to accomplish this is to provide a variety of written patient scenarios. These scenarios, while referring to fictitious patients, can be developed from clinical information derived from actual hospital records. The learners can then be evaluated on their ability to use the new PCS to actually classify patients based on information provided in the scenarios. Whatever method of training is used, it is imperative to evaluate the learning. Before individuals are allowed to classify patients, they must demonstrate the ability to use the system accurately.

The responsibility for training does not end when the initial educational classes conclude. During the initial stages of implementation, appointed and specially trained experts, preferably from each unit, need to monitor the accuracy of classification and be available to the individuals classifying patients to answer the questions that will undoubtedly surface. Periodic written updates and inservice classes will help clarify commonly asked questions and misconceptions as they arise from using the system. If clarification is not provided, nurses, who are highly creative, will invent their own answers.[14] Inconsistent use could threaten the reliability of the entire system.

Nurse administrators

In addition to understanding how the system was developed and how to classify patients, it is imperative for nurse administrators to understand how to best use the information generated by the PCS. Education for this group should focus on interpreting and monitoring the PCS data regarding daily staffing decisions as well as analysis of staffing trends. Emphasis should be placed on how the PCS can be used as an adjunct to other information when making decisions about staffing. For example, nurse administrators need to recognize discrepancies between the PCS staffing recommendations and what the nurse administrator observes and hears from nursing personnel. Attention to possible inconsistencies should alert the nurse administrator to investigate reasons for them and to initiate corrective action to ensure system reliability.

Educational efforts can bring other uses of the PCS to the attention of nurse administrators. The nurse administrator might consider using the PCS to establish admission

The nurse administrator might consider using the PCS to establish admission and transfer criteria for critical care units.

and transfer criteria for critical care units.[15] Furthermore, trend analysis could provide clues regarding cyclical changes in workload, and guide changes that would maximize the effectiveness of nursing resources. For instance, a cardiac stepdown unit may show a consistent rise in acuity levels on the weekend because of a policy that encourages transferring patients from coronary care units prior to weekends. Evidence of such peaks in workload can be used to negotiate policy changes in concert with physicians; in this case, it might be wise to stagger transfers from coronary care units throughout the week.[16]

Educational programs must also teach nurse administrators to use PCS information to establish collaborative bonds with physicians and hospital administrators. To achieve institutional goals, the PCS must be used in a positive, proactive manner, rather than as an adversarial tool. When patient demands exceed nursing resources, closing beds may be considered a ready solution to inequalities in supply and demand. Because bed closures result in lost revenue as well as loss of needed services to the community, other solutions must be taken into consideration. Alternate solutions include shifting resources between units, shifting patients to different units, authorizing overtime for nursing staff members, supplementing staff with agency nurses, and relieving the nursing staff of performing nonnursing tasks.

Physicians and hospital administrators

Because the staffing of nursing units affects the work environment of physicians and hospital administrators, specific educational programs concerning the PCS should be developed for these individuals. Objectives of the programs should be to familiarize physicians and hospital administrators with the PCS and to gain their acceptance

and support of the system. To accomplish this, educational efforts should be directed to demonstrating how physicians and hospital administrators can use the PCS to help them achieve their goals.

In addition, these individuals need to fully understand how the PCS was developed, how instrument validity and reliability were established, how interrater reliability is maintained and evaluated, and why the information derived from the system is important to them. Physicians must also understand that their orders exert a considerable influence on nursing staff requirements because medical orders strongly influence nursing practice.

ONGOING EVALUATION OF THE PCS

Concurrent with implementing a PCS, a proactive evaluation plan must be initiated. The plan might address a variety of elements that concern long-term, ongoing assessment of the system to include evaluating (a) the fit between nursing practice, patient needs, and what the PCS measures, (b) how interrater reliability is calculated, and (c) how interrater reliability is checked when a multihospital system uses a PCS.

The fit between practice and measurement

The importance of assuring that PCSs accurately represent nursing practice and patient needs was mentioned previously. Because of rapid changes in health care technology, it is imperative that PCSs undergo periodic evaluation to assure their congruence with the practice setting. This congruence concerns both the completeness of the PCS in reflecting nursing practice and the accuracy of measurements used in the PCS.

Practice in the labor and delivery setting provides examples of both of these situations. First, a PCS developed in the latter part of the 1970s would most likely not reflect changes in practice common to the latter part of the 1980s, such as amnioinfusions and external versions. Second, the time needed to assemble internal monitoring equipment in the late 1980s could either be shorter than that needed a decade earlier due to improving and simplifying the monitoring equipment, or longer due to increasing the complexity of the equipment. To sustain accuracy in the PCS, either variation would need to be corrected to more accurately reflect current practice conditions.

Interrater reliability

Another critical part of ongoing evaluation of a PCS involves examining the system's reliability. Consistent use among the classifiers is essential so that patient acuity information can be used to project staffing requirements and monitor productivity. There are various ways to evaluate interrater reliability; percentage agreement and the Kappa statistic are the two that will be considered here.

Many patient classification systems use percentage agreement to determine reliability.[2,3,5,17,18] Although this statistic is relatively easy to calculate, it does not correct for chance agreement. The opportunity for artificially high reliability values due to chance alone occurs notably in two ways.[19] First, agreement due to chance increases as the number of PCS categories decreases. In a three-category PCS, for example, there is a 33% opportunity for chance agreement per category as compared with only a 20% opportunity for chance agreement in a five-category PCS.

Secondly, the interrater percent may be inflated by chance alone if most of the nurs-ing activities contained in the PCS are either infrequently selected (less than 20 percent of the total) or frequently selected (greater than 80 percent of the total). In both instances, nursing staff quickly learn to either select only a few items or to select most of the items in the tool. Thus, artificially high interrater reliabilities can occur due to the rater's knowledge of the items in the PCS rather than due to knowledge of a patient's care needs.

Understanding the inaccuracies inherent in using percent agreement to determine interrater reliability, the nurse administrator should adapt a reliability method that corrects for chance agreement. The Kappa statistic represents one such option. Kappa is a reliability value that reflects the degree of agreement between two raters after agreement accounted for by chance alone has been eliminated.[20] Although mathematical computations for Kappa are more complex than percent agreement, the use of appropriately programmed computers simplifies the use of this statistic. Most importantly, the use of the Kappa statistic provides a more accurate reflection of reliability that is not unduly inflated by chance agreement. Prior to using the Kappa statistic, the nurse administrator should review guidelines for interpreting the values derived from Kappa. Because the opportunity to capitalize on chance is removed when using Kappa, the reliability coefficients will be understandably lower. The lower values, nevertheless, are actually more accurate and more meaningful; the values should be interpreted in this light.

Interhospital use

Just as interrater reliability is important to assess consistency in using a PCS on a particular nursing unit, so interhospital evaluation becomes important when PCSs are used systemwide in healthcare corporations, which are becoming more common. Writings concerning PCSs suggest that classification systems need to be specific to each facility.[21-22] Although, in the purest sense, facility-specific PCSs may be desirable due to subtle or even overt differences in practice among institutions, it would not be unreasonable for a corporation to purchase or develop a PCS for use throughout its system. In such a case, it would be essential for the corporation to consider how it might establish reliability among the hospitals comprising the corporation.

The notion of interhospital reliability may appear preposterous initially, but in fact it represents one way to control drift in the PCS. Just as interrater reliability is essential to assure that bias does not creep into the unit-level rating system, so interhospital reliability checks can help to reduce inconsistencies among institutions. It is possible that users at one facility might consistently (in other words, reliably) use the PCS in a way that distorts information. Such interhospital inconsistencies might be manifest in excessive conservatism whereby individuals, and thus the institutions they represent, inadvertently minimize patient needs; this in turn would underrepresent staffing requirements. Conversely, there might be facilities that, when compared with PCS data from other hospitals in the corporation, appear to use a more liberal approach to classifying patients, which might actually inflate the staffing profile.

In either case, it would be important to discern why one facility may be reporting staffing needs that are considerably different than the needs reported by similar institutions. To correct for these occurrences, which are to be expected considering the human element inherent to patient classification, it is important to build a method of interhospital reliability into the PCS. For example, interrater reliability coefficients can be compared among facilities to identify places with solid reliability parameters and places where reliability values might be improved. Similarly, PCS data from like units in different hospitals can be compared to identify trends in resource consumption that suggest excesses in either direction. Efforts can then be initiated to evaluate possible user discrepancies. By evaluating use of a PCS among hospitals within the corporation, administrators can realign the systemwide application of the classification tool when its use appears to be inconsistent among the facilities.

Frequency of classification

Another issue regarding ongoing evaluation of a PCS concerns how often patients need to be classified. It is important to ensure that the valuable information derived from PCSs is not offset by a too cumbersome approach to data collection. Frequency of classification raises the issue of how the information will be used. If the purpose of the PCS is to determine staffing needs for each subsequent shift, then the PCS must be completed each shift. Conversely, if staffing requirements are essentially similar over time, then patients may be classified less frequently (e.g., monthly) in order to provide trend information.

Some facilities collect PCS data from every unit on every shift; some collect information daily from most units but reevaluate only those units with rapidly varying patient situations each shift; some collect PCS data only once for each patient at the time of discharge; and still other facilities collect PCS information only a few times a month in order to staff according to unit trends. There is no right way to collect and use PCS data. The important point is to use the right information in the right way, to ensure that all relevant information is being captured.

As users become more sophisticated in collecting PCS data and managers become more sophisticated in interpreting PCS data, it may be worthwhile to reevaluate how often the information is collected, and to what end. To maximize the efficiency of the system, it is important to match requirements for completion with how the information is being used by managers. Once staff are comfortable with the system and managers have devised ways to optimize the use of the information derived, it is valuable to reconsider whether the same outcomes could be achieved in a more efficient way. This tactic was used in two studies, both of which supported reducing patient classification from multiple times a day to once a day.[3,23]

ADDITIONAL USES OF THE PCS

Finally, in order to maximize the use of data derived from PCSs, it is important to briefly consider various additional uses of PCS information. For example, because PCSs reflect productivity, it has become common to use data derived from PCSs to assess charges based on patient's acuity and nurse resource consumption, as opposed to using traditional billing approaches based on a set daily charge.[24] Another often-mentioned use of PCSs concerns quality of care. Less frequently addressed but equally relevant uses of PCSs relate to their relationship with diagnosis related groups (DRGs) and adequate staffing versus nonproductive time.

Quality of care

Although PCSs have been linked to quality of care issues, this connection is tangential at best.[3,11,25] Giovannetti and Haas both caution against this approach.[1,5] Although Giovannetti believes PCSs can be used to match patient workload with nursing requirements, she finds, "There is no evidence, however, that the effective utilization of nursing personnel hours has any direct relationship to the quality of care."[1(p.8)]

The whole issue of quality care, although important, is filled with ambiguity and imprecisely defined terms. The goal of quality care remains a desirable outcome. It appears, however, that it would be best not to further cloud this important goal by attempting to use existing PCSs as measures of quality. In other words, measuring the quality of care is *not* a wise additional use of PCSs.

Relationship to DRGs

Since DRGs were instituted as a prospective payment system, nurses have expressed concerns regarding the homogeneity of DRGs as related to nursing resource consumptions.[6,8,26,27] PCSs, however, *do* identify nursing resource consumption by patients. Consequently, linking this patient acuity data with DRG categories can provide invaluable information related to the similarity or dissimilarity of nursing resource consumption within any specific DRG.[28]

To establish this linkage, patient classification information should become part of the biomedical data set collected on each patient. If wide variations are found in nursing resource consumption within given DRGs, then nurse administrators, in concert with the hospital administrator and physician staff, need to examine patient

Measuring the quality of care is not a wise additional use of PCSs.

records to determine the cause of the fluctuating acuity. As an example: Certain medical orders may be more nursing intensive than others. If, in fact, these variations in medical orders reflect appropriate differences in medical treatment, the disparity in nursing resource consumption within the same DRG needs to be addressed at the national policy level to avoid cost overruns.

Adequate staff versus nonproductive time

Inseparable from the examination of productivity is the need to utilize patient classification information to set staffing guidelines. A simple way to derive the total number of staff is to calculate nursing requirements using the average number of patients in each acuity category. Such an approach, although appealing in its simplicity, may be appropriate only for situations in which extra staff can be easily mobilized when the patient census exceeds the average. Conversely, it might not be adequate for those patient care areas where specialized knowledge precludes "floating" in extra staff quickly (for example, labor and delivery, critical care units, emergency care areas). In these cases, nurse administrators might weigh the costs and benefits of staffing at a higher-than-average census level. The trade-off involves ensuring adequate staffing when the census is high, but also potentially increasing nonproductive time when the census is at the average or lower.

Displaying this trade-off between adequate staff and nonproductive time graphically may indicate the point where a small increase in personnel will substantially reduce the risk of insufficient staff coverage with only a small increase in nonproductive time. Thus, the nurse administrator should not automatically approve the use of the average patient census as the basis for staffing calculations. Rather, the decision that sets the appropriate patient census level to drive the PCS should be influenced by an appraisal of how easy it is to mobilize additional staff, as well as the effects of nonproductive time.

•   •   •

Selecting, implementing, and evaluating a PCS for use in any facility are not activities that can be carried out in isolation. Rather, they constitute a dynamic process that requires careful thought and collaborative exchange. A plan that is proactive from its inception will enable nurse administrators to properly monitor the system during all phases of its lifecycle, and thereby preclude reactive responses to startling changes in practice, information derived from the system, or user reaction to the system.

Because nursing practice is dynamic and the health care environment is undergoing considerable change, the need for fine tuning and modifying any PCS should be expected. There is no one PCS that will work in all facilities to serve as an expression of nursing productivity. Nevertheless, it is clear that concerns about cost and productivity are not likely to subside in the near future. It therefore behooves nurse administrators to exercise business savvy, along with their nursing knowledge, to select, implement, and evaluate a PCS that will reflect nursing productivity to the greatest extent possible.

REFERENCES

1. Giovannetti, P. "Understanding Patient Classification Systems." *The Journal of Nursing Administration* 9, no. 24 (1979): 4–9.
2. Giovannetti, P. and Mayer, G.G. "Building Confidence in Patient Classification Systems." *Nursing Management* 15, no. 8 (1984): 31–34.
3. Grant, S.E., Bellinger, A.C., and Sweda, B.L. "Measuring Productivity Through Patient Classification." *Nursing Administration Quarterly* 6, no. 3 (1982): 77–82.
4. Pardue, S.F., and Dick, C.T. "Patient Classification." *Journal of Psychosocial Nursing* 24, no. 12 (1986): 23–30.
5. Haas, S. "Patient Classification Systems: A Self-Fulfilling Prophecy." *Nursing Management* 19, no. 5 (1988): 58–62.
6. Prescott, P.A., and Phillips, C.Y. "Gauging Nursing Intensity to Bring Costs to Light." *Nursing and Health Care* 9, no. 1 (1988): 17–22.
7. Reitz, J.A. "Toward a Comprehensive Nursing Intensity Index: Part I, Development." *Nursing Management* 16, no. 6 (1985): 21–30.
8. Reitz, J.A. "Toward a Comprehensive Nursing Intensity Index: Part II, Testing." *Nursing Management* 16, no. 9 (1985): 31–42.
9. King, I.M. "Patient Aspects." In *Operations Research in Health Care. A Critical Analysis,* edited by L.J. Shuman, R. Dixon Speas, Jr., and J.P. Young. Baltimore: Johns Hopkins University Press, 1975.
10. Aydellotte, M.K. *Nurse Staffing Methodology. A Review and Critique of Selected Literature.* Washington, D.C.: U.S. Government Printing Office, 1973. DHEW Pub. No. 73–433.
11. Gallagher, J.R. "Developing a Powerful and Acceptable Nurse Staffing System." *Nursing Management* 18, no. 3 (1987): 45–49.
12. Chagnon, M., et al. "A Patient Classification System: By Level of Nursing Care Requirements." *Nursing Research* 27, no. 2 (1978): 107–13.
13. Misener, T., Frelin, A.J., and Twist, P. "Sampling Nursing Time Pinpoints Staffing Needs." *Nursing and Health Care* 8, no. 4 (1987): 233–37.
14. Unger, J. "Building a Classification System that Works." *The Journal of Nursing Administration* 15, nos. 7,8 (1985): 18–24.
15. Adams, R., and Johnson, B. "Acuity and Staffing Under Prospective Payment." *Journal of Nursing Administration* 16, no. 10 (1986): 21–25.
16. Rosenbaum, H.L., et al. "Costing Out Nursing Services Based on Acuity." *The Journal of Nursing Administration* 18, nos. 7,8 (1988): 10–16.
17. Poulson, E. "A Method For Training and Checking Interrater Agreement for a Patient Classification Study." *Nursing Management* 18, no. 9 (1987): 72–80.
18. Williams, M. "When You Don't Develop Your Own: Validation Methods for Patient Classification Systems." *Nursing Management* 19, no. 3 (1988): 90–96.
19. Suen, H.K., and Ary, D. *Analyzing Quantitative Behavioral Observational Data.* Hillsdale, N.J.: Lawrence Erlbaum Associates, 1989.
20. Soeken, K.L., and Prescott, P.A. "Issues in the Use of Kappa to Estimate Reliability." *Medical Care* 24 (1986): 733–41.
21. Jackson, B.S., and Resnick, J. "Comparing Classification Systems." *Nursing Management* 13, no. 11 (1982): 13–19.
22. Vanputte, A.W., et al. "Accounting for Patient Acuity." *Nursing Management* 16, no. 10 (1985): 27–36.
23. Kinley, J., and Cronenwett, L.R. "Multiple Shift Patient Classification: Is It Necessary?" *The Journal of Nursing Administration* 17, no. 2 (1987): 22–25.
24. Nagaprasanna, B. "Patient Classification Systems: Strategies for the 1990s." *Nursing Management* 19, no. 3 (1988): 105–12.
25. Rieder, K.A., and Lensing, S.B. "Nursing Productivity: Evolution of a Systems Model." *Nursing Management* 18, no. 8 (1987): 33–44.
26. Andro, R.J., Robertson, S., and Glandon, G.L. "Financial Implications of an Acuity-based Periodic Staff Adjustment Model." *Nursing Management* 18, no. 10 (1987): 21–25.
27. Giovannetti, P. "DRGs and Nursing Workload Measures." *Computers in Nursing* 3, no. 2 (1985): 88–91.
28. Green, J., et al. *Severity of Illness and Nursing Intensity: Going Beyond DRGs.* Final report on grant #N00014–86–C–0272. Naval Medical Research and Development Command, 1987.

Perspectives on costing nursing

Marion Johnson, Ph.D., R.N.
Assistant Professor
College of Nursing
University of Iowa
Iowa City, Iowa

*T*HE CONTINUED escalation of health care costs, despite cost containment efforts, has led to increased demands for cost control, quality control, and equity on the part of third party payors, consumers, and businesses.[1] Faced with the need to contain costs, health care organizations are applying efficiency models designed for industrial production to the health care sector and replacing service-oriented operations with business-oriented approaches. In such a setting, the need to measure nursing productivity and determine the cost of nursing care is increasingly important for nurse administrators, and will remain so for the forseeable future.

Predictions about the economic future of health care indicate the health care sector will continue to experience stringent resources in relation to demand. As a result, the following are projected:

- Cost pressures will continue to be the principal driving force underlying change in the health care sector.[2]
- As cost containment pressures continue to grow, pressure will mount to develop effective methods for evaluating and ensuring the quality of care.[2]
- Shifts in payment will occur from third party payors to direct contracting, and from health insurance to integrated health plans.[3]
- Regional differences will be eliminated, and a national reimbursement rate will be instituted.[3]
- Prospective pricing will expand to all payors and all care settings.[4]
- A business-oriented approach to health care will intensify.[4]

In such an environment, it can be anticipated that health care organizations will continue to operate under a system of economic constraints and incentives similar to those found in industry. The need to determine the cost of nursing services, to price nursing services, and to determine produc-

Nurs Admin Q, 1989, 14(1), 65–71
©1989 Aspen Publishers, Inc.

tivity is imperative if nursing is to compete successfully for limited resources. In addition to supporting resource requests, determining nursing costs has potential benefits for both nursing and the organization.

THE VALUE OF DETERMINING THE COST OF NURSING

Literature on costing nursing identifies a number of ways that the profession can benefit if nursing costs are identified. Frequently mentioned is the value of identifying nursing as a revenue center rather than a cost center. Determining the cost of nursing permits a price to be placed on nursing services, and forces recognition of nursing's contribution to the organization. Knowing both the cost of nursing, and the contribution of nursing to patient care relative to other health care disciplines, can serve as a basis for decisions about pay equity among workers, an issue of increasing concern with the current and projected nurse shortage.[5,6] It also enables nurse administrators to identify areas where nursing subsidizes other occupations by providing a service for which others are reimbursed.[5] In addition, the cost of investing a nurse's time in nonnursing activities can be readily identified.[7] Although these outcomes are positive for nursing, they have potentially negative effects for other occupational groups; therefore, nurse administrators must be able to identify the value of costing nursing services for the organization.

The need to manage resources effectively suggests a number of reasons for an organization to cost and price nursing services. To manage costs, nurse administrators must know where costs are generated and how the cost of specific nursing services relates to the identified priorities of the organization and the nursing department. Only with this information can nurse administrators make informed decisions about the effective allocation of scarce resources and the productivity of the department.

As patient acuity and the intensity of nursing care have increased in acute and community settings, organizations that charge a flat rate for nursing care are in danger of losing money.[8] To obtain adequate reimbursement for nursing services as prospective pricing extends to all health care payors, organizations need to know the outcomes of nursing care relative to its cost.

COSTING AND PRICING ISSUES

Unfortunately, concurrence among nurses about the value of costing nursing services does not include agreement about how to cost and price these services. The tasks of measuring productivity and costing products are complex in a service industry, and they are more so for nurse executives because of unresolved issues related to the quantification of nursing services. However, the importance of identifying nursing costs and pricing nursing makes it imperative that problems hindering the process be identified and addressed. Given the current economic climate, now is the time to justify nursing costs and assure nursing input into future health care pricing. To do so, nursing must address a number of issues related to costing its product.

Cost accounting issues

There is an urgent need to standardize components of the costing process, the most basic being the cost accounting method used to identify and measure nursing costs. Cost accounting methods currently used in nursing, and identified in the literature, describe differences in classification and terminology as well as differences in methodology, as shown in Table 1.[9–11]

There is an urgent need to standardize components of the costing process, the most basic being the cost accounting method used to identify and measure nursing costs.

The use of a standard cost accounting method facilitates comparisons of nursing costs across institutions; this is information that will be vital if regional differences in reimbursement are eliminated. To obtain meaningful comparisons across institutions, a standardized methodology is needed to avoid cost variances related to the methodology. Barhyte and Glandon[12] found differences among nursing costs using three cost accounting methods, and Wilson and associates[13] found that methodological differences accounted for some of the variance in reported nursing costs.

The majority of reported cost studies use patient classification systems to measure patient requirements or nursing workload as the method of determining nursing costs.[11,14] The use of patient classification systems (PCSs) has several immediate advantages for costing nursing care. Foremost is the fact that they are available and pro-

vide information about nursing care requirements in the form of units of care, or hours of care, that can be translated to personnel costs. Faster start-up is possible with a known system than with a new system, and more information is available about this method than about other methodologies.

There are, however, a number of problems with the use of PCSs to cost nursing that should be considered in the development of a costing system. Of major concern is what the PCS measures. Most PCSs quantify tasks or procedures and are, at best, "only primitive measures of patient demands for nursing care time."[15(p.57)] They do not take into account either the knowledge or the time required for clinical decision making, the core activity for which a professional is paid. If nursing is an intellectual endeavor, costing methodologies must account for the application of nursing knowledge. To do otherwise is to negate the need for professional judgment and open the way for less knowledgeable care providers. Either PCSs must be designed to account for professional nursing activities or the cost of these activities must be captured in another way.

Ideally, any nursing intensity measure should consider the necessary skill level of the caregiver as well as the service provided.

Table 1. Cost accounting methods used for nursing

Hoffman[9]	Mullinix[10]	Edwardson and Giovannetti[11]
Global	Flat per diem	Per diem
DRG-based	Per patient	Per diagnosis
Patient-acuity based	Per service or intervention	Per relative intensity measure (RIM)
Procedure-based	Per provider	Per nursing workload unit (PCS)
Relative intensity measure (RIM)		

Although this problem is addressed by some PCSs, a majority do not account for skill levels. As the use of "nurse extenders" becomes more prevalent, the problem of separating the cost of professional judgment and technical skill becomes more acute. Estimating the cost of care provided by a nurse extender does not provide information about the cost of planning, monitoring, and evaluating that care.

Another concern when using a PCS for costing is the need to measure delivered care versus prescribed care. Although most patient classification systems measure prescribed care, information about delivered care can be obtained from the patient record if not from the PCS. The problem, however, is the amount of time required to obtain this information in a manual system. As computerized nursing information systems are developed, attention should be given to ways of indicating the delivery of prescribed care.

The problem of establishing and maintaining reliability and validity has been addressed in numerous articles on PCSs. A system with predictive validity is essential if the PCS is to be used for determining costs, but this information is often not available if the organization has developed or adapted its PCS. Standardizing PCSs would allow information about the reliability and validity of current systems to be obtained and shared among various settings.

In addition to standardizing the measurement of nursing care, there must be agreement on the activities included in nursing costs and how these activities are to be classified. Currently, clerical, management, and education functions are reported as both direct and indirect costs or are not addressed as a component of nursing costs. Nonproductive time and unit supplies may be included in direct or indirect costs or may constitute a separate category. To avoid these problems and facilitate the inclusion of nursing costs within the organization's accounting system, nursing should define direct and indirect costs as they are defined for accounting purposes. Direct costs are all costs that can be traced to a specific unit or activity, in this case the nursing unit or designated patient, and indirect costs are those costs that cannot be directly traced to one unit or one client.[16,17] For purposes of costing nursing, direct costs would include the cost of supplies and personnel used in the delivery of nursing care on a unit or for a particular patient. Because the allocation of supply costs is not standardized and the immediate need is to determine nursing personnel costs, supply costs and personnel costs should be separated. Indirect costs include administrative, educational, and other nursing costs that cannot be allocated to a specific unit or patient. These costs can be determined for the department and allocated to individual patients as a per diem rate or can be based on the intensity of required nursing care. Defining nursing costs in this manner makes it possible to compare nursing personnel costs in one unit or cost center with total unit costs and revenues.

Data issues

The information needed to determine nursing costs has not been identified and stored for ready access in most nursing departments. A nursing minimum data set should identify the minimum, essential information required by nursing and should include information about nursing diagnosis, nursing outcome, and intensity of nursing care—information that can be used in conjunction with workload measures and personnel costs to study relationships between cost and quality.[18]

Each department can add to the minimum data set if patient information needed for costing cannot be readily obtained, for example, the diagnosis related group (DRG) category, if costs are to be determined for DRGs. In addition, the information needed to determine costs, such as hours of care or personnel wages, should be identified and stored for use with individual or group information from patients. As computerized nursing information systems are developed, it is essential that the information needed for costing has been identified so it can be stored for easy retrieval and linked to other information systems, such as the personnel system.

Quality issues

Donabedian has argued that the issue of cost must not be separated from the issue of quality, but few studies have attempted to link quantitative measures of cost, such as hours of care, with qualitative standards or with patient outcomes.[19] In a review of costing studies, Sovie identified the lack of information about quality as one of the serious weaknesses of the studies.[14] Outcomes need to be identified and evaluated in relation to severity of illness and nursing interventions. Until outcomes, as well as cost, are identified one cannot speak of cost-effective care.

Currently, there is no system in place that can determine how effectively, in clinical and economic terms, a patient was treated during a given care episode.[20] As nursing works toward a method for costing its product, systems that measure both the cost and outcome of nursing care must be developed, and the resulting information must be used to evaluate delivered care against accepted standards of care. The issue of quality must be addressed because quality and access will remain key concerns in a capitated health care system, and health care professionals are in the best position to assure quality.

Issues in pricing

Determining costs is only one side of the equation; the other side is setting a price for nursing services. Current prices, if set at all, tend to be based on the determined cost of care for an individual patient, and allocated indirect costs and a profit are then added. This, however, fails to deal with a number of current nursing concerns. The need to adjust nursing salaries to adequately compensate nurses who provide direct patient care has been recommended as one strategy for recruiting and retaining nurses. Prices should be set at a level that will allow the necessary adjustments in wage structures. Although nursing services may remain one of the best buys in health care, the costs identified to date may be low if equitable salary structures are initiated.

Another issue that must be considered in pricing is how charges are generated for a service; for example, is the charge for a bed bath given by a registered nurse the same as the charge for a bed bath given by a nursing assistant, or should the patient be charged more if the service is provided by a more highly skilled and highly paid individual? Also, how will prices be determined in an organization that provides more than one level of care? Will the cost of nursing care vary, and, if so, will these differences reflect differences in standards and outcomes? To resolve these and other issues related to pricing, nursing will need to resolve current dilemmas concerning the functions of the professional nurse relative to nurse extenders and the functions of registered nurses who have varying educational backgrounds.

The issues presented in this article suggest a number of actions that need to be taken to realize the benefits of costing nursing services. The following recommendations are proposed as one means of addressing problems in costing nursing care and, hopefully, will generate other and better solutions.

RECOMMENDATIONS

- Nurse administrators, nurse researchers, and nurse educators need a common forum for discussion and resolution of administrative concerns. The American Organization of Nurse Executives represents the largest body of nurse administrators, and, therefore, might be the best organization to bring these groups together.
- Models that can be used to describe the relationships among nursing functions, cost, quality, and price need to be developed as a framework for further research. One model for costing nursing has appeared in the literature and can serve as a base for future development.[21]
- PCSs should be used as the current method for costing, but other methodologies, such as nursing diagnosis, should be studied, and those costs compared with those from PCSs.
- The data sets needed for costing nursing should be identified and should be based on the current minimum data set

identified by Werley and her colleagues.[18]

- A system that accounts for professional decision making needs to be developed and incorporated into cost accounting methodologies.
- Outcomes that measure the effectiveness of nursing care need to be identified and related to the cost of nursing care. This information can be used to specify relationships between levels of care, cost of care, expected outcomes for differing levels of care, and the price of nursing care.
- Prices for nursing care need to reflect adjustments in nursing salaries and differences in levels of care.

The identification of nursing costs can serve to increase professional accountability in an era focused on economic accountability. However, as one of the major providers of health care, nurses cannot use efficiency as a substitute for quality. As Donabedian noted, "health care professionals today are caught between the opposing pulls of two implacable imperatives: to maintain quality and to contain cost."[19(p.142)] The challenge for nursing is to develop measures of cost-effectiveness rather than of cost alone.

REFERENCES

1. "Who Will Fall Off Health-Care Highwire?" *Des Moines Register,* 16 April 1989, p. 1c.
2. Council on Long Range Planning and Development. *The Environment of Medicine.* Chicago: AMA, 1989.
3. Colle, R.S. *The New Hospital: Future Strategies for a Changing Industry.* Rockville, Md.: Aspen Publishers, 1986.
4. Spiegel, A.D., and Kavaler, F. *Cost Containment and DRGs: A Guide to Prospective Payment.* Owings Mills, Md.: National Health Publishing, 1986.
5. Jacox, A.K. "Determining the Cost and Value of Nursing." *Nursing Administration Quarterly* 12, no. 1 (1987): 7–12.
6. Namerow, M.J. "From Salary Measurement to Equity Measurement Through Uniform Data Reporting." *Nursing Administration Quarterly* 12, no. 1 (1987): 39–43.
7. Joel, L.A. "DRGs and RIMs: Implication for Nursing." *Nursing Outlook* 32, no. 1 (1984): 42–49.
8. Overfelt, F.C. "The Fixed-Reimbursement Perspective on Patient Care Services: An Enlight-

ened View of Nursing." In *Patients & Purse Strings II*, edited by J. Scherubel and F. Shaffer. Pub. No. 20-2191. New York: National League for Nursing, 1988, pp. 27–38.

9. Hoffman, F. *Nursing Productivity Assessment and Costing Out Nursing Services.* Philadelphia: Lippincott, 1988.

10. Mullinix, C.F. "Research on Influences Affecting Availability of Resources of Patient Care Delivery." In *Nursing Resources and the Delivery of Patient Care,* edited by National Center for Nursing Research. NIH Pub. No. 89-3008. Washington, D.C.: Government Printing Office, 1988: 11–15.

11. Edwardson, S.R., and Giovannetti, P.B. "A Review of Cost-Accounting Methods for Nursing Services." *Nursing Economics* 5, no. 3 (1987): 107–17.

12. Barhyte, D.Y., and Glandon, G.L. "Issues in Nursing Labor Costs Allocation." *Journal of Nursing Administration* 18, no. 12 (1988): 16–19.

13. Wilson, L., Prescott, P.A., and Aleksandrowicz, L. "Nursing: A Major Hospital Cost Component." *Health Sciences Research* 22, no. 6 (1988): 773–96.

14. Sovie, M.D. "Variable Costs of Nursing Care in Hospitals." In *Annual Review of Nursing Research Vol. 6,* edited by J.J. Fitzpatrick, R.L. Taunton, and J.Q. Benoliel. New York: Springer-Verlag, 1988, pp. 131–50.

15. Haas, S.A. "Patient Classifications Systems: A Self-fulfilling Prophecy." *Nursing Management* 19, no. 5 (1988): 56–62.

16. Strasen, L. *Key Business Skills for Nursing Managers.* Philadelphia: Lippincott, 1987.

17. Neumann, B.R., Suver, J.D., and Zelman, W.N. *Financial Management: Concepts and Applications for Health Care Providers.* Owings Mills, Md.: National Health Publishing, 1984.

18. Werley, H.H., Lang, N.M., and Westlake, S.K. "The Nursing Minimum Data Set Conference: Executive Summary." *Journal of Professional Nursing* 4, no. 2 (1986): 217–24.

19. Donabedian, A. "Quality, Cost, and Cost Containment." *Nursing Outlook* 32, no. 3 (1984): 142–45.

20. Barnard, C. "Revolution or Evolution in Health Cost Management." In *Patients and Purse Strings II,* edited by J. Scherubel and F. Shaffer. New York: National League for Nursing, 1988, pp. 5–11.

21. McCloskey, J.C. "Implications of Costing Out Nursing Services for Reimbursement." *Nursing Management* 20, no. 1 (1989): 44–49.

Alternative caregivers: Cost-effective utilization of R.N.s

Sandra C. Hesterly, R.N., M.S.
Associate Director
Nursing Services
Alta Bates-Herrick Hospital
Berkeley, California

Margaret Robinson, R.N., M.S.
Assistant Administrator for Patient Care
  Services
St. John's Regional Medical Center
Joplin, Missouri

ALTA BATES-HERRICK Hospital (AB-H) is a prestigious community hospital in Berkeley, California. Named as a magnet hospital by the American Nurses' Association in 1985, located in a desirable community, and able to boast salaries among the highest in the nation, AB-H had for many years been able to select new employees from numerous highly qualified candidates for its vacant positions. Temporary agency staff were used only on rare occasions and only to fill positions typically very difficult to staff, such as night positions in the intensive care unit and labor and delivery.

An erosion of this enviable status began to occur late in 1986. The use of registry personnel escalated and bed closure occurred when staffing demands could not be met. Morale of the staff plummeted to an all-time low as patient needs became more acute. The quality of care that was the hallmark of AB-H nursing was felt by many to have been compromised. Staff expressed extreme discontent with their inability to meet the instructional and comfort needs of patients due to the amount of time spent performing sophisticated treatments and therapies.

Discussions regarding possible approaches to remedy this critical situation began with the Nursing Leadership Council, a group composed of nursing administrators, nursing unit directors, and clinical specialists.

Several areas of disagreement required careful examination and consensus building. The first of these was to accept the reality that vacant positions could not be

When this article was written, Margaret Robinson was Vice President, Clinical Operations, at Alta Bates-Herrick Hospital, Berkeley, California.

Nurs Admin Q, 1990, 14(3), 18–23

filled. The returns on expenditures for recruitment simply were not there. Second, lowering qualifications for staff added additional stress to an already frustrated staff and further undermined quality of care. Finally, an overwhelming philosophic commitment to the provision of total patient care by the R.N. had to be examined. Through the process of open, honest communication, nursing leadership arrived at the consensus that the staff should be offered an opportunity to consider an alternative patient care model.

DEVELOPING AN ALTERNATIVE PATIENT CARE MODEL

The process of developing the model that would sustain the hospital into the 1990s began in October 1987. Three concurrent task forces were established. Each group was given the same goals and assumptions but had flexibility in developing alternatives that would best meet the needs of their unit. All three groups developed a similar conceptual model, which introduced a nonlicensed caregiver to assist the R.N. in providing patient care. The job title of patient care assistant (PCA) was chosen to provide clear identity to the role.

The groups first reviewed a variety of patient care delivery models including functional nursing, team nursing, primary nursing, total patient care, and case management. This review helped identify current methods of practice, provided an opportunity to clarify important elements of practice for nurses at AB-H, and gave the groups the same opportunity to build consensus that the nursing leaders were afforded. The groups were assured that they would receive full administrative support for continuing to provide any aspect of care that they believed must be performed by the R.N. Nurse managers requested several items:

- The resultant model had to be easy to administer in day-to-day operations.
- Clarity of role definitions and expectations was mandatory.
- The model had to support the existing collaborative approach between physicians and R.N.s to care planning.
- The R.N. was to remain the overseer for coordination and delivery of all aspects of nursing care.
- A model that would ensure that the comfort needs of patients were met was highly desirable.

DEFINING THE ROLE

The staff nurses on the task forces were asked to identify tasks they were willing to give up. Items identified fell into two major groups, nonnursing functions and selected nursing functions. The nonnursing functions comprised two categories, general unit operations and transportation of people and things (see Box entitled "Tasks that R.N.s Would Give Up"). Once these items were identified, the groups acknowledged that the items that R.N.s were willing to give up were ones that could be performed by a nonlicensed practitioner. The three groups then began to collaborate on defining the new caregiver's role.

It became clear during discussions that many of the duties and responsibilities of the PCA would be similar to those of the "nurse's aide" in a team model. However, it was important to create a new image for this level of caregiver, since the image that existed was that of a minimally competent individual with little motivation. The new image was created by the development of stringent qualifications that included performance standards, a training program, and either prior certification by the state in its 150-hour course for certified nurse attendants or completion of the first semester/ quarter of an R.N. program.

introductory period of employment (90 days) and annually thereafter on the basis of these standards. Emphasis is placed on criteria for which development is needed (see Appendix).

TRAINING PROGRAM

The training program was designed to prepare the patient care assistant to function as a member of the nursing care team. Classroom sessions are devoted to reviewing expectations and to providing an opportunity to ensure competency prior to clinical placement. Adjunct clinical activities provide the PCA with a preceptor who reinforces expectations, provides an opportunity to practice skills under supervision, and begins to integrate the PCA into the unit team.

Formal instructional content is presented by lecture, audio-visual material, and demonstration. Return demonstrations of selected skills are conducted to validate competencies. A learner manual was prepared that includes articles and handouts that are required readings for all participants. The training program is divided into modules that emphasize the key components of the role (see Box entitled "Key Components of Patient Care Assistant Training Program"). All disease-oriented topics emphasize the importance of observations within the disease category and provide guidelines of what is critical to report to the R.N.s. Content is presented by nursing administrators and clinical nurse specialists.

In the task force discussions, it had become clear that R.N.s who practiced in a total patient care model were not prepared to direct the activity of others. Therefore, training was provided to all R.N.s on the units that were to be incorporating patient care assistants into the nursing care delivery team. This training included a formal

---

Tasks that R.N.s Would Give Up

Nonnursing functions
Transportation
  Trips to pharmacy
  Trips to central supply
  Moving furniture
  Moving patients
  Delivering water pitchers, dietary
    trays
Unit operations
  Cleaning utility room
  Stocking supply carts
  "Stuffing" charts
  Answering telephone
  Nursing functions
    Selected aspects of patient care
  Routine vital signs
  Ambulating patients
  Bed baths
  Morning care
  Bedtime care
  Assisting patient to bathroom
  Turning patients
  Feeding patients
  Oral hygiene
  Answering call lights

The performance standards reflect hospitalwide nursing expectations for practice. Each standard has performance criteria for outcomes that are observable and measurable. Performance appraisal of the PCA is conducted at the completion of the

Stringent qualifications for the patient care assistant included performance standards, a training program, and either prior certification by the state or completion of the first semester/ quarter of an R.N. program.

Key Components of Patient Care Assistant Training Program

Being a team member
Safety needs of the patient
Infection control
Positioning and transfers
The elderly patient
The stroke patient
The hypertensive patient
The diabetic patient
Meeting nutritional needs
Skin care
Bowel and bladder care

presentation of the PCA role and how it was to be incorporated on their unit. Skills training on delegation and other leadership skills was provided to give the R.N. tools that would enhance communication and listening skills, that would help subordinates solve their problems, and that would pro-vide a process for monitoring and providing feedback to subordinates.

COST ANALYSIS

A cost analysis was done to determine the cost-effectiveness of this role. The patient care assistant represents a $20 per hour savings over the use of outside R.N. agency salaries. This represents an annual savings of $32,000 for each full-time PCA. Conservative estimates project a savings of $1.3 million during the first year of the project.

• • •

The first patient care assistant training program was held in March 1988. Eighteen employees successfully completed this initial program. They have been fully integrated into the unit operations. Informal feedback suggests that this caregiver can be a cost-effective and valuable member of the patient care team who is accepted by nurses and physicians.

Appendix
Patient care assistant performance standards

Standard I

All nursing personnel are responsible for carrying out the patient's plan of care as it relates to the patient's physical needs. The assistant does the following:

A. Takes vital signs and reports changes from established baselines.

B. Following consultation with R.N., contributes to plan of care based on interaction with patient or family.

C. Makes appropriate decisions that reflect both knowledge of facts and good judgment and reports actions to R.N.

D. Demonstrates knowledge and accuracy in nursing procedures while following established policies and procedures.

E. Initiates and plans for provision of patient comfort and hygiene measures.

F. Actively keeps informed of the ongoing patient database and applies it appropriately.

G. Recognizes symptoms of cardiac or respiratory distress and shock and initiates emergency action.

H. Demonstrates knowledge of and adherence to infection control and isolation policies and procedures.

I. Completes appropriate documents in the medical record concisely and legibly.

J. Provides shift reports to the R.N. that are concise and specific with pertinent observations and occurrences.

Standard II

All nursing personnel are responsible for carrying out the patient's plan of care as it relates to the patient's emotional and instructional needs. The assistant does the following:

A. Reports observations to assist in the evaluation of the patient's movement toward optimum health as evidenced by
  - patient's ability to deal with his or her problem,
  - patient participation in self-care activities, and
  - patient achievement of optimum level of activity or dying trajectory.

B. Maintains patient confidentiality.

C. Participates in patient/family teaching follow-up as delegated by R.N.

D. Demonstrates adherence to principles of body mechanics and uses mechanical lifting devices appropriately.

Standard III

All nursing personnel are responsible for minimizing cost through early discharge planning, safe and efficient use of supplies, and appropriate utilization of other hospital services. The assistant does the following:

A. Seeks assistance from appropriate resources to aid in delivering care.

B. Maintains state of current knowledge regarding nursing policies and procedures.

C. Participates in staff meetings and uses problem-solving approach effectively for dealing with unit concerns.

D. Participates in educational inservices as indicated.

E. Assists with orientation of new personnel.

F. Reads bulletins and implements appropriately supporting hospital policies.

G. Adheres to dress code.

H. Maintains an appropriate attendance record:
   - Arrives at work and returns from breaks on time,
   - Remains in appropriate work areas for duration of shift,
   - Endeavors to remain healthy and use sick leave appropriately, and
   - Follows guidelines on use of overtime.

Standard IV

All nursing personnel are responsible for fostering a cooperative work environment. The assistant does the following:

A. Initiates problem-solving process with appropriate follow-up.

B. Recognizes limitations and asks for assistance when needed.

C. Displays honesty, congeniality, and mutual respect when communicating with other departments.

D. Conducts self in a helpful manner.

E. Gives and accepts constructive criticism in a positive manner and in the proper setting.

F. Channels suggestions and criticisms to appropriate persons.

G. Completes tasks as assigned.

H. Uses time appropriately:
   - Organizes work to account for work load, priorities, and emergencies;
   - Works in an orderly and systematic manner;
   - Asks for assistance when necessary and offers to assist co-workers willingly;
   - Spends free time with patients or in another constructive manner; and
   - Recognizes needs and voluntarily initiates appropriate action in regard to environment.

Adapted with permission from Alta Bates-Herrick Hospital, Berkeley, California, 1990.

Part I
Study and discussion questions

1. Describe the basic financial responsibilities assumed by the nurse manager and the nurse executive.
2. Discuss the value of patient classification systems in the monitoring of clinical resource allocation and in the maintenance of fiscal credibility.
3. Develop a ten point plan to communicate and support budgetary decisions with your patient care staff.
4. Review the major issues related to the costing of nursing services and describe the value of knowing costs in developing a competitively priced delivery system.
5. Using a current unit personnel budget (or build a hypothetical budget), create financial scenarios for labor costs ranging from 100% RN staff to a 50% staff. (Analyze costs for each 5% change/reduction.)

Part II
Nursing human resource management

Patricia O'Connor, R.N., M.B.A., Ph.D., C.N.A.A.
Executive Director of Nursing
Duke University Medical Center
Durham, North Carolina

Nurses are about as sophisticated as "human resources" can become. Managing nurses calls for some special considerations because of who we are and how our life and work experiences can interact.

Emphasis here should be on the human part. It is our very humanity that makes it possible for us to care for others; we have human needs and responses that need attention if we are to sustain our caring for others. Our service to others can have personal costs. Astute managers recognize and support the human dimensions of nurses' experience. Dealing with our needs and feelings is essential for professional growth and our ability to care for others. Otherwise, we can end up supporting ineffective coping within nursing practice. Managing depression and emotional impairment in nurses and the implications for nurse managers are just two of the subjects discussed in the following articles.

While this human support usually occurs at the first line level between the practice nurse, peers, and the manager, nursing administrators are responsible for evaluating and developing organizational systems so that it can happen. This means developing managers to support staff and developing supporting programs. Ultimately, this is an investment in our professional vitality and in our future that we cannot afford to forego.

Depression in hospital nurses: Implications for nurse managers

Gwen Marram van Servellen, R.N., Ph.D.
Associate Professor, School of Nursing
UCLA
Los Angeles, California

Elizabeth A. Soccorso, R.N., M.N.
Instructor, Psychiatric Nursing and
*   Nursing Research*
Department of Nursing
Mt. St. Mary's College
Los Angeles, California

Karen Palermo, R.N., M.N.
Mental Health Counselor
Department of Mental Health
Los Angeles County, California

Kathleen Faude, R.N., M.N.
Administrative Nurse I
Neuropsychiatric Institute
UCLA
Los Angeles, California

"STRESSED" AND "burned out" have become popular phrases describing the fate of staff nurses in the hospital setting. Recently the phenomenon of burnout has been observed in nurse managers and the faculties of nursing schools.

By implication, it would seem that no single group of nurse professionals is insulated from the prospects of burnout; yet, very little is known about the phenomenon. It has been defined as the failure to effectively cope with the difficulties and anxieties of the work setting. Symptoms associated with burnout are fatigue, irritability, distancing, denial, recourse to drugs and alcohol, and eventually termination of employment.[1] Many of the symptoms attributed to burnout are also symptoms of the affective disorder, depression.

While selected studies have addressed stress and burnout in nurses,[2-7] no studies have focused on depression as an underlying condition in hospital nurses. Most noteworthy is the fact that no studies to date have focused upon the phenomenon of depression exclusively, in an attempt to assess the severity and the nature of this condition in nurses. Is syndromic depression, that is to say, affective illness, a condition found in

Nurs Admin Q, 1985, 9(3), 74–84

hospital nurses? And, if so, does the prevalence in nurses suggest that nurses are a group vulnerable to affective illness?

Questions such as these prompted an investigation of the incidence of depressive symptomatology and depressive illness in hospital nurses. The findings of the study provide specific implications for nurse administrators in designing effective employee health care programs. Nurse administrators must assess the relative importance of specific programs in assisting staff with the full range of depressive experience, beginning with subsyndromal episodes of depression, for example, those observed in cases of burnout and culminating in episodes of major depressive disorder.

DEPRESSION: PREVALENCE AND INCIDENCE

Depression manifests itself in a variety of biological, psychosocial and behavioral symptoms. The central symptoms of depression differentiating it from all other emotional disorders are the preponderance of sadness, pessimism and self-dislike, with a loss of energy, motivation and concentration.[8] Arieti and Bemporad defined depression as an affective disorder that spans a continuum from mild depressive moods to major depressive illness.[9]

Affective illness, and particularly depression, are considered the most prevalent major mental illnesses and the leading cause of psychiatric hospital admissions in the United States.[10] It has been estimated that one out of four individuals will experience at least one significant depressive episode in his or her lifetime.[11]

A higher incidence of depression disorders in women has been substantiated by several researchers. Weissman and Klerman established the difference as a 2:1 female-to-male ratio; that is, women are twice as likely as

men to evidence depressive symptomatology.[12] Craig and van Natta's study[13] indicated that, although women are more likely to report transient symptoms of depression, both sexes are equally likely to report evidence of syndromic depression.

The epidemiological studies cited here consistently point to a concern that women are particularly vulnerable to depression. Although other demographic variables such as education, age, socioeconomic and marital status may play a part in individuals seeking treatment, sex differences as a discriminating factor still remain an important concern.

Theories explaining the high incidence of depression in women have relied on both sex-role explanations and biological predispositions. That is, either the socialization of women in our society or a biochemical vulnerability, or both, may be associated with evidence of higher rates of depressive symptomatology in women.

Researchers are not, however, in agreement that syndromic or illness-related depressions can be grouped with subsyndromic depressive episodes. It is possible that two different theoretical explanations are valid; one for subsyndromic depression and another for depressive illness. The issue of whether depressive symptomatology eventually leads to full-blown depressive illness (the continuum theory) still must be decided. It has been documented that persons who exhibit depressive symptomatology are more likely to have a depressive illness in their lifetimes.

PROFESSIONAL VULNERABILITY

Studies of the prevalence of depression in health care professionals suggest that women health care providers are vulnerable to depressive illness. In a study of professional women, Welner and associates, using an expert-administered diagnostic interview, found that 51 percent of the physicians and 32 percent of the Ph.D.s in a community sample had a primary affective disorder.[14(p.169)] The researchers tested several factors that they felt were important in understanding the high incidence of depression among these professionals. More than 50 percent of the women reported gender prejudice in training and employment, and depressed subjects reported this more often than nondepressed. Women with children were found to have significantly more career disruption compared to those with no children. And in 80 percent of the depressed female professionals, career disruption occurred at the time of the depressive episode. In support of a genetic contribution, it was reported that a significantly higher number of first-degree family members had a history of affective disorder among the depressed group.

Studies of physicians in particular have raised the issue of specific vulnerability for depressive illness.

In a review of American Medical Association records of physician deaths from 1965 to 1967, women physicians had a significantly higher rate of suicide-related deaths.[15] This analysis showed that 17 (5.7 percent) of the 297 consecutive deaths of women physicians were suicides. A similar study conducted for the period 1967–1972 revealed a slight increase in suicide as the cause of death in 49 (6.5 percent) of 751 consecutive deaths of women physicians.[16] These findings indicate a suicide rate for women over age 25 in the general (U.S.) population. It is also approximately twice the rate for divorced women over age 70—that group of women exhibiting the highest known suicide rate.

In a study of suicide among physicians in the United States over a 5½-year period (March 1965 to August 1970), Steppacher and Mausner concluded that women physi-

cians have a higher suicide rate than their male peers.[17] Reviewing the obituary listings in the *Journal of the American Medical Association,* they attributed suicide or possible suicidal death to 530 deaths. The rate for male physicians was 1.15 times that for males in the general population. However, the calculated rate for women physicians was 3 times the estimated rate for females in the United States. High rates of suicide were correlated with the high rate of primary affective disorders attributable to these professionals. Although these researchers did not offer specific explanations of the high rate of both suicide and affective disorders in female physicians, some inference was made about the self-selection for professional careers of women with affective disorders. That is, depressed women could be attracted to work oriented to the relief of pain and suffering of others.

DEPRESSION IN NURSES

Although numerous studies have focused on the incidence and prevalence of affective disorders in physicians, and particularly female physicians, little focus has been aimed at the analysis of these emotional problems in nurses. Nursing, a predominantly female occupation, would seem to have its fair share of affective illness. It is possible that this group of health care professionals—primarily female and wishing to help others—especially when confronted with frustrations in achieving these goals, would exhibit high levels of depression.

Currently the primary nursing literature addressing the profession's emotional problems cites the incidence of burnout. Burnout has been said to be a serious problem contributing to high turnover rates, absenteeism, accidents, overutilization of sick leave, and general deteriorating quality of nursing practice. Burnout is defined as a syndrome of physical and emotional exhaustion involving the development of a negative self-concept, negative job attitude, and loss of concern and feelings for clients.[18] In addition to these symptoms, feelings of helplessness, hopelessness and a lack of enthusiasm about work and even about life have been reported by individuals suffering from burnout. Burnout is said to be insidious in nature, striking those whose career profiles were once idealistic and enthusiastic—the opposite of the negative, apathetic, sometimes agitated, burned-out nurse.

Burnout has been attributed to nurses' failure to effectively cope with the stressors of the hospital environment. In a cross-cultural study of burnout, Pines, Kafry and Etizion found that American nurses reported significantly more burnout than Israelis.[19] The researchers attributed this variance to different coping styles, charging that American nurses' coping patterns were more inactive and indirect. American nurses were said to internalize blame for personal failure whereas Israelis were more likely to externalize blame for personal failure and were also observed to have a stronger supportive family network than American nurses.

Burnout has also been attributed to the type of role and the numbers (and kinds) of stressors that play a part in the work environment. For example, direct care givers are believed to be more likely candidates, suggesting that the bedside staff nurse is most vulnerable to burnout. Research has also shown that burned-out staff nurses often seek administrative positions to escape this fate.[20]

High rates of burnout have also been attributed to intensive care nursing[21] and emergency department[22] nursing. High stress, constant anxiety, costly mistakes and the threat of object loss triggered by exposure to the critically ill are pervasive in

> *Burnout is said to be insidious in nature, striking those whose career profiles were once idealistic and enthusiastic—the opposite of the negative, apathetic, sometimes agitated, burned-out nurse.*

the intensive care unit (ICU) and are said to relate to high levels of stress-related depression.

An important study examining the incidence of depression and other psychological phenomena in intensive care nursing found significant differences between ICU and non-ICU nursing. Gentry, Foster and Froehling administered the Zung Depression Scale, the Tennessee Self Concept Scale, the Buss-Durkee Hostility Inventory and the Minnesota Multiphasic Personality Inventory to a group of ICU and non-ICU nurses.[23] ICU nurses reported significantly more depression, hostility and anxiety than was evident in the non-ICU nurse. The groups did not differ significantly with respect to basic demographic variables (age, marital status, longevity on the unit or total years of nursing experience). Consequently, the researchers attributed the differences to situational and work stressors (i.e., overwhelming workload, too much responsibility, poor communication between nurses and physicians, limited work space, too little continuing education) and not to specific personality features of the nurses.

CONCEPTUAL FRAMEWORK OF THE STUDY

Depression manifests itself in a variety of biological, psychological, behavioral and social symptoms. Although recognized for over 2,000 years, numerous aspects of the condition remain unclear. The term "depression" may designate reactions varying from a single episode of depressed mood to a symptom complex to a well-defined disease entity.[24] Yet to be determined is whether depression is a continuum of increasing severity, or rather a unique disease process in which episodic subsyndromal symptoms are clearly different in origin from syndromic depression. While theorists continue to argue whether depressions are of biochemical or of psychological causation, current theorists are not likely to dismiss any or all explanations. Akiskal and McKinney indicate that depression, in proportions to be designated "illness," is more likely than not the outcome of a complex interaction of multiple phenomena.[25]

Based upon this understanding of depression and a review of the literature by the authors of this article, the following framework and assumptions guided this study:

1. Depression is a term used to describe both subclinical episodes of depressed mood as well as affective illnesses.
2. Subclinical depression may be a precursor of affective illness; persons experiencing depressive symptomatology in their lifetimes are prone to depressive illness.
3. Nurses, as females who frequently choose nursing to relieve the pain and suffering of others, may have a premorbid predisposition to depression.
4. Once situated in an environment conducive to high levels of work stress, this assumed predisposition may result in more severe levels of depressive illness diagnosable as clinical depressive syndromes.
5. Whereas burnout may be a phenomenon describing the presence of stress-related depression in hospital nursing, it does not sufficiently explain the presence of all depressive episodes.

6. The role of the nurse administrator in projecting adequate employee health programs encompasses recognizing and planning for the full range of depressive problems that can arise in nursing staff.

STUDY DESIGN

This exploratory (descriptive) study measured the incidence of depression (subclinical and clinical) in a sample of hospital staff nurses. A convenience sample of 64 registered nurses (RNs) was selected from a sample of three hospital settings in a metropolitan area in southern California. The hospitals were general medical-surgical hospitals varying in size: 151 beds, 347 beds, and 412 beds. All three hospitals were JCAH (Joint Commission on the Accreditation of Hospitals) accredited and members of the American Hospital Association. Registered nurses with a minimum of three months of hospital nursing experience were sought. Nurses were self-selected in that all those who attended a workshop on "Communicating with Patients and Their Families" were included in the study.

Six standardized survey instruments and an expert-administered diagnostic interview for depression were used. The instruments measuring depression included: (1) the Center for Epidemiological Studies—Depression (CES-D) Scale,[26] (2) the Diagnostic Interview Schedule (DIS)[27] based upon the DSM III diagnostic categories for depression (National Institute of Mental Health) and (3) the Symptom Check List—90 Revised (SCL-90R).[28] All 3 research instruments have undergone extensive testing for reliability and validity. Additionally, the researchers administering the Diagnostic Interview Schedule underwent extensive preliminary training. Interrater reliability was established using an experienced researcher; 95 percent agreement in several trials was sufficient to establish reliability. The entire survey packet was also presented with a sample of eight RNs, in which clarity of directions and format was sought.

Research questions

The following research questions guided the analysis of the survey data:

1. What is the incidence of depressive illness in this sample of hospital nurses?
2. What type of depressive illness is more prevalent in the sample?
3. What are the critical symptoms most frequently exhibited by these nurses?
4. What is the incidence of current depressive phenomena of the subclinical variety?
5. How do these rates of depressive illness and current depressive features compare with community samples using the same research instruments?

Findings

Results from each survey instrument were examined separately and are displayed in Table 1.

Sample characteristics from the demographic data sheet revealed the following statistics. The mean age of the sample was 38.8 with 51 percent of the sample falling below age 39; 61 percent had less than 5 years of work experience and reported their longest time employed by any one hospital was under 5 years (mean = 3.14 years). Forty-one percent of the nurses reported having an associate degree; 31 percent, a diploma, and 28 percent, a B.S. degree in nursing. Most worked full time (87 percent) on either days (55 percent) or evenings (34 percent); 36 percent worked in either medical or surgical nursing or both. Only 2 were

employed in oncology and 12 in intensive care nursing.

Results of the Diagnostic Interview Schedule indicated that 77 percent (49) of these nurses exhibited either symptomatic or syndromic depression (current or history of). Only 23 percent (15) were both syndrome- and symptom-free. Of the group with symptoms, 18 met the criteria for major depressive disorder and 1 met the criteria for dysthymic personality representing 30 percent of that group. This rate of illness-related depression is significantly below that for the normal population [Z of 12.8 ($p <$ .001)] where 11.8 percent of a female community sample was tested for dysthymic or major depressive disorder. Results of the CES-D measuring current depressive symptomatology (within the last week) indicated that only 14 percent (9) scored above 16, the cut-off score used to designate currently depressed persons. The mean CES-D score for the nurse sample was 9.9 (standard deviation [S.D.] = 7.5). Lastly, results of the SCL-90R, depression subscale, indicated that the sample's mean score was .56 (S.D. = .46), compared to that of normals, .36 (S.D. = .44), $p < .0005$.

In summary, the incidence of clinical depression (syndromic depression) in the sample was significantly higher than that found in females in the population at large. Major depressive illness was more prevalent than dysthymic disorder. While these nurses could not be deemed currently depressed (CES-D), their rate of depressive symptomatology was greater than that for the female population in general (SCL-90R).

An additional 47 percent of these nurses exhibited depressive symptomatology currently or at some point in their lifetimes. The 5 critical or most frequently exhibited symptoms are displayed in Table 2. Thoughts of committing suicide ranked sixth (23 or 36 percent) and wanting to die was evidenced

Table 1. Incidence of depression in sample—DIS and CES-D

Factor: Depression		Frequency	Percent
I. DIS (DSM III)			
a. Syndromic		19	30
b. Symptomatic		30	47
c. Neither syndromic nor symptomatic		15	23
Totals	N	64	100
II. CES-D			
a. Above 16		9	14
b. Below 16		55	86
Totals	N	64	100
CES-D Mean 9.85; Standard deviation = 7.54			
III. SCL-90 (Depression subscale)			
Mean score, sample .56		Mean score, normals .36	
Standard deviation .46		Standard deviation .44	

in a little over a quarter of the sample (17 or 27 percent).

Considerations

There is reason to assume that staff nurses may suffer higher rates of affective disorders in proportion to the female population at large. As revealed in this study, the rate was indeed significantly higher in these nurses. Female physicians have been found to exhibit higher rates of affective illness compared to females in general and compared to their professional male peers. It would appear that staff nurses are similar, although it is too early to suggest that the

Table 2. Most frequently expressed symptoms (currently or history of)

Depressive Symptoms (DIS)	RN sample (n = 64)	
	Frequency	Percent
1. Continually tired	43	67
2. Trouble sleeping	42	66
3. Thoughts about death	40	63
4. Depressed mood (2 weeks or more)	36	56
5. Trouble concentrating	35	55

reasons are the same. The prevalence of affective disorders among physicians has been related to a self-selection process. That is, medicine, and possibly nursing, may attract individuals with higher rates of affective disorders, those interested in relieving the pain and suffering in others. This study also suggests a need to clarify the manifestation of burnout. Many of the most frequently reported symptoms in the sample have also been related to burnout. Symptoms of trouble sleeping, continually tired, trouble concentrating, and depressed mood would seem to correlate with the general malaise, emotional, physical and psychological fatigue, feelings of helplessness, hopelessness and detached concern and withdrawal described as burnout by Pines and Maslach.[29] Certainly, there is a need to differentiate burnout from what is clinical depression, or for that matter, subsyndromic depressive illness. Is what has been described and measured by untrained mental health care professionals really depressive illness or symptoms of a subclinical expression of the illness? And is the depressive symptomatology such as revealed in this study really a manifestation of burnout?

RECOMMENDATIONS

Obviously, there are many recommendations for research that can be made. Most specifically, additional studies to measure the incidence and prevalence of depression in nurses is a high priority. Of great importance is the need to distinguish evidence of burnout from depressive illness. Longitudinal studies that show the incidence of illness that arises over time in a symptomatic group

Medicine, and possibly nursing, may attract individuals with higher rates of affective disorders, those interested in relieving the pain and suffering in others.

of nurses and depict the influence of personal stress, work stress and coping would be extremely valuable.

Nurse administrators must be aware of the tendency of staff to evidence symptoms and syndromes. Most importantly, they must recognize that attempts such as staff support groups, while believed important in preventing and relieving burnout, will not be enough for the nurse with a full-blown depressive illness. Rather, psychotherapy and, in some cases, medication will be needed for these nurses. Those organizing a broad-range employee health care program must consider both peer support groups for potentially burned out nurses and also psychological services that assess for referral and treatment nurses who report major depressive disorders. An example of such a program at Northwestern Memorial Hospital in Chicago was described in the spring issue of *Nursing Administrative Quarterly* by Fleming and Van Cura.[30]

In an era where stress and burnout are receiving a great deal of attention, one would assume that the troubled nurse is getting more recognition and more support. Still, it would be disastrous to assume that all nurses are manifesting a single phenomenon—burnout—and one that is poorly defined at that. Careful consideration of what staff are manifesting, in what proportions, is very important. Staff, as well, must be helped to understand the different types of problems, lest they minimize (or exaggerate) their experiences of depressive symptomatology.

REFERENCES

1. Pines, A., and Maslach, C. "Characteristics of Staff Burnout in Mental Health Settings." *Hospital Community Psychiatry* 29, no. 4 (1978):233.
2. Olsen, M. "OR Nurses' Perception of Stress." In *Burnout in the Nursing Profession,* Edited by E. McConnell. St. Louis: Mosby, 1982.
3. Kanner, A.D., Kafry, D., and Pines, A. "Conspicuous in Its Absence: The Lack of Positive Conditions as a Source of Stress." In *Burnout in the Nursing Profession,* edited by E. McConnell. St. Louis: Mosby, 1982.
4. Pines and Maslach, "Characteristics of Staff Burnout."
5. Conselvo, C.A. "Nursing Turnover in the Newborn Intensive Care Unit." In *Burnout in the Nursing Profession,* edited by E. McConnell. St. Louis: Mosby, 1982.
6. Jacobson, S.P. "Stressful Situation for Neonatal Intensive Care Nurses." In *Burnout in the Nursing Profession,* edited by E. McConnell. St. Louis: Mosby, 1982.
7. Oskins, S.L. "Identification of Situational Stressors and Coping Methods by Intensive Care Unit Nurses." *Heart and Lung* 8, no. 5 (1979): 953–60.
8. Mendals, J. *Concepts of Depression.* New York: Wiley, 1970.
9. Arieti, S., and Bemporad, J. *Severe and Mild Depression.* New York: Basic Books, 1978.
10. Teuting, P., Koslow, S., and Hirshfield, R. *Special Report on Depression Research.* Rockville, Md.: The National Institute of Mental Health, 1981.
11. American Psychiatric Society, Task Force on Nomenclature and Statistics, 1980.
12. Weissman, M., and Klerman, G. "Sex Differences and the Epidemiology of Depression." *Archives of General Psychiatry* 34 (1977): 98–111.
13. Craig, T., and van Natta, P. "Influence of Demographic Characteristics on Two Measures of Depressive Symptoms." *Archives of General Psychiatry* 36, no. 2 (1979): 149–54.
14. Welner, A., et al. "Psychiatric Disorders among Professional Women." *Archives of General Psychiatry* 36, no. 2 (1979): 169–74.
15. Craig, A.G., and Pitts, F.N. "Suicide by Physicians." *Diseases of Nervous System* 29 (1968): 763–72.
16. Pitts, F., et al. "Suicide among U.S. Women Physicians," 1967–1972. *American Journal of Psychiatry* 136, no. 5 (1979): 694–96.
17. Steppacher, R.C., and Mausner, J.S. "Suicide in Male and Female Physicians." *Journal of American Medical Association* 228 (1976): 323–28.
18. Pines and Maslach, "Characteristics of Staff Burnout."
19. Pines, A., Kafry, D., and Etizion, D. "Job Stress from a Cross-Cultural Perspective." In *Burnout in the Helping Professions,* edited by K. Reid. Kalamazoo, Mich.: West Michigan University Press, 1980.
20. Maslach, C. "The Burnout Syndrome and Patient Care." In *Stress and Survival: The Emotional Realities of Life-Threatening Illness,* edited by G.A. Garfield. St. Louis: Mosby, 1979.
21. Godfrey, M.A. "Job Satisfaction—Or Should That Be Dissatisfaction?" *Nursing '78* 8 (1978): 89–102.
22. Mytych, K.M. "Burnout in the E.D. Nurse." *Journal of Emergency Nursing* 25 (1981): 265–68.
23. Gentry, W., Foster, S., and Froehling, S. "Psychologic Response to Situational Stress in Intensive and Nonintensive Nursing." In *Burnout in the Nursing Profession,* edited by E. McConnell. St. Louis: Mosby, 1982, pp. 262–66.
24. Usdin, G. (ed.) *Depression: Clinical Biological and Psychological Perspectives.* New York: Brunner/Mazel, 1977.
25. Akiskal, H.S., and McKinney, W.T. "Overview of Recent Research in Depression." *Archives of General Psychiatry* 32 (1975): 285–305.
26. Radkoff, L. "The CES-D Scale: A Self-Report Depression Scale for Research in the General

Population." *Applied Psychological Measurement* 1, no. 4 (1977): 385–401.

27. Robins, L., et al. "National Institute of Mental Health, Diagnostic Interview Schedules, Its History, Characteristics and Validity." *Archives of General Psychiatry* 38, no. 4 (1981): 381–89.

28. Derogatis, L., Lipman, R., and Covi, L. "The SCL-90: An Outpatient Psychiatric Rating Scale—Preliminary Report." *Psychopharmacology* 9, no. 1 (1973): 13–27.

29. Pines and Maslach, "Characteristics of Staff Burnout."

30. Fleming, M., and Van Cura, B.J. "Producing a Resource Booklet for Stress Management," *Nursing Administration Quarterly* 8, no. 3 (1984): 71–82.

Managing impaired nurses

Patricia O'Connor, R.N., M.S.N., M.B.A.
Associate Administrator
University of Cincinnati Hospital
Assistant Professor
College of Nursing and Health
University of Cincinnati

Rhonda Seawright Robinson, R.N., M.S.N.
Clinical Nurse Specialist
Employee Assistance Program
University of Cincinnati Hospital
Cincinnati, Ohio

JANE D., THE EVENING charge nurse, was arrested yesterday for prescription forgery. When the supervisor accompanied the police to the arrest, she saw, for the first time, an obviously impaired and physically wrecked person. Today the supervisor and the unit's staff are in shock. They do not know how they could have missed what was going on, but they now realize they have been contributing to and glossing over problems on the unit.

Mary S., the supervisor of the medical units, is at her wit's end about 9 East, her most dysfunctional unit. The unit staff obviously do not communicate well. Some staff members provide deficient nursing care, yet others are very protective and make excuses for them. The head nurse identifies with the staff and responds to their expectations of her; she finds it difficult to manage the unit. Morale and attendance problems are obvious.

An estimated 40,000 to 75,000 chemically impaired nurses are in the work force.[1] According to Zahourek, approximately 5 percent of the 1.5 million registered nurses in this country are dependent on alcohol and other drugs.[2] Ten to 12 percent of the entire work force have serious personal problems—over half of which are related to alcohol or other mood-altering chemicals. Thus nursing administrators have no alternative but to manage this pervasive issue.

The cost of employee chemical dependency are staggering. An employee who earns $18,000 per year can cost an institution $50,000 to $75,000 per year in decreased job efficiency, through sick leave abuse, unnecessary overtime, overuse of

Nurs Admin Q, 1985, 9(2), 1–9
©1985 Aspen Publishers, Inc.

health insurance claims, possible workers' compensation claims resulting from injuries on the job, and retraining and payment of replacement personnel.[3] It is impossible to place a cost on the human suffering of the impaired professionals and their families, friends, coworkers, and patients, whose emotional needs are neglected. Fortunately, however, this destructive cycle can be reversed.

The problem of impaired nurses can be approached at several levels. First, nursing management must identify troubled employees and work groups. Second, nurse managers can follow structured approaches to confront and manage impaired nurses, motivating them to seek help, usually through progressive discipline. Finally, nursing administrators can structure management approaches, treatment options, and employee program alternatives designed to rehabilitate and manage impaired nurses.

WORK GROUP DIAGNOSIS

The impaired nurse affects many other people. This nurse disrupts and manipulates family, social and professional interaction systems to support continuing addictive behavior. Codependency symptoms are evident in families, friends and coworkers until the problem is confronted and the relationships that enable the impaired behavior are changed.

In most units with an impaired nurse, staff group dynamics evolve into an enabling pattern. An "enabler" (often unknowingly) allows the chemically dependent individual to continue inappropriate, nonproductive and detrimental behaviors.[4] This happens quite easily, since many nurses have not been taught to recognize or handle alcoholism and addiction, even in their patients. Few have learned how to initiate positive confrontation with colleagues. Because of our culture of nurturance and caring, when nurses consider confrontation, it evokes feelings of guilt.

Staff often excuse the impaired nurse from full responsibility simply by failing to deal with inappropriate behavior, and thereby sanctioning it. The impaired nurse is exempted from constructive criticism; gossip, grumbling and criticism are instead passed on to others. Some staff take on additional duties to cover for the impaired colleague. Thus the nurse is prevented from facing the situation and improving his or her performance. Through identification, denial or reaction formation, the staff manage to contain and enable the impaired nurse's inappropriate behavior.

Eventually, the enabling staff feel responsible or even guilty themselves. They may respond to a supervisor's confrontation of the problem by rushing to the defense of the impaired nurse—providing excuses for his or her behavior or reinforcing the idea that the nurse is being picked on. The staff also may fear what will happen when an impaired colleague is caught. Their fantasy (alas, sometimes it happens) is that the nurse will be arrested on the unit, hauled off in handcuffs, publicly embarrassed in the media, sent to jail and prevented forever from working as a nurse. Staff will work to hide the problem if they fear such excessive punishment.

Supervisors experience similar fears and guilt in dealing with impaired nurses. The rest of the unit staff may deny the situation and defend the impaired nurse. Supervisors, however, must not only overcome their own emotions and professional identification with the impaired nurse but also refocus the whole work group on their own enabling role. Enabling is unsupportive to the impaired nurse, damaging to the professional practice climate, and detrimental to the patients and the community.

Initially, a supervisor may be unaware of the exact nature of the problem. Faced with an employee who exhibits problem behaviors and who fails to meet standards, and with a unit unable to confront and solve problems, a supervisor should focus initial efforts on breaking the staff's enabling patterns.

INTERVENTION FOR THE WORK GROUP

When critical incidents do not occur, the work group's enabling behavior can usually be interrupted, though not always quickly. One impaired nurse on a unit can manipulate and distort relationships and block communication. Nursing leaders who are uncomfortable in management roles often complicate these work groups. In fact, impaired nurses may seek out these leaders as supervisors, knowing that they can be manipulated.

To intervene with the work group, a supervisor should question the enabling conspiracy by challenging its assumptions. Attempts to identify the problem as drug addiction or alcoholism will only provoke denial and defensiveness from the staff and the impaired nurse. A blaming, critical, or judgmental approach will fail. Instead, the supervisor should begin by asking the work group such questions as do you think that is a plausible story? Does that story really excuse the resulting poor patient care? Is this what you expect of a professional? Do you believe that? How do you feel when that nurse disappears from the unit? Is that what the nurse told others, too? Have you told that nurse how you feel? Should you?

When the staff realize they are being conned, they will be ready to work together for constructive confrontation and improved working relationships. They can provide their own examples of problems, but they may need a group facilitator. Information about how the administration will handle chemical dependency can reduce guilt feelings and allow the staff to risk confrontations.

Supervisors can make other obvious interventions. They can work with the head nurse to resolve any management role ambivalence and human relations deficits. The unit's deficiencies in meeting standards of care can be used to open communication. Problem-solving work groups can try to improve unit communication in response to other identified problems.

When an impaired nurse is suddenly "discovered," the unit work group usually reacts intensely. Some staff members realize for the first time how they may have been enabling and contributing to the problem; they feel guilty for not having realized it sooner and not having done something. Others direct their feelings at the impaired nurse in the form of blaming, scapegoating and fear; they want to feel that the impaired nurse is at fault. Some staff will want swift retribution; others will be troubled by any form of punishment, particularly if they have seen impaired physicians protected and treated (or not), rather than punished.

Most units need help with these intense feelings. Supervisors who work with the staff usually find that confidentiality constraints are balanced by the staff's shared awareness of the problems. They often need information about what happens to impaired nurses and how to prevent these problems in the future.

INDIVIDUAL DIAGNOSIS

Impaired nurses can function undetected for years. As the disease progresses, the symptoms become more visible. Absenteeism is sometimes the most obvious indica-

Impaired Nurses: Professional and Ethical Issues for Nursing Leadership

Nursing administrators and managers have a number of overlapping and conflicting obligations in dealing with impaired nurses. However difficult the choice of appropriate intervention, the worst alternative is to ignore the existence of substance abuse.

It is unquestionable that patients must be protected from substandard care and other risks caused by the impaired nurse. However, if this is done by quiet termination or encouragement of turnover, will patients of the impaired nurse's next employer be protected until the problem becomes obvious at that institution? Will the next employer in turn simply allow the nurse to leave and take the problem elsewhere, thus exposing another group of patients? Failing to face the problem exposes the public to risk and accomplishes nothing for the profession.

As persons responsible for the patient milieu and the work climate, managers cannot overlook the effect of the impaired nurse on colleagues. Units that shelter an impaired nurse will have many problems with teamwork, responsibility, assertiveness, and powerlessness issues. Frequently, nurse colleagues have no experience in providing constructive criticism, confrontation, or support or no confidence in their ability to do so. Nursing managers must intervene to help the group establish collegial work relationships and a professional practice climate in which the impaired nurse can face the truth and seek treatment without condemnation.

If the impaired nurse has a problem with drugs, state law will also influence how deeply the nurse is cast in the criminal role. Ideally, some states permit open communication and treatment in lieu of conviction for health care professionals. In the worst cases, states use public embarrassment, foster criminal prosecution with heavy penalties, and use nonprofessionals to conduct humiliating investigations. The latter process emotionally maims and professionally destroys people who can become productive again; it also gives added incentive for impaired nurses to keep their problems hidden and untreated.

Nursing administrators should meet with local law enforcement officials and find out exactly how impaired nurses will be treated and how far officials are able and willing to go to help these nurses obtain treatment. Will the criminal system be a support or a limitation in dealing with impaired nurses? The same issue must be explored with the Board of Nursing. The answers are important in deciding how to structure intervention and treatment alternatives to maximize patient confidentiality and minimize the employer's knowledge and legal obligations when there are punitive and destructive enforcement systems.

By recognizing the elements of occupational exposure and normal incidence of problems, nursing can identify and manage the impaired nurse as a professional issue. Doing so will deemphasize the punitive and criminal factors that contribute to tragic losses. Nurses have the resources to take responsibility and facilitate rehabilitation. They cannot afford to abdicate the management of impaired colleagues.

tion. A sick leave pattern may develop around days off; the nurse may appear confused about work schedules and may bargain with coworkers to change hours. The individual may request vacation or time off at the beginning of a shift, take extended lunch periods, or have frequent, unexplained absences from the unit during the shift.[5]

The impaired nurse's overall work output usually changes from willingness to accept new challenges to doing only the minimum necessary. The nurse's charting may become sloppy and undecipherable, reflecting irrational thought processes. A routine task may seem overwhelming and impossible to accomplish on time. The nurse makes judgment errors, particularly in the use of controlled substances. If the nurse is addicted to drugs, patients may receive large amounts of pain medication with little relief or problems may develop with narcotic counts and wastages.

Other personality changes occur as the illness progresses. General irritability and mood swings are noticeable. The impaired nurse withdraws from relationships and becomes socially isolated. Poor personal grooming also becomes apparent. The nurse may also be forgetful and make inappropriate responses, which may indicate blackouts or complete memory loss.[6]

INTERVENTION FOR THE IMPAIRED NURSE

Too often, management's response to an impaired nurse is to dismiss the nurse immediately, particularly if problems are suspected but unavoidable confrontation has not yet occurred. Some impaired nurses adopt low visibility and remain in one job. Others change jobs frequently to stay one step ahead of responsibility. They seem to be interested in positions with little day-to-day continuity, such as in supplemental staff agencies and float pools. Nursing service organizations might encourage this turnover through inability to recognize the problem, lack of management and treatment alternatives, and reluctance to give a bad or doubtful reference (also enabling behaviors). Impaired nurses can move from place to place without anyone confronting the problem and forcing them to seek treatment.

The supervisor begins by dealing with problem behaviors until the impaired nurse accepts the problem and seeks treatment. Each behavior should be confronted imme-diately but without strong emotions. Professional skills and resources need to be mobilized for what is often a life-or-death struggle. The supervisor is often in the most powerful position to persuade the impaired nurse to enter treatment. Few things are as important to an alcoholic or an addict as keeping a job. It is usually the last thing between them and utter ruin. In some cases the job is also the primary drug supply source. In all cases it is a strong motivator toward treatment.

Although early efforts to confront a troubled employee must focus on the problem behavior rather than its probable causes, at some point the cause often becomes apparent. Critical incidents of drug theft, obvious intoxication, discovery of caches of alcohol or other drug supplies, confession, accidental overdose, and so forth, may make it impossible for supervisors and coworkers to overlook or excuse the real situation. These critical incidents are sometimes precipitated by impaired nurses in the hope that someone else will be able to bring the situation under control, because they cannot. The impaired nurse often experiences a sense of relief once caught, because the problem can no longer be denied. Critical incidents do not always occur, however, and the supervisor may need to create a confrontation.

Impaired nurses usually enter the disciplinary process because of failure to meet performance standards; failure to correct problems after counseling; or specific acts

---

Critical incidents are sometimes precipitated by impaired nurses in the hope that someone else will be able to bring the situation under control, because they cannot.

of negligence, drug theft, absenteeism, or tardiness. The authority of the disciplinary proceedings should be used to create a controlled confrontation about the performance issue so that the nurse can no longer deny the need for treatment. These confrontations can also be precipitated by employee assistance counselors and families in a nondisciplinary setting. The manager's control of employment is often a vital tool in these confrontations, too.

It is necessary for managers to work with problem behaviors rather than the cause, which must come from the nurse. It is useless to offer help for a "drinking problem" if the nurse does not believe one exists. The disciplinary process must make it clear that serious problems exist and that the nurse is responsible for correcting them. The employer is obligated to ask for and is entitled to a response.

Disciplinary actions can include required participation in a treatment program or mandatory counseling, as well as the traditional penalties (reprimands, suspensions, etc.), which are important symbols (see boxed material). In no case, however, should management settle for substandard behavior as the outcome because the person is "sick" or being treated. It is impossible to avoid firing a nurse who cannot meet minimal standards of care or who will not accept treatment.

PROGRAM INTERVENTIONS

To manage impaired nurses, it is important to have treatment alternatives available. Drug addiction is an occupational hazard for health professionals, and alcoholism in endemic in our society. A hospital seemingly without impaired nurses probably has hidden problems. Management should educate the staff so that problems can be recognized and treated.

Constructive confrontation through the disciplinary process

Step 1*
- Inform employee of deficiencies and problems
- Communicate clear performance expectations
- Offer voluntary referral for personal problems
- Document actions
- Follow up in two to four weeks

Step 2
- Enter written reprimand in employee's record
- Identify consequences of continued poor performance
- Reiterate performance expectations
- Make voluntary or mandatory referral for counseling
- Follow up in two to four weeks

Step 3
- Hold a disciplinary hearing (more than one may be required)
- Use accumulated data to counteract denial of problems
- Identify consequences of continued poor performance
- Reiterate performance expectations
- Make mandatory referral for employee to keep job

Step 4
- Terminate employee

*Serious infractions are grounds to start the process at a higher level.

Definitive treatment of the disease is best handled by mental health professionals in alcoholism and drug treatment programs. Gettint an impaired nurse into treatment keeping him or her chemically free, however, requires special resources or commitment. Managers who deal infrequently with substance abuse in their staff need someone trained to consult, assist, and support their efforts to manage an impaired nurse. Fortunately, many treatment alternatives are available for large and small institutions.

The smallest of hospitals can afford to allow at least one nurse to develop specialized knowledge and skills in treating substance abuse in addition to his or her regular duties. The specialized skills will not be wasted, considering the frequency of substance abuse problems in patients.

It is also possible for several institutions to develop consortium resources. Substance abuse is a problem in other hospital departments, other professional groups, other hospitals and even other industries. Shared resources may be one of the most efficient approaches; other industries might be willing to fund the program in return for staff management and clinical expertise.

Another approach is to hire an outside mental health consultant, preferably one with experience and special training in substance abuse. It should also be possible to contract with institutions that have already developed resources.

Several state nurses' associations have peer assistance programs that are available to any nurse. These may be the best solution for hospitals in sparsely populated areas.

Larger hospitals frequently have at least one clinical nurse specialist who manages psychosocial aspects of care for medical-surgical patients. This person can work with unit group dynamics and is usually in a good position to consult with management in identifying and helping problem employees.

An employee assistance program for the entire hospital is ideal. It can be started by one mental health nurse, with additional preparation in handling chemical dependency, who provides a broad range of problem-solving support to employees and managers. The program can be operated through the nursing or employee health department, or both, and can be instrumental in broadening community treatment and support responses (e.g., it may facilitate establishment of a nurses' Alcoholics Anonymous group and sensitize substance abuse treatment programs to the special needs of health professionals).

Regardless of how resources are structured, a program should identify mechanisms for:

- education of managers and staff;
- consultation with the managers of impaired staff;
- facilitation of confrontation and intervention for impaired staff;
- professional support of colleagues;
- consultation with employee labor unions for support of troubled employees involved in disciplinary processes;
- placement of impaired employees in treatment programs;
- continuity of effort between employment and treatment; and
- treatment follow up to maintain the employee's compliance.

Such a program can protect the institution from liability while providing an appropriate response to impaired staff. The problem is so large that referrals from all departments should be anticipated. Chemical dependency is no respecter of class, race, economic status, or job level. A broad-based program can be made available to all staff, including those in managerial and administrative positions.[7]

• • •

Impaired nurses are colleagues. No one knows why they respond to life stress in this particular way. Alcoholism is rampant throughout American society, and because of their jobs, nurses are exposed to drug addiction opportunities. Nurses with these problems are people desperately in need of professional help. Nursing administrators can choose to support them through confrontation or can blame and punish them.

When the impaired nurse is confronted and helped, there is relief at several levels: (1) the individual nurse is relieved to be caught; (2) the peer group is relieved of the burden of enabling and protecting the nurse and can redirect their efforts toward professional practice; (3) nursing managers are relieved from assuming a punitive role, such as firing the nurse, because successful treatment alternatives are available; and (4) the profession is relieved from denying that the problem exists. Rather than allowing other authorities to punish nurses, nurses can be responsible for seeing that their colleagues are treated and their patients are protected.

REFERENCES

1. Jefferson, L.V., and Ensor, B.E. "Help for the Helper: Confronting a Chemically-Impaired Colleague." *American Journal of Nursing* 82 (April 1982): 574–77.

2. Zahourek, R.P. "Even 'People Helpers' Need Help—Stress and Addictive Behavior in Nurses." *Imprint* 28, no. 3 (1981): 30–33.

3. Wrich, J.T. *The Employee Assistance Program—Updated for the 1980's.* Center City, Minn.: Hazelden, 1980, pp. 22–23.

4. Lee, D.K., and Ventres, S. "The Nurse: The Enabler." *American Journal of Nursing* 81 (March 1981): 506–508.

5. Jefferson and Ensor, "Help for the Helper," 576.

6. Ibid.

7. Wrich, *The Employee Assistance Program.* 47–55.

Retention: Has it obstructed nursing's view?

Genevieve E. Chandler, R.N., Ph.D.
Assistant Professor
School of Nursing
University of Massachusetts, Amherst
Amherst, Massachusetts

WEBSTER'S DICTIONARY defines "retain" as "to hold back, to keep from departure or escape, to keep in a fixed state, to restrain."[1] The literature is replete with descriptions of hospital programs geared to retain nurses.[2-5] In this day and age do health care organizations still want to hold nurses back? Has that not been a consistent theme in nursing history for long enough? How can nursing move forward if nurses are held back?

Consider the following cases: One dynamic nursing administrator remarked: "My pattern is to stay in one place maybe four to five years at the most, then I have to move on. By that time I usually feel like I have done my thing and need a change." A former excellent staff nurse stated: "When I was a staff nurse I had to move every 15 to 18 months. I got bored with the routines. I was good while I was there, but for me moving up meant moving on and learning more to keep interested." A head nurse states:

> Two years was the max for me. After that I was ready to leave. I liked the idea of doing something new and different. I was known as a nurse enthusiast and that's how I did it—a new situation energized me. I recognized when my energy was getting low, I would feel demoralized. I suppose I could have stayed and worked to change things but systems don't change that fast so it worked better for me to change instead.

These nurses are speaking to the issue of progression within the nursing profession, which does not necessarily mean retention in one organization. The work patterns of these three typical nurses belie a major assumption of nurse retention programs (i.e., keeping people working in the same place is beneficial and cost-effective). With the combination of shrinking hospital budgets, the depletion of the pool of available nurses, and the cost of recruitment at $3,000 to $5,000 per nurse, retention certainly appears to be desirable.[6] This assumption, however, is worth examining. This author

Nurs Admin Q, 1990, 14(4), 70–75
©1990 Aspen Publishers, Inc.

maintains that there is a difference between organizational and professional retention and that trying to promote both may be counterproductive.

Organizational retention is defined as keeping a nurse working in the same facility over time. Professional retention is defined as keeping nurses in the nursing profession. Organizational retention may be as obstructive to the nursing profession as the definition of the word retain implies. The push to keep nurses in one organization may work against the ultimate goal of retaining nurses in the profession. To expound on this point, the concepts of organizational and professional retention are addressed in the following sections.

ORGANIZATIONAL RETENTION

With the limited supply of student nurses combined with an increased demand for acute care nurses, it is no wonder that retention is a primary concern of nursing administrators. The organizational retention of nurses has been a popular topic in both the nursing literature and at nursing conferences. Clearly, there is research, theory, and anecdotal information available on turnover and retention strategies. Yet, as Prescott[7] observed, there has been limited implementation of retention strategies due to economic reasons. The bottom line is that providing ongoing management training, offering competency-based rewards, budgeting realistic salary incentives, and structuring effective work environments is expensive. It may be time to reconsider retention from a different perspective.

Retention: The myth

Most businesses, including hospitals, still yearn for what was termed the "organization man." In the 1950s Whyte described the phenomenon of the organization man as "the ones who have left home, spiritually as well as physically, to take the vows of organizational life."[8(p.3)] These workers lived and died for the organization. They personalized the success or failures of the organization. They were the committed and loyal followers of company policies. Recruitment into a bureaucratic system that was based on male military model fit the expectations of the organization man.

Today, hospitals still cling to the organization man myth in the belief that the retained employee develops competency and proficiency, which will lead to a more productive organization. The assumption is that the retained employee will benefit the employer by becoming the prototype of the organization man myth: a selfless, loyal, and committed member of the team. The reality, however, may be different from the myth.

Retention: the reality

With the overwhelming demand for change and innovation in today's health care environment, staff with considerable tenure may be more interested in holding on to the comfortable routines of the past than in committing to an uncertain and ever-changing future. The reality is that individuals with seniority must actively support the organization in moving forward while they are stuck on hold. The retained nurse must wrestle with the realities of feeling stuck and being "plateaued."

Plateauing is a term Bardwick[9] uses to describe the situation in which employees reach a point in their career where they are no longer advancing up the career ladder. Instead, they remain at the same hierarchical level. With an organizational structure shaped like a triangle, where there are many positions at the bottom and few at the top, plateauing is inevitable. Bardwick[9] termed reaching the top and leveling off as the "plateauing trap." One can either be "content plateaued" or "structurally plateaued." Content plateauing occurs when the individual is no longer challenged by the job and knows all there is to know. Structural plateauing occurs when there are no further rungs to climb on the ladder. Structural plateauing can occur at any level: from the bottom of the triangle at the staff level, where the bedside nurse has limited promotional opportunities, to the top of the triangle at the vice president level, where there are no other positions to advance to.

With nursing's flat hierarchy, plateauing is predictable. Bardwick[9] states that because few people are prepared for the end of the climb, whether it happens early in their career or much later, most experience depression when they realize that they are not advancing any further. If those that are plateaued do not understand what has happened to them, their depression is compounded by anxiety. The response to the plateauing trap is manifested in a variety of nonproductive behaviors. Kanter[10] described the individual's response to being "stuck" as an experience of powerlessness.

Kanter[10] found that employees who felt they were stuck in terminal jobs were likely to develop a cautious attitude toward new ideas. These individuals were interested in maintaining the status quo and did not want to "rock the boat." They viewed themselves as the keepers of the culture keys and were committed to keeping their workplace the same. They became the passive resistors.

Employees who felt they were stuck in terminal jobs were likely to develop a cautious attitude toward new ideas.

Those that were "stuck" did not directly confront change, but they were so slow to adapt that the value of the new idea was lost. The stuck employees still got the job done but were less likely to take risks while doing so.

In order to tolerate dead-end jobs, the stuck employees developed their own criteria for on-the-job success, such as taking long breaks or getting out on time. Outside of work, where there were no new promotions to indicate success, accumulating material goods, such as new carpeting or a new car, became the symbols of success.

Kanter[10] and Bardwick[9] both suggest that the structure of the work environment, the lack of promotional opportunity, and the limited definition of success lead to a sense of being stuck or being plateaued. Though nursing leaders have called for a change in the structure of the traditional hospital work environment, dramatic organizational change takes time. Granted, there are some shared governance models and case management approaches to patient care that have altered the traditional structure. For the most part, however, changes have been gradual and slow. Many nurses will not wait. It is time to confront the organization man myth of the '50s and recognize the cost of plateauing.

The patterns of today's mobile work force are quite different from those of previous generations. That most nurses are not men who leave their families to take the vows of organizational life means that nurses' relationship to work may be different from the accepted norm as defined by the white, middle-class male standard. The other norm has yet to be described, but it is safe to say that the place of work in women's lives may be different from the accepted norm. Moving between workplaces, a concept different from the traditional work norm, may offer alternatives to nurses. There may be options to remaining in one workplace. Currently, however, progression by moving on is not condoned.

THE DILEMMA OF LEAVING

Leaving a nursing unit can be analogous to leaving home. When children are old enough to leave the nest, secure parents recognize that children with wings to fly independently can also choose to fly home. Other parents cling to the adolescent, taking every step toward independence as a personal insult. In this situation, as adolescents make attempts to move on, they feel guilty for leaving their parents and respond by acting out their anger. Obsession with retention regarding staff nurses may place nurses in the latter scenario. They feel guilty about wanting to leave and act out by leaving abruptly, giving some canned excuse about family commitments rather than scheduling a planned career transition that can be expected by both management and staff. Guilt-ridden leave taking does not always have to be the case, however. Consider the following case example:

While interviewing a new nurse, a nurse manager worked through the typical questions. She then asked the interviewee, "Now, what can Valley Hospital do for you while you are working on our unit?" The nurse had not considered what the hospital could do for her. She expected to explain what she could do for the hospital.

With some assistance from the manager the nurse was able to formulate a potential career plan. When the nurse suggested that she would like to consider graduate school within the next five years, the manager recommended that she send for the school application so they could see what sort of experience the program expected. With this information they could formulate goals and objectives for her current position that would include the required experience for graduate school. The new nurse left the interview walking on air. She felt she

was respected as an individual and could be honest with her new manager.

This manager reported that staff members actually stayed longer, possibly because they were encouraged to think about their future. She identified a number of her staff members who had designed some very creative positions for themselves both within the institution and after they had left. When the staff members did leave the unit it was not unusual for them to refer other nurses to Valley Hospital or return to work part time while they attended school.

As with children who are leaving home, when staff members were given permission to plan for their next career move they felt more comfortable in staying, knowing they were working toward a personal goal. When staff did leave, it was a planned, negotiated step.

Retention in the profession may mean moving within and between organizations. In order to create opportunity for advancement, acquire new knowledge and skills, and be recognized and rewarded, nurses may need to actively formulate their own career ladder rather than passively depend on the hospital. The individual nurse's career ladder would consider the plateauing trap and would probably include many career moves. If nurses are supported in developing an individualized career plan, they become the directors of their own careers. In this way the hospital does not plan for them, but provides proactive support and information for career planning and progression.

With a different view of retention, one that encourages nurses to move on within the profession, new avenues emerge that can facilitate professional growth rather than stifle it. Vogt et al.[11] observed that turnover allows people to move up, assume new roles, and take on new responsibilities. With new employees, organizations can gain fresh perspectives, new insights, and new questions. A too stable work group might lapse into what Janis[12] called "group think," in which the group tends not to disagree in order to maintain cohesion and the status quo. A planned program of progression and turnover could lead to a more productive organization.

PROFESSIONAL RETENTION

Based on the information presented, the following is an evolving list of plans for professional retention that range from the unit level to the national level:

Employee interviews, with an eye toward the future, can assist staff in developing long-range career plans. As in the case example, the individualized career plan can begin during the hiring interview.

Field trips for staff nurses to other clinical units similar to their own could be arranged to expose staff to a variety of situations. For example, when the census was down in the dialysis unit in a local community hospital, two staff nurses were sent to a city medical center's dialysis unit for one day. The staff returned with new ideas and at the same time were more appreciative of the positive qualities they observed in their home unit.

Lateral transfers are a way to expose nurses to the various types of care given within the same facility. Often staff perceive their own unit as *the* hospital and have no idea how other units function. By facilitating lateral transfers, managers can give nurses cross training of the nurses' own choice within one facility.

Exchange programs have already been initiated in some facilities. Sharp et al.[13] reported an exchange program between a hospital in Minnesota and one in Florida. The program addressed the needs of the nurses as well as the facility. Both of the hospitals were faced with fluctuating staffing needs due to peaks and valleys in patient admissions. This article described the process of instituting a successful nurse exchange program, a model that other hospitals could follow.

Outplacement is a concept that has been in the business community for years. Outplacement offices could be established within hospitals so that nurses who are considering leaving could obtain accurate information about other job possibilities within the facility and in other facilities. The office would also have up-to-date information on educational programs available, such as returning R.N. programs, graduate schools, and funding sources.

State and national centers for career opportunities might be established. Nurses could consult their local and state organizations for accurate information about job possibilities and educational information. These centers could provide career information beyond the typical journal advertisement and have the hard data that nurses need to make a career decision.

Career days are already an intrinsic part of undergraduate programs, but their focus is limited to different types of agencies recruiting nurses. Undergraduate, graduate, and doctoral students could all use career days that include information on career planning, particularly on developing career pathways. Examples of successful nurses' career pathways would be very useful to a new graduate on all three levels.

External educational programs that are based within the profession rather than the organization would be very beneficial. Currently, the different factions of nursing professional organizations offer educational opportunities, but aside from specialty certificate programs most of the professional organizations tend to present a disjointed menu of current issues. It is left to individual hospitals to provide such education as management training, research development, and clinical updates. It may be more profitable for professionals organizations to initiate a sequential agenda of topics, for example, a course in middle management offered for nurses from several hospitals. This is only a beginning list of new horizons that emerge when the prospect of organizational progression is considered as an avenue for professional retention.

• • •

It is no accident that every résumé of the recent senior class taught by the author stated as career objective, "to pursue a career with the opportunity for advancement." These intelligent, forward-thinking novice nurses are the profession's hope for the future. Their goal is a healthy, fulfilling one, consistent with that sought by professionals in other fields. Organizations need to accept that turnover has always been a part of nursing and may not be something to fight against but rather to work with. Progression and career planning should be the watchwords for the next generation and for those nurses who are stuck on hold. Plateauing need not be the end of a career but rather a symptom of the need to move on. Health care organizations need to recognize this opportunity to support professional growth and reap the benefits of letting go. Nursing leaders need to make the hopes for career advancement a reality and not let their views be obstructed by retention methods.

REFERENCES

1. *Webster's New Twentieth Century Dictionary.* New York, N.Y.: Simon and Schuster, 1983, s.v. "retain."
2. Weisman, C. "Recruit from Within: Hospital Nurse Retention in the 1980's." *Journal of Nursing Administration* 12, no. 5 (1982):24–31.
3. Scherer, P. "Hospitals that Attract (and Keep) Nurses." *American Journal of Nursing* (1988):34–40.
4. Hoffman, H. "A Nurse Retention Program." *Nursing Economics $* 7, no. 2 (1988):94–97.
5. Hinshaw, A.S., Smeltzer, C., and Atwood, J. "Innovative Retention Strategies for Nursing Staff." *Journal of Nursing Administration* 17, no. 6 (1987):8–16.
6. Donovan, L. "The Shortage." *RN* 8 (1980):21–27.
7. Prescott, P. "Another Round of Nursing Shortage." *Image* 19, no. 4 (1987):204–09.
8. Whyte, W.H., Jr. *The Organization Man.* New York, N.Y.: Simon and Schuster, 1956.
9. Bardwick, J. "The Plateauing Trap. Part 1: Getting Caught." *Personnel* 10 (1986):46–51.
10. Kanter, R.M. "Men and Women of the Corporation." New York, N.Y.: Basic Books, 1977.
11. Vogt, J., et al. *Retaining Professional Nurses: A Planned Process.* St. Louis, Mo.: Mosby, 1983.
12. Janis, I.L. "Victims of Group Think: A Psychological Study of Foreign Policy Decisions and Fiascos." Boston, Mass.: Houghton Mifflin, 1972.
13. Sharp, J.Q., Fredrick, B., and Voss, R. "Nurse Exchange—A Creative Approach to the Nursing Shortage." *Nursing Management* 5 (1989): 92–93.

The moderately troubled nurse: A not-so-uncommon entity

Jane Halsey, R.N., M.N.
Director of Nursing Services
St. Joseph Hospital
Bellingham, Washington

"LEAVE YOUR troubles on the door step when you come to work" is a trite and well-known adage. Some nurses even believe they can carry out such a directive. But for many, it is impossible. The stresses and strains of personal problems subtly and insidiously seep into the work place and manifest themselves in various behavioral patterns.

Troubled nurses run the gamut from one so severely distraught that he or she cannot function to one who goes on for months or years without arousing a great deal of alarm. As a director of nursing services, I have seen both extremes and many in the middle. The troubled nurse who appears to function relatively well often causes the most damage to himself or herself and to the organization, because of the length of time the problem continues without being detected or dealt with. The moderately troubled nurse is not an uncommon entity. Thus the nurse manager needs the skills to identify problems and intercede to resolve them for the well-being of the unit.

Job-related stressors can cause significant problems for the individual nurse and his or her unit. However, this article is limited in scope to the moderately troubled nurse who is plagued by home or personal problems, which have an impact on on-the-job performance.

RECOGNIZING THE MODERATELY TROUBLED NURSE

The troubled nurse's problems from the nurse manager's point of view are behavioral manifestations that surface on the job. Such behaviors as the following can point to a moderately troubled nurse:

- numerous or repeated errors;
- frequent use of poor judgment;
- decreased productivity;
- increased absenteeism;
- expressions of negativism or subversive activities;
- increased physical or psychological illness; and

Nurs Admin Q, 1985, 9(2), 69–76
©1985 Aspen Publishers, Inc.

- failure to contribute to the unit or to professional growth.

Any one of these problems does not automatically indicate a troubled nurse, but each in itself, when identified as a pattern or trend, should serve as a red flag for the nurse manager to further explore the situation. Further exploration is especially necessary when the behavior pattern is a decided change from the nurse's previous and usual level of practice. However, even a nurse who chronically fails to function and contribute at the level of his or her peers may fall into this category.

The nurse manager can obtain objective measures of work performance from direct supervision of the nurse's adherence to policies and procedures and audits of charts and files. Such a systematic approach allows the nurse manager to clearly identify deviations from acceptable standards.

In addition, a less used method of evaluation that approaches measuring performance from a patient satisfaction model is extremely pertinent.[1] Comparing the satisfaction levels of a nurse's patients over time with those of other nurses' patients is another method of confirming that a problem exists. It is expected that patients will, for the most part, be satisfied with the care they receive. However, a nurse who routinely receives poor ratings from patients is in need of improvement.

Why should a nurse manager care that a moderately troubled nurse is on his or her staff? Clearly a nurse who functions below the accepted level of performance can present a variety of problems. A nurse who makes numerous medication errors or uses poor judgment in reporting patient status changes is unsafe. A nurse who is not able to complete assignments on time or has an unacceptable absenteeism record has a negative impact on unit productivity. A nurse who does not treat patients, families,

and staff with courtesy and respect is making a statement about interpersonal relations that is sure to clash with the philosophy of care of most hospitals.

Allowing a nurse's unacceptable behavior to continue gives a clear message to the nurse and other members of the unit. It says to all that the behavior is okay and that management doesn't care if it continues. Role models are accepted and promulgated by default. All nurse managers have witnessed the devastation to unit organization caused by an unhappy nurse. Negativism is contagious, and when allowed to spread, can cause deep wounds in the cooperative team spirit. Thus widespread poor nursing practice and poor morale can result when a nurse manager chooses to ignore unacceptable behaviors thinking (and wishing) that they will go away when the troubled nurse "gets himself or herself back together."

The effects of a moderately troubled nurse fall into two categories. The first category I have already discussed, that is, performance or behaviors that fall below accepted standards. The second category is less frequently discussed but nonetheless of vital concern to the nurse manager. A moderately troubled nurse will fail to contribute positively to unit growth. He or she will not have the energy and motivation to strive for improved or ideal performance. Such a nurse will be the weakest link in the chain, the individual who is holding the unit back from greater achievements. Not only will this nurse not have the psychic energy to devote to unit progression, his or her own professional growth and enthusiasm will stagnate.

The nurse who "puts in time" and "does the work" may meet the minimum standards of performance required. Yet professional and unit growth require a level of motivation that allows the nurse to make positive contributions. Such contributions improve unit functioning and patient care and thus provide a revitalizing force. Nurse managers appreciate those who make such contributions, but often do not identify it as a problem when someone stops making or has never made such contributions. A team effort is mandatory for moving a unit forward. A nurse who does not participate has a negative impact on the organization.

PERSONAL PROBLEMS THAT SURFACE ON THE JOB

The nurse manager's job or interest should not be to pry into the private lives of his or her staff. Yet depending on the duration and quality of the nurse-supervisor relationship, the nurse manager may already be aware of personal problems that could be affecting work performance.

The nurse manager is responsible for ensuring that patients receive high-quality and loving care. When he or she sits down with staff to discuss problems that interfere with the delivery of such care, one or more of a wide variety of stressors may surface. The following are examples of the most common stressors nurses share:

- financial burdens or being the sole source of income;
- guilt or concern regarding child rearing;
- divorce or marital strife;
- death of a loved one;
- trouble with the law; and
- chronic illness in the nurse or a family member.

A study by Gulack of nearly 3,000 registered nurse respondents revealed that 58 percent of those working were the sole support of themselves or their families.[2] Therefore it is not surprising that financial difficulties are frequently the cause of the nurse's stress.

If Gulack's population can be seen as representative, about 97 percent of all actively working nurses are women.[3] Thus childbearing and child rearing are common life events during the career years. The most important reason Gulack cited for leaving nursing was to raise a family.[4] For those families able to manage on one spouse's income, this is not a problem. However, the nurse who must leave an infant or small children behind each day often feels guilt for having done so. A nurse may also experience physical exhaustion if she returns to work too soon after the birth of her child.

Another stressor related to child rearing is the inability to conceive or carry a fetus to term. Stressful reactions to such a situation are feelings of failure and disappointment. A nurse who desperately wants a child and whose biological clock is rapidly running out appears more and more obsessed as time elapses.

Marital strife is a common occurrence in American society, and one that nurses are not immune to. Gulack stated that 15.5 percent of the nurses actively working in the profession were divorced.[5] Whether or not marital strife results in divorce, the resulting family and individual problems are burdensome.

The stress caused by the death of a loved one, including an unborn child, can be expected to result in a period of grieving. If a nurse is unable to cope with the loss, he or she may carry this burden to the work place.

Trouble with the law is not an expected problem for most nurses or their families. Such problems as a spouse jailed for child abuse, a child in juvenile hall for burglary or a nurse or his or her spouse arrested for driving while intoxicated create great personal and family stress and are a source of embarrassment.

A chronic illness or handicap brings with it a special set of stressors. It requires great personal and family adjustments and often results in severe life plan limitations. Whether the nurse or a family member is ill or disabled, the nurse's coping energy can become exhausted.

Not all nurses who experience the previously discussed stressors suffer behavioral problems. To the contrary, many possess the coping skills necessary to help them survive and even prosper in the process.[6] However, for many the burden is too great, and work performance suffers. Physical exhaustion often results and leads to further cycling of the problem.

DEALING WITH THE MODERATELY TROUBLED NURSE

The approaches to dealing with the moderately troubled nurse can be divided into three steps: identification of the problem; referral to a professional counselor; and making alterations in the work setting or schedule.

Identification of the problem

It is the nurse manager's responsibility to evaluate job performance. When the nurse manager ascertains that areas for improvement exist, he or she needs to determine what action to take to correct the performance deficit and specify the consequences of continued failure. It is the nurse manager's job to ensure early identification and implementation of a means to resolve the problem.

Use of tools such as those mentioned previously can assist the manager in identifying what the problems are. Sitting down with the troubled nurse and having a one-to-one fact-finding session is a good way to begin. Here the nurse manager's interpersonal expertise is invaluable. In this setting the nurse manager can present in a factual manner the unacceptable performance or practice (e.g., frequent errors, decisions involving poor judgment, decrease in productivity, increase in absenteeism).

It is especially important for the nurse manager to present only the facts. Ascribing motives to behavior is not productive and can lead to alienation of the nurse. During the fact-finding session, the nurse manager, with the input of the nurse, can rule out training needs or work environment problems as factors that are interfering with expected performance.

During the fact-finding session, an unsolicited personal problem may surface. The nurse manager's first impulse may be to suggest a solution; however, that is not his or her role. The nurse manager cannot be expected to address the source of the problems (e.g., marital strife or financial difficulties); he or she should address only the symptoms that have surfaced on the job.

The nurse manager's job is to insure excellent patient care through supervision and early problem identification and resolution. Listening, allowing the nurse to vent feelings and displaying a caring attitude are helpful. However, the nurse manager cannot accept lesser standards of patient care from a nurse who is experiencing personal problems. Rather, the nurse manager must clearly state the performance improvement required.

Referral to a counselor

The next step the nurse manager may implement is referral of the troubled nurse

The nurse manager cannot accept lesser standards of patient care from a nurse who is experiencing personal problems.

to a counselor. Historically the role of nurse involves the expenditure of psychic energy to comfort, console and counsel patients, their families and even other members of the health care team.[7] But who is there to comfort, console and counsel the nurse when he or she becomes overburdened?

Support groups and continuing education seminars have sprung up to meet the needs of the nurse who is overstressed from work burdens. However, the nurse experiencing personal disorganization needs a more private and individualized assistance mode. Some hospitals provide counseling in the form of an employee assistance program (EAP).[8] EAPs offer the nurse manager and the nurse an opportunity for direct referral. If an EAP is not available, a referral to a social worker, minister or counselor is usually an option.

By referring the troubled nurse to a qualified counselor, the nurse manager has directed the nurse toward help while maintaining his or her own position. By seeking professional counseling, the nurse will have an opportunity to explore his or her work problems in relation to his or her personal problems.

If the work problem is in need of immediate improvement in order for the nurse to retain his or her position or avoid disciplinary action, the nurse manager may want to make the referral mandatory. If this is the case, the nurse manager may want to send a written summary of performance problems to the counselor or call the individual directly. This would be done with the full knowledge of the nurse. At no time could the nurse manager expect a report from the counselor that violates client-counselor confidentiality. However, the nurse manager could reasonably request verification of kept appointments and an indication at some point from the counselor as to whether the

nurse will be able to rectify the work problems identified.

Altering the nurse's schedule or assignment

The final step that may be followed in the problem resolution stage is to make changes in the nurse's schedule or assignment. This is the least desirable option, since it may be disruptive to the functioning of the unit. However, if the nurse manager wants to retain the nurse, it may be a good step to consider.

Such alterations as a decrease in work hours or a change of shift or work unit may be of benefit to the troubled nurse. If the nurse needs more personal time off and is financially secure, a personal leave of absence may give the nurse the time he or she needs to focus on the problem while still maintaining the security of his or her seniority.

In some situations a more drastic approach may be necessary. It may be best for the nurse manager to suggest that the troubled nurse transfer to a less stressful environment, either within the institution or elsewhere in the community. If handled correctly, such suggestions can be a positive avenue for the nurse to explore. These suggestions are highly preferred to the devastation of termination if the nurse cannot reverse the negative trends in his or her performance.

EVALUATING RESULTS

By using the same objective criteria assessments he or she employed to determine that a performance problem existed, the nurse manager can evaluate the nurse's level of improvement. By having and using objective performance evaluation tools, the nurse manager can provide positive reinforcement for meeting job requirements as well as recognize the need for further improvement.

Time frames should be set for improvement, and plans for follow-up sessions at specific intervals should be established. The nurse then has a time frame in which to better his or her performance and knows when to expect periodic evaluations. These evaluations must be based on the same criteria on which the original concerns were based. For example, if the nurse has poor attendance and a low patient satisfaction rating, then these two criteria must be addressed. If additional performance problems surface, they need attention in addition to, not to the exclusion of, the original problems.

The nurse deserves credit if he or she has rectified the initial set of problems. Reinforcement methods foster a positive approach and decrease feelings of inadequacy and failure. In addition, through his or her caring approach, the nurse manager is role modeling the caring aspect of patient care expected of nurses.

However, a pattern of correcting one problem and replacing it with another is not acceptable. At some point the nurse manager must examine the need to take a hard look at the probability of getting the results he or she needs for the unit. The nurse manager's energy is not boundless, and by focusing vast amounts of attention on one individual, the nurse manager may be denying others with positive contributions to make the attention they need.

FOSTERING A LESS STRESSFUL WORK ENVIRONMENT

In themselves, work environments are stressful for nurses. There are steps the nurse manager can take to foster a less stressful environment for all nursing personnel on his or her unit. The nurse manager who espouses the philosophy that nurses need time and space to periodically retreat from the job can work to create such relief sports either on the unit or somewhere else in the institution. When renovations or expansions occur, the nurse manager can diligently lobby for such space, knowing its importance to individual and unit mental health. In addition, the nurse manager can encourage staff to use the retreats and not routinely skip breaks or meal periods.

If the institution offers exercise classes or space to walk on breaks, the nurse manager will do well to encourage his or her staff to participate. Exercise in itself can be a valuable stress reliever. Vacations and personal time away from the job allow a time for refreshment and revitalization. Encouraging nurses to use their time and granting requests whenever possible pay off.

Besides offering and encouraging physical retreats, the nurse manager can, via his or her management style, reduce work stress. A nurse manager who is nonreactive and supportive will contribute immensely to decreasing stress on his or her unit. On the other hand, a nurse manager who is reactive and volatile will only add negatively to an already stressful environment. Subordinates will mirror this behavior and further increase the stress level.

Reacting calmly in a stressful environment or situation is a learned behavior for many but one that is well worth the effort to acquire. Those nurse managers who recognize that they need assistance in this area are well advised to obtain help. Their employees and unit functioning as a whole will be better served.

REFERENCES

1. MacStravic, R.S. "Being Patients' 'Personal' Hospital Is Survival Strategy in Hard Times." *Modern Healthcare* 14 (July 1984): 182–87.
2. Gulack, R. "Why Nurses Leave Nursing." *RN* 46 (December 1983): 32–37.
3. Ibid., 36.
4. Ibid., 35.
5. Ibid., 36.
6. Ross, J.K., and Halatin, T. "When Family Stress Affects Worker Productivity." *Supervisory Management* 27 (July 1982): 2–8.
7. Taylor, P.B., and Gideon, M. "Day In and Day Out You Minister to Others—But Who Will Minister to You?" *Nursing 81,* no. 11 (October 1981): 58–61.
8. Steinberg, S.L. "Employee Assistance Program Conserves Human Resources." *Hospital Progress* 62 (February 1981): 50–51.

Part II
Study and discussion questions

1. Identify ways that nurses' personal lives can interact with their professional practice.
2. To what degree can managers and administrators realistically wear a "therapist" hat?
3. How might a nurse's depression and burnout interact or overlap, and how might a manager intervene?
4. In what ways do individuals' problems become a group practice problem for nurses?
5. How can a nurse executive differentiate healthy and unhealthy turnover; how would a nurse manager optimize turnover?
6. Nurses (and women in general) have high rates of depression. Nurses have high rates of substance abuse, burnout, and turnover. To what extent is this demographics (women's life experiences), and selection (who decides to become a nurse) and to what extent does the nursing work experience shape these results?

Part III
Marketing: Enhancing patient outcomes and organizational effectiveness

Joan O'Leary, R.N., Ed. D.
President
O'Leary and Associates, Inc.
Port Jervis, New York

The quality revolution mandates that nursing adopt new sets of skills. One of those skills is to identify customer needs and meet those needs in an organized manner. Adopting a market framework within a nursing organization can enhance organizational effectiveness and profitability. Applying the knowledge of the marketing processes effectively within our organizations can position us in identifying customer needs and wants. Defining ways to satisfy customer expectations and implementing effective marketing strategies can assure quality outcomes of care.

Staff nurses, nurse executives, and national nursing leaders have unique opportunities to capitalize on our customer needs and wants, and overall improve our public's view of the service that we render. Understanding our public, defining our markets, and identifying our products can influence our effectiveness, our outcomes of care, and our profitability.

Adopting the critical elements of the marketing process into nursing organizations can improve responsiveness to our clients, enhance nursing's position in hospital organizations, maximize profitability, and positively impact the perception of the public that we serve.

In order to cope with the changing economic environment, health care organizations are restructuring. Developing a business posture requires that nurses examine the purposes of their business and determine from that examination viable products. Delivering those products in a quality manner further requires nursing to determine the role and the function of the product manager. Implementing the role of the product manager requires an expertise in meeting customer needs and services as well as an understanding of internal and external environments, management information systems, and planning mechanisms.

Managing and organizing a product line can effectively result in an increase in quality and production of services. Incorporating business concepts into the practice of nursing can demonstrate to our public that we are a revenue generating business. Nursing has a unique opportunity to demonstrate its value by positioning itself through implementing nursing as a product line.

The role of nursing in marketing health care

Barbara Norkett, R.N., B.S.N.
Director, Support Functions
Division of Nursing
Saint Francis Hospital
Evanston, Illinois

NURSES CAN NO longer remain passive, perceived by patients as caring individuals who attend to their comfort while implementing physicians' orders with technical competence. Nurses must discover exactly what patients—consumers of health care services—want from them and what consumer needs they can meet. Once they have that information, nurses must learn how to persuade consumers to come to them for those services.

Marketing is the process by which an individual or an organization comes to know the consumer's needs and how to meet them. The concept of marketing for the nonprofit organization was introduced in 1969 by Kotler and Levy.[1] The volume of literature has increased since 1975, and some hospital administrators have integrated marketing into their management functions. Because the concept is relatively new to the health care industry, few nursing administrators are knowledgeable about marketing or have incorporated it into their roles.

Marketing does not try to be all things to all people but rather selects a target or segment of the market. A formal definition is that "marketing is the analysis, planning, implementation and control of carefully formulated programs designed to bring about voluntary exchanges of values with target markets for the purpose of achieving organizational objectives."[2]

The objective of marketing in the commercial sector is profit. Profit is the reward for providing distinctive services that satisfy customers. To identify these services, a set of tools called the marketing mix is used: product, promotion, price, and place.[3] A product is something offered to satisfy a need; promotion is advertising, selling, and publicity; price is the fee; and place is how the service is made available to the consumer.

Three elements are critical to marketing: public, market, and exchange.[4] The first, a public, is a distinctive group of people who have an interest in an organization. Each health care entity, for instance, deals with a

Nurs Admin Q, 1985, 10(1), 85–89
©1985 Aspen Publishers, Inc.

variety of publics that are related not only to it but also to each other—patients, physicians, communities, donors, third party payers, staff members, trustees, and regulatory agencies. The attitudes of one public often affect those of another.

The second element, a market, is different from a public. A market is a potential arena for trading resources. When an organization begins thinking of a public in terms of trading values, that public becomes a market. For example, when an organization recruits staff nurses to volunteer for a health promotion program, the staff nurses become a market.

And the third element, exchange, requires two separate parties, each having something valued by the other party. The something that might be valued by the other party is called the product—having a product does not necessarily guarantee an economic exchange. The product could be comfort, socialization, personal satisfaction, or a feeling of social contribution.

From a competitive point of view, everything should be differentiated. It is not a superior generic product that accounts for IBM's success; it's the marketing. IBM's product is differentiated from the competition's product, and the markets are segmented. This is a basic marketing strategy: targeting distinct groups of consumers. The values of a particular segment or group of consumers influence the approach used to promote products. Marketing requires constant awareness, looking for gaps in market coverage and for new ways to influence buyers to choose one's product over those of one's competitors.[5]

ETHICAL ISSUES

Marketing health care raises ethical questions. Marketers in general are accused of causing people to buy products they do not

> *To develop marketing strategies for the family nurse practitioner (FNP), Smith and Shamansky analyzed the characteristics of potential users of FNP services.*

want and do not need. Marketing is said to be responsible for unnecessary services. For instance, a hospital might cater to physicians by adding facilities, equipment, and personnel in order to make their health care agency seem superior to others in the community. Marketing is also considered manipulative, and market research is considered an invasion of privacy.

Health care providers must be sensitive to these ethical concerns and be prepared to defend the cost-benefit ratio of marketing activities. Nonprofit organizations should inform their publics of the purpose and benefits of marketing. The sign of the true professional is having a service to offer the public, being sensitive to the wants and needs of clients, and meeting those needs. This is the definition of marketing.

THE ROLE OF NURSING

Private practice

Marketing in the health care industry is an opportunity for all nurses, those employed by health care agencies as well as private practitioners. Nurse practitioners must understand consumers' needs and how consumers select health care providers. To develop marketing strategies for the family nurse practitioner (FNP), Smith and Shamansky analyzed the characteristics of potential users of FNP services. In a random sample of 239 Seattle residents, they found that one-quarter of them intended to use FNP services. Potential users, it turned out, were primarily young women, professionally employed or homemakers, middle or upper income, single or with small families. The authors found that FNP care could be presented as being compatible with family norms and especially advantageous to this group of women.[6] As a result, this segment became the marketing target. Knowledge of who intended to use the service helped the nurse practitioners in this study decide how to present themselves.

Staff nurses

Staff nurses are an important public in the health care system. They have an exchange relationship with the organization. Their value in marketing an ambulatory care program was described by Stahl. Nurses were asked to conduct an informal marketing survey and were included in the marketing mix. Although the program was advertised, presentation of the program to the nurses resulted in word-of-mouth promotion. Program evaluation showed that the patients identified nurses as a major source of promotion.[7] The interest nurses took in the program and their enthusiasm for it brought patients into the system.

Market analysis really begins with the nursing assessment the staff nurse performs when the patient enters the health care system. Segmentation occurs with the nursing diagnosis, and the individual care plan designed to meet the patient's needs is the product. As interventions are being implemented, systematic monitoring determines whether the product is actually meeting those needs.

However, there is a problem with the exchange relationship between the nurse and the patient. The patient exchanges money for primary, secondary, or tertiary care. The nurse is skilled in assessing the patient's needs and designing a service to meet them. But does the patient know the price of the product, that is, nursing care? Third party reimbursement obscures the product's monetary value. Nursing charges are billed as room and board; thus the public is not aware of the cost and nursing cannot price its services competitively. Since the usual point of entry into the system is the physician, the voluntary exchange portion of the relationship is also violated.[8] Nurses employed by health care agencies and their patients cannot choose their exchange relationships. Nursing must identify its services and translate those services into costs in order to enter into an exchange relationship with patients.

Nurse executives

Traditionally, the nurse executive's planning begins with the organization's goals and objectives. Today the nurse executive is also a marketer, and planning begins with an analysis of consumers' needs. Marketing is coming to be thought of as a management discipline. "At its most basic level, marketing is the organizational function that manages the relationship between the organization and the consumers of its products and services."[9] It is the systematic monitoring of exchange relationships with the organization's publics. In order to be effective, the nurse executive must identify all the publics that have an impact on the nursing division and know what is valued and what is exchanged by each.[10]

The nurse executive is probably the health care manager most strongly oriented to the needs of consumers; yet, with little or no formal education in marketing, he or she must function as the marketing advocate within the organization. In the absence of a marketing consultant, the nurse executive can take an informal approach, using the existing information systems, such as the patient satisfaction survey, to gather information for a market analysis.[11] When the nurse executive takes the lead and institutes marketing, staff nurses realize that their actions have an effect on patient satisfaction. If an organization is truly oriented to meet the consumers' needs, each member of that organization will attempt to know and satisfy the consumer.

National nursing leaders

On the national level, nursing leaders have begun collaborating with consumer groups. In December 1983 the National Consumers League brought together business, labor, and insurance executives, consumer activists, and health care providers to discuss health care issues. Claire Fagin, professor and dean of the School of Nursing at the University of Pennsylvania, working under a scholarship from the American Nurses Foundation, will develop a model for effective collaboration between organized consumers and the nursing profession.[12] What services does the consumer need from the nurse? What do consumers want? These are questions the profession must address. The issue is not what services the nurse should provide, but rather what is valued by different groups of consumers. The use of marketing consultants on a large scale will promote nursing's differentiated service.

● ● ●

John Naisbitt, in *Megatrends,* predicts two trends for the 1980s and 1990s that relate to the kinds of services and products nurses can supply: the shift from short-term to long-term care, and the shift from institutional care to self-help, including fitness programs, home diagnostic kits, and corporate fitness. He also predicts a shift from a managerial society to an entrepreneurial one.[13]

Marketing is a legitimate professional activity for nursing at both the macro and the micro levels. Nurses can contribute to this process both directly and indirectly; specifically, they can conduct research that identifies consumers' needs and design services to meet those needs. Nurses' services must be identified and promoted in order to ensure the economic survival of the profession. Since other health care providers are competing for turf in the health care industry, nurses can no longer be reluctant to promote their services. These are times of great change in health care. Nursing's potential power is enormous.

REFERENCES

1. P. Kotler, and S.J. Levy, Broadening the Concept of Marketing. *Journal of Marketing* 33 (January 1969), 10–15.
2. P. Kotler, *Marketing for Nonprofit Organizations.* 2nd ed. (Englewood Cliffs, N.J.: Prentice-Hall, 1982), 6.
3. R.R. Alward, "A Marketing Approach to Nursing Administration: Part 2." *Journal of Nursing Administration* 13 (April 1983): 18–22.
4. P.R. Loubeau, "Marketing as a Health Care Concept." *Nursing Economics* 2 (January–February 1984): 37–41.
5. T. Levitt, "Marketing Success through Differentiation—of Anything." *Harvard Business Review* 58 (January–February 1980): 83–91.
6. D.W. Smith, and S.L. Shamansky, "Determining the Market for Family Nurse Practitioner Services: The Seattle Experience." *Nursing Research* 32 (1983): 301–305.
7. D.A. Stahl, "Developing and Marketing Ambulatory Care Programs." *Nursing Management* 15 (May 1984): 20–24.
8. Alward, "A Marketing Approach to Nursing Administration: Part 2."

9. LaTour, S.A., Calder, B.J., and Burns, L.A. "Marketing Hospital Ambulatory Care Services." In *Hospital Ambulatory Care: Making It Work,* edited by K. Meshenberg and L.A. Burns. Chicago: American Hospital Association, 1983, p. 65.

10. Alward, R.R. "A Marketing Approach to Nursing Administration: Part 1." *Journal of Nursing Administration* 13 (March 1983): 9–12.

11. Ibid.

12. "National Consumers League and Nurses to Work Together on Health Care." *Nursing Economics* 2 (March–April 1984): 92.

13. Naisbett, J. *Megatrends.* New York: Warner Books.

Products and product-line management in nursing

Ruth A. Anderson, R.N., M.S.N., M.A.
Doctoral Student
University of Texas at Austin
School of Nursing
Austin, Texas

*T*HIS IS AN ERA of change in the financing of health care that will provide many opportunities for the enterprising nurse administrator. Product-line management is one opportunity. It provides a mechanism for recognizing the many contributions nurses already make to the hospital product. It also offers expanded opportunities for influencing patient outcomes. Nurses must be prepared, however, to step into new positions as product-line managers and to take an active role in making decisions related to the product and to marketing it. Health care administrators must be convinced that nurses are prepared to be managers who understand the process of product-line management and of marketing methods that enable the health care agency to maintain its competitive edge in the health care market-

place. The first step is to think of nursing care in a business environment.

Nurses are part of the major restructuring of health care delivery that began in the 1980s with the era of the new federalism. New federalism economics and its philosophy stimulated major restructuring of health care services financing, bringing prospective reimbursement to hospitals and a demand in the health care system for cost containment, efficiency, and competition. These changes offer nursing an unequaled opportunity to demonstrate its contributions to the delivery of health care services. The nursing profession can establish its worth by understanding and becoming active in product development, product-line management, and marketing—the business environment.

Hospitals, physician practice groups, and nursing corporations are developing business acumen in order to survive—and even thrive—in the changing economic environment. This business acumen is influencing the structure and practices of health organizations. Increasingly, hospital services are defined as products and product lines, indicating a shift in health

Nurs Admin Q, 1985, 10(1), 65–72
©1985 Aspen Publishers, Inc.

care from service to product.[1] To success-fully make this transition, nursing service administrators must define nursing's place in a competitive health care delivery system. Nursing must offer an effective patient service that is both efficient and cost effective. Nursing must establish that it has a product that can be defined, priced, marketed, and sold.

Nursing is developing business acumen of its own, as indicated by the increasing num-ber of models for costing nursing services.[2-6] Authors discuss patient care units as profit centers with revenue-production goals.[7,8] Recently, the terms product and product-line management have been applied to nurs-ing.[9-11] This trend to use business concepts is expected to continue.

WHAT IS A PRODUCT?

Before defining a product, it is important that the purpose and mission of the business be appropriately conceived.[12] The impor-tance of this point is demonstrated by the railroad industry. Had the industry been conceived as the transportation business, rather than as strictly railroading, it might have mitigated today's financial problems by investing in air and ground transporta-tion. Tuberculosis sanatoriums are another example. In the 1950s, these institutions defined their product too narrowly to sur-vive.[13] After the advent of drugs for treating tuberculosis, many sanatoriums closed in-stead of developing and marketing new products.

Nursing can learn from these examples. The profession must first consider itself a business. Second, this nursing business must be broad enough to offer a variety of products. For instance, nursing can be in the patient care business or in the wellness business. The wellness business provides many more options for products and is not bound to any particular service agency or type of client.

WHAT PRODUCTS CAN NURSES MARKET?

A nurse's products vary depending on many factors, including demographics and whether the nurse is in an industrial, corpo-rate, business, or health care facility. Many types of products can be offered by nurses. For example, consumer wellness programs can be packaged and sold (or provided through contract) to health maintenance organizations and industry. Home health services and nurse practitioner services can be packaged to meet the needs of communi-ties. Continuing education services can be packaged in a variety of ways to meet the needs of different purchasing groups. Nurs-ing care is also a product. Thus, as Strong describes, "Nursing care is the product of nursing judgement and techniques—nurs-ing process."[14] If organized properly, nurs-ing can profit from this product; this would mean contracting with hospitals to provide nursing care for a fee, which would produce a profit.

The most important step in product defi-nition is describing its quality.[15] Describ-ing the quality of the product provides a mechanism for determining whether the product meets its own standards. In nurs-ing this is imperative in order to ensure that activities such as emotional support, patient and family education, and other "intangibles nurses insist are essential to quality health care"[16] are assigned a value in the product definition.

THE HOSPITAL (HEALTH CARE AGENCY) PRODUCT LINE

A broad definition of a hospital (health care agency) product is that it is health care.[17] Cleverly defines a hospital's product line as a clinical service area such as cardiology, pediatrics, or obstetrics.[18] Hospital products (e.g., patient care services) can be organized into product lines in a variety of ways, for example, according to diagnosis related groups (DRGs), patient demographics, physician specialty groups, programs (usually directed toward a specific category of diagnoses or according to clinical specialty), and specific procedures particularly for outpatient services.[19] The definition of the hospital's product line can be refined to the most specific designation: each diagnosis or patient care.

Nursing care can be a separate product or a component of a hospital product. For example, if nursing care is a component of the total product, other health professionals contribute to the final product. According to this definition of nursing's product, nursing's role becomes the management of an intermediate product.[20] Effective management of material and human resources in producing the intermediate product determines the quality and the marketplace value of the final product. Whether nursing is a separate product or a component of a product, it must be defined as a production function. Because nursing coordinates patient care in the acute care hospital, it is reasonable that nurses become product-line managers. In this case, product-line management becomes another nursing product.

MANAGING A PRODUCT LINE

History and evolution

Product-line management is a business management technique that originated in 1928, when Procter & Gamble employed a product manager for Lava soap.[21] It has been widely used only in the past 25 years.

Whether nursing is a separate product or a component of a product, it must be defined as a production function.

Product-line management evolved from the need to decentralize all decision-making information in operations in order to optimize profits. Management's goal was to produce a quality product at the least cost. This goal required timely decisions. One person close to the product had to know the product and to have the authority to make decisions relating to that product. Through this person, the product-line manager, companies with a diversity of products could respond quickly to the changing needs of consumers and remain competitive in the marketplace.[22]

Product management and product-line management are used interchangeably. Product management refers to a single product; product-line management refers to a group of similar products.

Role of the product manager

Dominguez offers this definition of the role of a product manager and in doing so describes product management:

The product manager is the central focus for all information relative to his product or product line. He is the repository of all such data, the source of information about his product, the planner, the profit controller and motivator, and the center of a large sphere of product influence that permeates every aspect of the business operation necessary for the accomplishment of his primary duty—the successful introduction, marketing and sale of profitable products and the continuous review and analysis of his product or product lines to assure continued overall profitable growth and marketing position.[23]

Product management was intended to create true profit centers.[24] The objectives of the product manager are, first, to develop strategies to continually improve and market the product; second, to develop the financial and operational plan for the product; and last, to monitor the implementation of the plan and evaluate results, instituting modifications as necessary. Six components of product management were defined by Dominguez: product, market, profit, coordination, forecasting, and planning.[25]

Product

The product manager must be an authority on the assigned product and must develop the "concept of product" rather than simply the product. The concept of product forces the manager to conceptualize the process of product development, production, and marketing (company image, customer service, the marketplace, and the internal environment of the organization are examples). These influences determine the nature and value of the final product.

Market

The market is the specific entity in which the product will be sold. The product manager must be knowledgeable about the target market. This knowledge is the basis for product planning and development. Aspects of the market that are of interest to the product manager are demographics, population density, social and psychological factors, and income levels.

The product manager must also analyze trends in the industry to ensure that products are kept current and that new product needs are discovered. Analyzing trends helps determine what products to offer. The most important consideration in planning is that the product plans are based on the needs of the market, not on what the company happens to be proficient at manufacturing. If the market is not using that product, it will not be profitable.

Profit

The product manager also has responsibility for the profit of an individual product. The product manager is responsible for gross profit, which includes the cost of the product sold. Cost factors include items such as labor, materials, equipment, and overhead. "The product manager is the corporate octopus with each of his tentacles reaching out to improve profit when and wherever this can be done."[26]

Coordination

Theoretically, the effective product manager has unlimited influence both vertically and horizontally within the organization. Conflict occurs in areas where the manager may have responsibility but no authority. Effective interpersonal skills are essential to smooth coordination. The product manager, as coordinator, is the primary source of information on the product, communicating and interpreting to others the objectives of the product plan. The product manager coordinates all the inputs in product development and makes the decisions about what inputs to incorporate into the product. Comprehensive knowledge of all aspects of the product is imperative.

Forecasting

The product manager forecasts trends and to do so, must have access to accurate, timely information. Management information systems can provide the manager with essential information, such as inventory levels, turnover rates, cash flow, expenses, and quantitative data from which trends can be established. In forecasting, the product manager uses this information to make decisions about the product. Managers must be thoroughly familiar with the organization's management information system capabilities.

Planning

The last of the six major principles in product management is planning. It is the responsibility of the product manager to develop a feasible operation plan, provide for the research and development of new products, and see that they are successfully introduced into the marketplace. Planning activity is continual, since the product manager is continually gathering information. The formal phase of planning involves writing objectives and establishing time parameters.

NURSE AS PRODUCT-LINE MANAGER

Organizing for product-line management

Product lines in hospitals can be organized according to subspecialties of the major diagnostic categories. In this approach, the large number of hospital products (467 DRGs) can be clustered into 10 to 20 product lines. Costs can then be applied to individual products, providing a means by which to measure the impact on the product of changes in volume, medical staff, nursing staff mix, and use of other resources. Product-line management cuts across traditional departmental lines, since the product manager must coordinate all the pieces that contribute to the product.[27]

Nurses as coordinators are product-line managers. Nurses possess current clinical data relating to patients. Nurses are informed about the activities of other departments in relation to individual patients. They are in a position to evaluate patient changes and can make timely clinical decisions based on their knowledge of the activities of other professionals and their own clinical judgments. Strange states, "Nurses are at the point in the hospital where key management decisions will be made.... [Nurses] are at the key point in the system, the production coordination point, managing the sequence of a variety of product lines, including nursing."[28]

Managing quality and cost in a product management environment

Product lines are the framework in which operations are evaluated. Quality, along with profitability of the clinical service, is a major objective of the manager.

As product managers, nurses must interact with staff from all other departments in the hospital to coordinate services and expedite quality patient outcomes. Linking cost and quality, nurse product managers must efficiently manage resources such as staffing and patient education and consider factors such as early discharge planning and coordination of services. Efficient planning avoids duplication, improves the turnaround time for lab and other diagnostic tests, and achieves smoother interunit transfer of patients.[29]

Control of inputs is part of the product-line manager's responsibility. Nurse product managers must develop a keen business sense and control inputs to the product production. As product-line managers, nurses must develop new relationships with physicians. Physicians' orders influence resource use and can add to the cost of the product. Collaboration with physicians is necessary to ensure that physicians' orders are correlated to the patient's clinical condition, which may change rapidly. In addition, the best professional staff mix must be established and justified. All production costs must be identified and linked to quality patient outcomes. Nurse product managers must have access to management information reports and must use them in planning budgetary, productivity, and quality care goals.

The nurse as product-line manager takes responsibility in marketing the hospital's product. Nurses, having always concerned themselves with quality patient care, will agree with Strange, who states, "Quality care with the human touch provides the superior competitive edge. Winners provide a product of superior value rather than one that simply costs less."[30]

The nurse as product manager becomes the most important person in the hospital's attempt to be competitive. The product manager must be familiar with the hospital's product lines. He or she must be familiar with what competing hospitals are doing. The product manager must ask the questions: How does the hospital measure up to the competition? What revision can provide a competitive edge? What new opportunities exist in the marketplace for a particular product line? What new products can be developed within a particular product line? Answers to such questions may lead to the development of new products, such as home care services, geriatric day care, or other specialized services for the elderly or other groups.

•   •   •

It is imperative that nurses add knowledge of business concepts to their nursing knowledge. Applying nursing knowledge effectively in this era of prospective pricing, cost containment, efficiency, and competition requires adept application of business and finance principles. Continuing education programs must provide practicing nurses with appropriate business knowledge and skills.

Nursing must be active in seizing the opportunities afforded by this time of change in the health care financing system. Now is the time to demonstrate nursing's value by documenting quantifiable results for nursing actions. Nursing's position as a hospital revenue generator must be made clear. Nurses must be prepared with a knowledge of business and economics and must step into emerging roles in the hospital system. Outside the hospital, nurses can establish a number of diversified, profitable nursing products, thereby maintaining a place in the competitive health care system.

REFERENCES

1. Strange, D. "Service to Product: A Transition of focus." Paper presented to the American Society of Nursing Administrators, Chicago, October 1984.
2. Caterinicchio, R. "Relative Intensity Measures: Pricing of Inpatient Nursing Services under Diagnosis-Related Groups Prospective Hospital Payment." *Health Care Financing Review* 6 (Fall 1984): 61-70.
3. Curtin, L. "Determining Cost of Nursing Services Per DRG." *Nursing Management* 14 (April 1983): 16-20.
4. Mitchell, M., Miller, J., Welches, L., and Walker, D. "Determining Cost of Direct Nursing Care by DRGs." *Nursing Management* 15 (April 1984): 29-32.
5. Riley, W., and Schaefers, V. "Costing Nursing Services." *Nursing Management* 14 (December 1983): 40-43.
6. Walker, D. "The Cost of Nursing Care in Hospitals." *Journal of Nursing Administration* 13 (March 1983): 13-18.
7. Higgerson, N., and Van Slyck, A. "Variable Billing for Services: New Fiscal Direction for Nursing." *Journal of Nursing Administration* 12 (June 1982): 20-26.
8. Riley, W., and Schaefers, V. "Nursing Operations as a Profit Center." *Nursing Management*

15 (April 1984): 43-46.

9. Piper, L. "Managing the Intermediate Product." *Nursing Management* 16 (March 1985): 18-20.

10. Strong, V. "Nursing Products: Primary Components of Health Care." *Nursing Economics* 3 (January-February 1985): 60-61.

11. Strange, "Service to Product: A Transition of Focus."

12. Levitt, T. "Marketing Myopia." *Harvard Business Review* 38, 4 (1960): 45-56.

13. Loubeau, P. "Marketing as a Health Care Concept." *Nursing Economics* 2 (January-February 1984): 37-41.

14. Strong, "Nursing Products: Primary Components of Health Care," 60.

15. Ibid.

16. Ibid., 60.

17. Cleverly, W. "Cost Accounting Pins a Value to DRGs." *Modern Healthcare* 14 (April 1984): 172.

18. Ibid.

19. Burik, D., and Duval, T. "Hospital Cost Accounting: Strategic Considerations." Part I, *Healthcare Financial Management* 39 (February 1985): 19-28.

20. Piper, "Managing the Intermediate Product."

21. Dominguez, G. *Product Management.* American Management Association, New York, 1971.

22. Fendrich, C. *The Industrial Product Management System.* American Management Association, New York, 1966.

23. Dominguez, *Product Management*, 4-5.

24. Luck, D. "Interfaces of a Product Manager," In *Product Planning,* edited by A. E. Spitz. New York: Auerbach Publishers, 1972.

25. Dominguez, *Product Management.*

26. Ibid., 2.

27. Strange, "Service to Product: A Transition of Focus."

28. Ibid., Tape No. 2-109.

29. Ibid., Tape No. 2-109.

30. Ibid., Tape No. 2-109.

Part III
Study and discussion questions

1. What is the marketing process?
2. What are the elements critical to the marketing process?
3. Describe how nursing can contribute to the marketing process.
4. Describe how product line management can positively affect the practice of nursing.
5. What is the role of a product line manager?
6. What are the products that nursing can market?
7. What are the benefits of organizing a nursing department for product line management?

Part IV
Nursing informatics

Roy L. Simpson, R.N., C.
Corporate Executive Director, Nursing
  Affairs
HBO & Company—Health Quest
Atlanta, Georgia

Nursing staffing continues to be the proverbial "bur under the saddle" of nursing management. As Barbara Brown—*Nursing Administration Quarterly's* editor since the publication's inception—wrote in 1974, "Staffing is the most written about, discussed, frustrated-over, agonizing situation, crucial problem, 24-hour dilemma confronting nursing service administration today." Obviously, little has changed in nearly 20 years.

Thankfully, much *has* changed over the decades in terms of our sophistication and understanding of the issues involved with nursing staffing. Authors McHugh and Dwyer do an excellent job of not only articulating the key issues in measuring patient acuity for nursing staffing, but also in reviewing the history (and inadequacies) of previous methods of measuring the consumption of nursing hours for staffing purposes.

Their historical review of the literature starts with a look at the popular model used in the 1940s and 1950s—"census staffing" based on patient occupancy—and takes us through a breakthrough period in the 1960s when researchers first began looking at the intensity of patient dependency upon the nurse as a model of staffing. The authors also review all the approaches and variations that followed from that perceptual shift, including models that were based on controlled variable staffing, float pool staffing, work sampling, standard and nursing times for tasks, and nursing staff records.

McHugh and Dwyer provide us with a cogent overview of the principles behind measurement of patient acuity—and all of the complexities, assumptions, and performance tasks that are involved.

In the end, they give us a healthy dose of reality by reminding us of the imperfection and limits of acuity based classification measurements. They do so, not to undermine our confidence in the measurement system, but to remind us that there is no perfect solution and that we must be forever vigilant in checking our assumptions and the validity of the tools and models we use.

Only with that kind of intellectual vigor can we hope to continue advancing in our search for a "perfect" classification system to support adequate nursing staffing.

Automation is another major change. Today, automated information systems—originally introduced in the early 1980s—help us monitor nursing consumption and the quality of patient care. But in the mid-1970s, there were no automated tools to help Carol Smith and her staff at the Children's Memorial Hospital in Chicago implement the first acuity-based patient classification system in a total pediatric setting.

Her 1977 article shows us the depth of commitment, time, and paperwork that was necessary to create a patient classification system in the early days. Yes, it still takes a great deal of commitment, time, and paperwork today, but we have the advantage of computerized data tracking.

In the end, Smith tells us that nursing management was very concerned about their classification program not becoming stagnant—which is why they continuously looked for ways to improve the methodology. This drive continues today, not only at Children's Memorial, but at health care organizations all over the country. It is a drive that is familiar to most nursing managers—one that will continue indefinitely—technology or no technology.

Measurement issues in patient acuity classification for prediction of hours in nursing care

Mary L. McHugh, Ph.D., R.N.
Director of Nursing Research and
Development

Vicki L. Dwyer, M.N., R.N.
Assistant Director, Staffing and
Scheduling
St. Francis Regional Medical Center
Wichita, Kansas

THE TERMS "PATIENT ACUITY" and "patient classification" have a variety of meanings in the contemporary hospital environment. Historically, the term "acuity" has been used when the variable being measured could conceptually be defined as "multiorgan system failure," "probability of death," or "medical or nursing resource consumption."[1,2,3] For nursing, patient acuity has long been used as a factor in nursing efforts to staff patient care units with the number of nursing hours required to provide appropriate, high-quality nursing care to individual patients. If terms used to measure a concept are to be useful, they must be defined in a way that all users can agree

upon. A short history of patient acuity will be presented along with a definition of how the term is to be used. This study also focuses on how acuity measurement affects utility of the concept for research and hospital nurse staffing.

The term "patient acuity system" is sometimes used to describe systems designed to predict a patient's probability of survival. The Acute Physiology and Chronic Health Evaluation (APACHE) measure was designed to categorize patients into "acuity classifications" for the purpose of comparing one hospital's patient population with another.[1,2] Therapeutic Intervention Scoring System (TISS[3]) was developed to measure and compare intensity of medical and nursing care across agencies. "Intensity of nursing care" may refer to amount of work or task difficulty, for example, "Should the work be performed by a nurse aide, licensed practical nurse (LPN), registered nurse (RN), or a clinical specialist?" Nurse managers will recognize Cullen's work as more closely related to their interests than the APACHE measures. In nursing, acuity has been of interest primarily as a means

Nurs Admin Q, 1992, 16(4), 20–31
©1992 Aspen Publishers, Inc.

to an end, specifically, the end of developing appropriate models of hospital nurse staffing.

For the purposes of staffing, the concept "intensity of nursing care" is concerned with numbers and types of nursing personnel required to deliver care to a group of patients. Measures of nursing care intensity are usually derived from measures of patient acuity. The combined measurement and nurse staffing system is often called a "patient classification system."

FACTORS IN THE CONSUMPTION OF NURSING HOURS

From a measurement perspective, one might ask, "How does measuring a patient's acuity tell us about a hospital's consumption of nursing time? What is the relationship between patient acuity and nursing time expenditures?" A review of the literature shows that estimating nursing hours from patient acuity is a relatively recent strategy.

During the 1940s and 1950s, variables used as the basis for determination of budgeted nursing hours included hospital bed capacity, peak or mean census, and average daily census.[4-6] A typical strategy was as follows: Managers determined the number of beds and average occupancy to determine the average daily census. Then they multiplied the average daily census by a predefined number of nursing hours (usually four to five) per patient, per day. For the purposes of this study, this type of staffing was labeled "census staffing."

Census staffing made several assumptions about hospital nursing, which research later proved invalid. First, it assumed a fairly constant number of patients; often 100 percent occupancy was assumed. Managers may have believed that the risk of depriving patients of adequate nursing care overshadowed the risk of excess staffing

costs. It should be noted that nursing wages were extremely low prior to the 1960s, so the financial costs of that decision may, in fact, have been quite modest. (It also should be noted that the study demonstrating the high rate of errors in chronically overstaffed units was not published until 1959 by New, Nite, and Callahan.[7]) Second, Census Staffing assumed that nursing care needs varied little among patients, *or,* that when averaged together, the required hours of nursing care changed very little from day to day. Third, Census Staffing assumed the most important factor in a hospital's consumption of nursing time was the number of filled beds. Several studies published in the early 1960s showed these assumptions to be incorrect.

In the early 1960s, Robert Connor[8-10] published the results of his doctoral dissertation and dramatically changed the health care industry's assumptions about the nature of the nursing department's workload. Connor found that the most important factor in a hospital's consumption of nursing time was intensity of patient dependency upon the nurse, that is, nursing care needs. He discovered that nursing care needs varied greatly among patients, and total nursing hours required in a single unit varied significantly from day to day. Connor also was able to demonstrate that those day-to-day variations occurred in a random pattern.

Connor's work showed that workload was not constant because both occupancy and patient care requirements changed from day to day, and these changes occurred randomly. Thus, the most important factor was not filled beds alone. A combination of numbers of patients and care requirements of each patient were the factors that determined nursing workload. At the same time, nursing wages were rising and the New, Nite, and Callahan[7] study demonstrated the danger of overstaffing. Managers were forced to reconsider the importance of nurse staffing levels. Connor concluded that any staffing pattern that provided a constant level of staffing achieved a very poor fit with the realities of nursing unit workload distributions.[8-10]

Connor's solution to the poor fit between existing staffing patterns and workload patterns essentially converted the entire nursing staff into one large float pool. Theoretically, any nurse could be floated to any unit, if the nurse was needed in the understaffed unit, and was excess staffing in his or her permanent work unit. Connor developed and tested a new staffing pattern that he named "controlled variable staffing." His research demonstrated that controlled variable staffing was able to produce substantial cost savings in the nursing department's salary budget by cutting consumption of nursing hours. Connor's work graphically showed that staffing practices of nursing departments significantly impact the consumption of nursing time and, therefore, the hospital's budget.[8-10]

Unfortunately, Connor's system assumed that all nurses are adequately prepared to function effectively in all of the various nursing specialties. The performance of controlled variable staffing has been questioned more intensely during the past 20 years. The degree of clinical specialization required of nurses has increased during the 23 years since Connor's study. His assumption that any nurse could safely be floated to any unit has become increasingly untenable.

Connor's study also ignored nursing morale issues through the tacit assumption that floating would be acceptable to nurses. Most hospitals find that at least some nurses are extremely resistant to being floated to other units. Equally as important, clinical managers today are more likely to understand the quality and risk management issues pertaining to orientation and experi-

ence levels of nurses who are asked to float. Quality and risk management considerations, the cost in damage to morale, and the resultant effects of nursing turnover make controlled variable staffing an increasingly costly solution to the workload variation problem.

Other staffing patterns have been introduced, which proponents claim produce cost savings that are comparable to controlled variable staffing but more palatable to the nurses. One such pattern is float pool staffing. In float pool staffing, minimum and mean workloads are calculated. (Minimum is the number of nurses for commonly occurring low workload times—usually about 10 percent less than mean workload.) The number of nurses required for minimum workload are employed and permanently assigned to the unit. The rest of the nurses needed to provide *mean* workload staffing are assigned to a float pool. Float nurses are assigned on a daily basis to whatever unit has the greatest need for their services. In this model, overall staffing is lowered, flexibility to meet varying workloads is provided, and stable work groups are not violated, thus improving morale. The effectiveness of float pool staffing is highly dependent upon having several different units, and the different units' workloads must be independent of each other. That is, a high workload in one unit will not be dependent upon, or related to, a high workload in another unit. When this is true, a high workload in one unit will often be offset by a low workload in another unit.

In addition to patient care needs and nurse staffing patterns, a hospital's organizational and task structures impact the consumption of nursing time. For example, a hospital that does not staff its respiratory therapy department (RT) 24 hours a day reassigns RT's duties to the nursing staff during the hours that the department is

---

In addition to patient care needs and nurse staffing patterns, a hospital's organizational and task structures impact the consumption of nursing time.

---

closed. If a hospital does not provide a ward clerk during the evening and night shifts, the nursing staff must perform clerical tasks in addition to their nursing duties. While these accommodations may prove cost-effective for the hospital's total budget, they do impact the consumption of nursing hours.

APPROACHES TO THE MEASUREMENT OF NURSING TIME CONSUMPTION

A patient acuity classification system is a secondary product of more precise measures of factors that consume nursing time. Connor was as famous for his use of work measurement studies in nursing as he was for some of his other findings. Although Wright[11] and Torgersen[12] had demonstrated the usefulness of one form of work measurement in the nursing department, their work had far less impact than did Connor's, perhaps because their work was published in the industrial engineering literature, which, at the time of publication, was a most obscure resource to nurses. Since the early 1960s, several approaches to the precise measurement of nursing time consumption have been used.

Work sampling

In work sampling, a single type of employee is chosen for study. Then, the work to be observed is divided into discrete, mutually exclusive categories. For example, Torgersen chose the 10 task categories pre-

sented in the box entitled "Torgersen's 10 Categories of Nursing Activities." After the categories are defined, observers are selected on the basis that they either understand, or readily can be taught to understand, the nature of the work they are to observe.

Work sampling techniques involve observations of individual nurses at randomly selected points in time. (Strict randomization of the time of observations is essential to the use of the technique.) The day must be divided into blocks of time from which the observation samples are drawn. At least 50 observation points must be obtained; Torgersen chose to obtain

---

Torgersen's 10 Categories of Nursing Activity

1. Administering medications or physical treatments (e.g., changing bandages).
2. All other patient contact time. This category consists of "nonprofessional" tasks such as making the bed, feeding, or bathing the patient, etc.
3. Preparation and conclusion to no. 1. This category includes all work or cleanup that nurses perform after professional, direct patient care activities.
4. Preparation and conclusion to no. 2.
5. Travel time, not including nos. 3 and 4.
6. Exchange of information about the patient.
7. Personnel work (e.g., employee management, hiring, performance evaluation).
8. Housekeeping.
9. Teaching other personnel (e.g., teaching a new aide to take a blood pressure reading).
10. Idle and personal time.

1,600 for a higher degree of confidence in his measures.

Continuous observation

One of Connor's first strategies involved continuous observation of selected patients to measure consumption of direct patient care hours. In this method, an observer is assigned to watch one patient (or the two patients in a semiprivate room). With a stopwatch, the observer simply counts the minutes during which a member of the nursing staff is in the room or near a patient's bed. In this method, patients are carefully selected by using a random or stratified random sampling strategy; however, the times of observation are not randomized since *all* direct care is measured. There is also no requirement for categorization of tasks. The method does not require the investigator to differentiate among the various types of direct care given. It is assumed that some a priori categorization or selection criteria exist for the patients' inclusion in the study.

Standard nursing times

Standard times for tasks are sometimes used to measure consumption of nursing time. This method involves identifying as many of the discrete tasks that nurses perform as possible, and then obtaining standard amounts of time required for performance of each task. The observer simply notes each task, and, at the end of the measuring period, standard times for each task are summed to obtain the amount of nursing time consumed for each patient studied. Standard times are obtained by observing many instances of the performance of each task, at least 30 to 50 observations of each task should be obtained. Once the times needed for each task are obtained, the "standard" amount of time needed for

that task is determined. Standard times may be based on the average time required, or on the amount of time that corresponds with a percentile of the sampled times, such as the 50th percentile or the 75th percentile.

When standard times are used in combination with work sampling studies, precise measures of the way nursing time is used in a unit may be obtained. However, it is time consuming and expensive to obtain the original standard time measures if they cannot be obtained from another source. If obtained from another hospital's studies, original standard time measures should be validated using the new hospital's nurses since different types of equipment, experience levels of the nurses, and the like may alter the values of "standard" task performance times.

Nursing staff records

Another method for measuring use of nursing time resources involves the staff as data collectors as they go about their work. This method usually is employed to measure direct care, although, sometimes, it is used to measure time for charging, and communicating with the family, physician, auxiliary departments, and other staff about a particular patient. A data collection sheet is usually placed on the door to the patient's room (or other spot convenient to the location where data are to be collected). Anyone who enters the room or provides any care to the patient is expected to record the time when the service was rendered, the nature of the service, and the professional level of person providing the service. Often, only nursing staff are asked to record data on the sheets. Information collected is used to prepare summaries of nursing time utilization patterns by type of patient (for example, diagnostic category, acuity class, and so forth).

Although this method may be the only form of measurement available, the hospital should realize that this method is the least reliable of the work measurement methods. It is inevitably biased toward *underestimating* the work performed. Nurses will frequently forget to write down activities—especially if the location of the activity is different from the location of the data collection sheet. Data collection will be especially poor when workloads are heavy because data collection will be the lowest priority task to the patient care personnel. Unfortunately, those high workload data, if lost, are the items that will have the most devastating impact on nurse staffing. Also, this method will underestimate a unit's direct care workload by a randomly varying amount. Adding a constant figure to compensate for lost, high workload data will not be a reliable correction factor. Nevertheless, this method will provide some information on nursing time consumption and should be used when the hospital is unable to obtain the assistance of specially trained data collectors.

PATIENT ACUITY CLASSIFICATION

Instrument development

All the fairly precise techniques for measuring a unit's consumption of nursing time are extremely costly to financial and human energy resources. Therefore, the precise methods are inappropriate tools for the measurement of daily nursing workloads and cannot be used to fine tune nurse staffing on a shift-to-shift basis. Patient acuity classification systems were developed to support day-to-day staffing decisions. They are derived from the more complex work measurement studies.

Work measurement techniques demand careful assessment of a large number of discrete tasks. However, many tasks tend to be components of task complexes. For example, the task "complete bed bath" implies a whole set of tasks closely related to actually washing the patient. The nurse must gather the materials (for example, soap, towels, bath pan, and so forth), draw the water, transport the materials to the bedside, wash the patient, empty the used water, clean the bath pan and the bedside area, and return the materials to storage. The nurse usually changes the bed at the time the bath is given, so that set of tasks also accompanies the "complete bed bath" task complex. Since all of these tasks must be performed as the nurse completes the bed bath, the entire complex may be represented by the single task label, "complete bed bath."

Subsets of task complexes are often needed rather than the entire complex, and patterns of demand for task complex subsets have been identified. In the bed bath example, patients vary in their needs for assistance with personal hygiene. Some patients can bathe themselves without help. Others need the nurse to bring supplies to their bedside but will bathe themselves. Still others need the nurse to assist with their bath but can do some things for themselves. Patient classification systems define these different levels of need as acuity levels and use these patterns to measure staffing needs. In this example, the nurse would identify one of the following four levels of patient independence in personal hygiene:

Acuity Level	Category of Need
I	Self-care
II	Simple assist bath
III	Partial bath
IV	Complete bed bath

A similar process is followed for a variety of care, in addition to hygiene. Nourishment, mobility, medications, and physical treatments are just a few of the areas of care that have been included in patient acuity classification systems.

Once the task complex groupings have been identified, the general classification for the patient must be determined. For each area of nursing care measured, the usual method involves assigning points to the various levels of care needed. Totals are calculated for each patient, and the final class assignment is a function of the number of care points earned. (High totals correspond to high consumption of nursing hours.) A patient's acuity is a function of care point totals, and care points correspond to nursing hours. Therefore, the staffing needed on a unit is easily calculated by counting the number of patients in each class and translating class totals into nursing hours from a prepared conversion table.

Roy Simpson[13] developed a simple and yet elegant method of determining a patient's acuity classification from task complex measures. It was based on the discovery that care complexity follows an orderly progression. The need for one very complex care task usually implies the need for a whole set of other tasks. Furthermore, certain tasks can be viewed as global indicators of patient acuity. For example, an order such as "measure the patient's vital signs every 15 minutes for the next 24 hours" is sufficient information to conclude that this patient will consume a great deal of nursing time and achieve a high acuity score. No further information is needed to classify that patient. As with other systems, the acuity scores are translated into nursing hours required for care.

The need for one very complex care task usually implies the need for a whole set of other tasks ... certain tasks can be viewed as global indicators of patient acuity.

The acuity score is determined by the highest acuity "indicator task" the patient requires in his or her nursing care.

Limitations of patient classification systems

Patient classification systems may be thought of as greatly reduced and simplified instruments for work measurement. They are useful tools for *estimating* nursing units' workloads. They are not precise measures, and the estimate will have rather large amounts of error because simplifying the measurement of workload sacrifices a great deal of precision. The loss of precision is a function of the essential task of patient classification, the effort to superimpose a multimodal distribution on what is essentially a normal distribution of patients' nursing needs.

Figure 1 offers an example of the variation in hours of nursing care per 24-hour day among individual patients. Such a distribution might assume a unit average of approximately 5 hours of care per day, with a self-care patient average of 3 hours of care and an absolute maximum of 24 hours of nursing care per day. (Theoretically, a patient could exceed the 24-hour maximum if he or she needed at least one nurse for 24 hours of care plus more nurses to assist from time to time.) In a patient classification system, an attempt is arbitrarily made to break up that distribution into several smaller but discrete (nonoverlapping) distributions.

Figure 2 shows an example of the hypothetical distribution for a "near-perfect," four-level patient classification system. Patients have been arbitrarily divided into 4 groups: the self-care patients, with an average of 3 hours of nursing care per day; low moderate care patients, with an average of 4.5 hours per day; high moderate care patients, with an average of 7.5 hours per day;

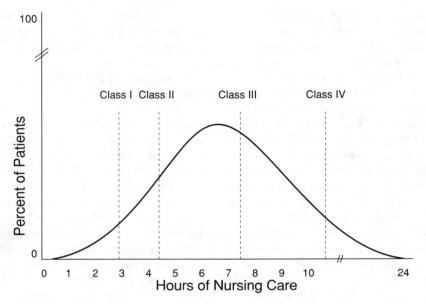

Figure 1. Actual distribution of hours of nursing care (exhibits a "normal distribution").

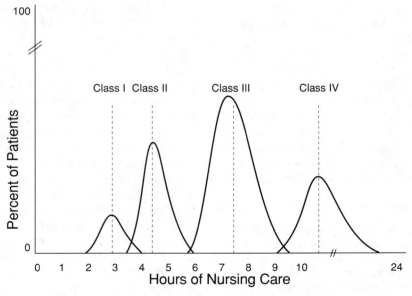

Figure 2. Ideal distribution produced by a "perfect" patient classification system.

and intensive care patients with an average of 15 hours per day. Of course in this "ideal" model, there is little or no overlap between the categories.

When the two distributions are superimposed, as in Figure 3, the fit between the hypothetical and actual distributions is not very close. Figure 4 shows the actual clinical distribution when hours of care by patient acuity class are graphed. There is a great deal of overlap at the edges of the distributions. This relatively poor fit is an expected consequence of moving from precise but complex work measurement to an imprecise but simple patient acuity classification system. The error in classifying patients, seen at the edges of the quadrimodal distribution, produces error in estimation of the nursing workload hours. However, if the error does not exceed eight hours of nursing care in any shift on one unit, the estimate will be correct within a hospital's ability to alter staffing. Therefore, a great deal of precision is not really necessary since hospitals usually cannot divide a nurse among two or three units during the same shift.

Patient classification systems can be used to fine tune daily staffing. They also can be used in annual budgeting processes. However, they may have limited value for long-term staffing predictions or when used as tools to evaluate long-term changes in average acuity. As care protocols change, the classification system may have to be adjusted or revised to take into account different care "items." Also, a trend toward increased acuity may be a function of increasing patient acuity, or it may be a function of loss of rater reliability in the direction of "overclassifying." Stable acuity may be a function of unchanged patient care requirements or of an instrument that was

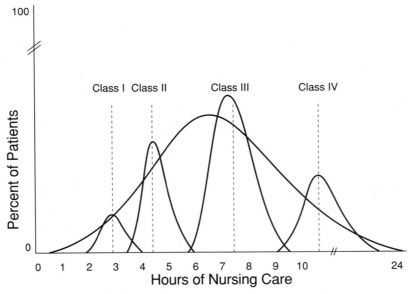

Figure 3. Ideal distribution produced by a "perfect" patient classification system (with Figure 1 superimposed).

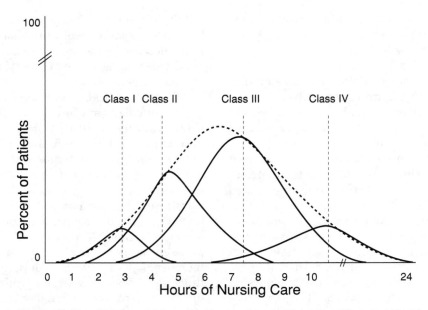

Figure 4. Typical distribution of hours of care by acuity classification (with Figure 1 superimposed).

not designed to measure the new types of care being delivered. External measures of change in average acuity may be of help. For example, the Medicus Company has reported that patient acuity is increasing at a rate of approximately 3 percent per year. However, an imprecise measure, such as the typical patient classification system in use today, should be retested for validity at least every three to five years, and for rater reliability annually.

CHARACTERISTICS OF THE CLASSIFICATION INSTRUMENTS

Measurement error

Measurement instruments are subject to a variety of reliability problems called "measurement error." Measurement error may be either systematic or random. Systematic

error means that the instrument consistently overestimates or underestimates what it has been designed to measure. Systematic error can be itself measured and compensated for by adding or subtracting a value equal to the size of the error from the measurement results. A yardstick 1 inch short of 36 inches is an example of a systematic error. The yardstick would be reliable—it would make exactly the same error every time. However, calculations using that yardstick would not constitute valid measures of how long an object (a piece of lumber, for example) actually is. If the deficiency were known, the user could correct for the error by subtracting one inch from the obtained measure of every three feet of result. Similarly, if a staffing system instrument consistently underestimated needed staff by two nurses per shift, the user could correct for instrument error by adding two nurses to the instrument estimate of staffing needed. This technique could assist the administrator to adapt a staffing system formula to a hospital other than the one in which the formula had been developed. For this reason, systematic error is not an insurmountable problem.

Random error is a much more serious problem. It means that errors in measurement of unknown size are sometimes made, but not always. Random errors are usually a function of unreliability on the part of people using the instrument, that is, rater reliability problems. These errors are caused by such things as writing a "two" when a "three" was intended, recording the information under the wrong patient's name, and so forth. Errors in addition are probably a frequent source of random error when the nurses are required to add up several figures for each patient—especially if they must perform manual calculations without the assistance of a calculator or computer. Another important source of rater unreliability includes poorly defined terms and directions on the data collection instrument. These problems will lead to situations in which the same nurse classifies different patients according to different standards (intrarater reliability problems), or situations in which no two nurses can agree upon one patient's proper acuity level (interrater reliability problems). To prevent or limit random error, the procedure should be kept as simple as possible. The nurse should be required to perform few, if any, mathematical calculations. The directions should be kept simple. If possible, directions should be clearly printed on the acuity classification instrument. If the nurse needs many rules and procedures to accurately complete the instrument, and the rules will not fit on the instrument, the random error rate may be so high that it renders results insufficiently reliable to use for staffing. As a general rule,

increased complexity in use generates an increased random error rate. Furthermore, a very complex instrument will probably demand a great deal of nursing time, thus increasing staffing costs rather than helping to control them.

Instrument validity

Validity refers to the question, "Does this instrument measure what we think it measures?" It is always necessary to confirm that the staffing estimates produced by the patient acuity classification system reflect the workload realities in the unit. It is especially important to check the validity of any instrument developed in another unit or hospital. The lowest level of validity to be examined is face validity. Face validity means that the instrument appears to measure what it was designed to measure. One way to obtain face validity might be to ask nurses who work on the unit to examine the instrument. They would be asked if it measures all of the most important factors in consumption of nursing time in their unit. An extreme example of poor face validity would be an attempt to use an instrument developed for the surgical intensive care unit in the adolescent psychiatric unit.

The instrument also should be tested for predictive or criterion-related validity. This type of validity involves correlating the estimates of staffing need, which are provided by the instrument at the beginning of the shift, with actual experience during the shift. Actual experience estimates could be provided by the charge nurse. For example, if the instrument is designed to estimate the number of staff needed so that no more than 10 percent of shifts will be overstaffed or understaffed, the instrument is valid to the degree that its predictions match the actual staffing needs on the sampled shifts.

• • •

Patient acuity classification systems have brought a degree of objectivity to the allocation of staffing resources. Whether they have improved staffing is not really known. There is some evidence that the best measure of a classification system's validity is the degree to which it matches the head nurse's judgment of what staffing the unit needs.[14] Regardless of their ability to improve staffing, the systems certainly help nurses defend staffing decisions to the hospital administration and may help in the explanation of consumption of nursing time.

REFERENCES

1. Knaus, W., et al. "APACHE II: A Severity of Disease Classification System." *Critical Care Medicine* 13 (1985): 818-29.
2. Knaus, W., et al. "An Evaluation of Outcome from Intensive Care in Major Medical Centers." *Annals of Internal Medicine* 104, no. 3 (1986): 410-18.
3. Cullen, D., et al. "Objective, Quantitative Measurement of Severity of Illness in Critically Ill Patients. *Critical Care Medicine* 12, no. 3 (1984): 155-60.
4. Cramer, G. "Analysis of Ward Nursing." Master's thesis, The Johns Hopkins University, 1955.
5. Gunn, M. *A Method for Developing a Master Staffing Plan for the Nursing Service Department*. St. Louis, Mo.: Catholic Hospital Association, 1960.
6. Howell, G. "A Hospital Solves Its Staffing Problems." *Hospitals* 29, no. 7 (1955): 54-56.
7. New, P., Nite, G., and Callahan, J. "Too Many Nurses May be Worse than Too Few." *The Modern Hospital* 93 (1959): 104-8.
8. Connor, R. "A Hospital Inpatient Classification System." *Dissertation Abstracts International* 21, (1960): 565.
9. Connor, R. "A Work Sampling Study of Variations in Nursing Work Load." *Hospitals* 35, no. 9 (1961): 40-41, 111.
10. Connor, R., et al. "Effective Use of Nursing Resources." *Hospitals* 35, no. 9 (1961): 30-39.
11. Wright, M.J. *Improvement of Patient Care*. New York, N.Y.: G.P. Putnam's Sons, 1954.
12. Torgersen, P. "An Example of Work Sampling in the Hospital." *The Journal of Industrial Engineering* 10, no. 3 (1959): 197-200.
13. Simpson, R. Verbal report from HealthQuest Company. Atlanta, Ga., January 1984.
14. Trivedi, V., and Hancock, W. "Measurement of Nursing Work Load Using Head Nurses' Perceptions. *Nursing Research* 24, no. 5 (1975): 371-76.

Adequate staffing: It's more than a game of numbers

Carol A. Smith, R.N., B.S.
*Assistant Director of Nursing for Inpatient
  Services*
The Children's Memorial Hospital
Chicago, Illinois

STAFFING FOR QUALITY of patient care has long been a concern of nursing administrators, and certainly has been and is a concern for us at Children's Memorial Hospital. A little over a year ago, we found ourselves extremely short-staffed, utilizing large numbers of outside agency personnel to fill the gaps, asking our own staff to work many hours of overtime, and obviously providing less than optimal patient care. Motivated by our deep concerns regarding this situation, we felt a need to provide the quality of patient care we wanted and felt we were obligated to give.

As we began our undertakings, one thing was apparent: our traditional use of "nursing care hours," while readily available for projecting staffing requirements and the personnel budget, had given us less than optimal results in the past and we, therefore, did not want to use this method again if something better was available. We all had "gut feelings" as to what type of personnel we needed and what kind of mix (RN, LPN, Aide) we would like, but had no good concrete data to support and communicate our viewpoint to the administration or the Board of Directors.

We have reviewed staffing studies done at other children's hospitals in the United States and Canada.[1] Most of these institutions had utilized consulting firms to do time studies to help them identify their staffing needs. We had, in fact, done time studies of our own on two units to determine how much actual time it took to care for acute versus chronically ill children of all age groups.

Our experience had shown that this approach was extremely time consuming and after reviewing the experience of others, we felt the resulting data provided little meaningful information which could be utilized by our institution. Since we felt our situation was critical, time was a key factor and it became obvious that we could not find the answers ourselves without considerable

Nurs Admin Q, 1977, 1(4), 15–25

time involvement effort. We therefore began looking for outside consultants to provide specific expertise and assistance.

FINDING ASSISTANCE

Wanting the very best assistance available, we reviewed several firms, looking in depth at their approach and services. This search led us to Medicus Systems Corporation who, fortunately, had their corporate offices in Chicago, and had worked with other hospitals in the Chicago area in nursing staffing and quality assurance. Due to this, it was possible for us to observe their work firsthand. After talking with and visiting several institutions where Medicus had provided services, we felt we would like to have them evaluate our situation and perhaps help us with our problem.

As a first step in developing a proposal, a multidisciplinary team of Medicus representatives visited the hospital and conducted interviews with individuals within our institution representing nursing, medicine, administration and staff development. These interviews were directed toward clear identification of our current situation as well as factors contributing to our problem. Following these interviews a proposal was submitted outlining Medicus' understanding of our problems and a suggested plan for action. Among objectives enumerated in the proposal were those leading to:

- Achievement of better management of staffing through workload monitoring.
- Reduction of the utilization of outside agency personnel.
- Improvement of the management skills of nursing administration.
- Introduction of quality of nursing care monitoring and obtaining baseline data.

- Development and implementation of nursing management information systems.

Having identified these needs and knowing what tools would be available, we established long- and short-term goals for the staffing project.

Since it is the philosophy of our department that as many people as possible should have a voice in change as it occurs, we proposed heavy participation by our staff in all aspects of the project. Although we would have a great deal of involvement by hospital and Medicus personnel, we felt that some one person within our nursing department was needed to act as coordinator for the project. This individual would actively participate and work as liaison between those working within the institution and the consultants and would be a key individual for continuing the project at the end of outside support.

ESTABLISHING A STAFFING SYSTEM

The staffing system which was to be established at The Children's Memorial Hospital was aimed at providing a measurement of nursing workload as a basis for long-range and variable (daily) staffing. Workload determination is based upon the nursing activities performed in the actual delivery of nursing care to the patient. The amount of work associated with the performance of these activities is derived from the level of

---

Since it is the philosophy of our department that as many people as possible should have a voice in change as it occurs, we proposed heavy participation by our staff in all aspects of the project.

---

self-sufficiency of the patient and the nurse's perception of the difficulty of performing each activity.

To determine patient self-sufficiency, a classification tool needed to be developed specific to the care needs of children. Although Medicus had previously implemented patient classification systems in more than 50 hospitals throughout the United States and Canada, such a system had never been used in a total pediatric setting. Using a committee composed of four head and four staff nurses (representing medical, surgical, intensive care and infant care units) we looked at previously developed patient classification forms and realized that they wouldn't totally meet our needs.

After identifying usable portions from the forms, we struggled to construct our form by identifying common patient care needs based on the condition of the patient, the basic care each patient might require, and the therapeutic needs of a patient and/or his family. After several sessions and much discussion, we finally arrived at 34 "condition indicators" which would differentiate levels of patient acuity and would be applicable for any patient admitted to our hospital or any of our nine units.

We soon learned that agreeing on the list of indicators was the easiest part of the particular project. Coming to agreement on definitions for each indicator was much more difficult since we all had different opinions as to the meaning of specific terms. In order for the tool to be useful, we had to come to some consensus. The patient classification tool presented in Figure 1 is the result of that agreement.

Once we had established the format for the classification form, it was tested on the four units mentioned above. We quickly felt comfortable with the classification tool and expanded its use to all inpatient units. This expansion provided us with a clear example of the importance of including as many individuals as possible in changes as they occur. Implementation of the tool on all units meant a period of orientation for staff who were not originally involved in the tool's development. It was a little more difficult to "sell" the program to this group since they had less of a grasp of the reason behind the tool and tended to see only the fact that they were being asked to fill out additional forms. A great deal of orientation was needed for this group before they were able to "buy in" to the tool and recognize its worth. Once adequate data were collected to insure that the forms were being utilized correctly on all units, we were ready to move on to the next phases of the project— quality review and establishing workload measurement of each unit.

Determining staffing requirements

In the approach we utilized to determine staffing requirements, workload was not determined through the use of traditional time study techniques. While these approaches would add the number of elements to be accomplished on a particular unit, relate the element to patient type and multiply by the "standard time," our approach was based on the concept of assignment "difficulty."

As one looks at assignment elements (i.e., providing A.M. care for a group of critically ill patients, passing medications to a group of minimal care patients, etc.), it is apparent

> *In the approach we utilize to determine staffing requirements, workload was not determined through the use of traditional time study techniques . . . our approach was based on the concept of assignment "difficulty."*

Assignment Summary	Specialing																				
	Monitor/Treatments																				
	Medications																				
	Routine Care																				

Unit: _____
Shift: _____
Date: _____

Rm. No. / Patient's Name

Conditions	Admission and Discharge																				
	Age 0 to 8 Years																				
	Age 8 Years to Adult																				
	Incontinent																				
	Disoriented/Retarded																				
	Blind or Deaf																				
	Isolation																				
	Partial Immobility																				
	Complete Immobility																				
	Severe Respiratory Distress																				
	Tracheostomy																				
	Surg. Day of Surgery																				
	Surg. 1 Day Post-Op																				
Basic Care	Bed Rest																				
	Up With Assistance																				
	Bath With Assistance																				
	Bath Total																				
	Feeding Oral With Assistance																				
	Feeding Oral Total																				
	Feeding Tube Total																				
	Feeding Over 1/2 Hour Feeding																				
	Feeding Frequency Q^{4n}																				
Therapeutic Needs	I & O																				
	Specimen Collection																				
	Tube Care																				
	Suction Q^{4n}																				
	Wound or Skin Care																				
	Oxygen Therapy																				
	Vital Signs Q^{2} rr. or More																				
	Monitor up to Q^{15} Min.																				
	IV's																				
	Special Teaching Needs																				
	Special Emotional Needs																				
	Prepped for Procedure																				

Figure 1. Sample patient summary form

that some are more difficult to accomplish than others. Differences relate not only to what needs to be done to accomplish the element (i.e., provide A.M. care) but also difficulty relates to the level of acuity of the patient for whom an assignment element is performed.

Although time is certainly involved, other factors such as the skill and knowledge of the staff, organizational skills of the staff, their ability to problem solve, accessibility to supplies and equipment, usual methods of assignment, etc., contribute to the degree of difficulty of a task. Nurses are able to judge the difficulty of accomplishing one assignment element as compared to another.

In beginning to develop the method to determine workload, therefore, staff were interviewed by members of the Medicus staff to determine the structure of their usual assignment and "assignment elements" were developed (i.e., routine care for four patients). All combinations of elements were paired and staff were asked to complete questionnaires to determine their perceptions of the difficulty of accomplishing one element as compared to the other, if it were included in their assignment. For example, one pair was:

- Medications for two intensive care patients.
- Medications for five self-care patients.

Questionnaires were developed specific to each unit, shift, and personnel type (i.e., RN, LPN, Aide) and administered to a maximum number of personnel. Results of this questionnaire process then provided a numerical "value" for the difficulty of performing each assignment element, and values were specific to unit, shift and category of personnel.

QUALITY ASSURANCE

We felt that it was equally important when looking at the numbers of personnel

required to relate this to quality of care. Quality assurance played an important role in the Medicus approach and it was imperative that we began assessing quality early as we needed to develop a baseline. Such a baseline would assist us in knowing what and if any significant changes occurred in the quality of care as a result of changes in staffing and/or staff mix. Medicus proposed, and we agreed, that the most valid measure for comparing staff to the quality of nursing care is that which focuses on nursing activities performed in the actual delivery of nursing care to the individual patient: the process model of patient care. Medicus had previously developed a tool for measuring the quality of the care process and we chose to utilize this since it provided an assessment of direct care of the patient by the nurse and also the quality of support services in facilitating nursing care (i.e., unit management, dietary, etc.).

Again, we realized that to achieve acceptance, this must be done with available inhouse staff. The decision was made to train the already existing audit committee in conducting necessary observations based on the fact that they were (1) a group who was used to working together doing discharge outcome and auditing (chart review), and (2) the group was composed of head nurses and staff nurses representing several nursing units. The entire group of nine attended a three-day workshop on the system which for us not only involved learning the method of review but changing the wording of several of the questions to make them more oriented to a pediatric setting. During the month of March 1976, 178 reviews were done on all inpatient units for all three shifts—a commendable undertaking for a group of nine people who had other full-time commitments on their assigned units.

In March, we received the preliminary reports of our quality observations and in

April the recommended staffing. Believing we had the most accurate data available we projected budgeted staff for FY 1976–1977 (see Table 1). We chose to add a 1.5 factor to the suggesting staffing to provide coverage for employee orientation (important to us as we projected an increase in the number of new staff), vacation (each of our employees receives ten days after one year of employment, eight holidays, including two personal holidays) and ill time. While we felt our initial staffing projects were valid for the particular time we studied, we knew our needs might change based on projected or possible changes in patient acuity. This led us into the final project phase—establishing variable staffing and meaningful daily and monthly management reporting.

KEEPING STATISTICS

There are many methods available for keeping statistics, and we had in the past been using six different forms to give us such information as unit census, daily staffing, daily average patient care hours, vacation, illness and absence, pulling from one unit to another, utilization of outside agency help and finally a monthly average of all of the above. This has been reduced to one form which gives us everything but the monthly totals (see Figure 2).

There are almost as many ways of utilizing the classification forms. Some hospitals have the clerk on each unit add up the total points and classify the patients by hand before sending the sheets or totals to a control staffing office. Some hospitals have full computer capabilities and are able to readily transfer the information to the computer and have results within two or three hours (maybe longer in some settings). Some have utilized programmable calculators.

We have chosen the latter route, first of all because we do not feel our clerks should be used for the task of adding up the numbers of as many as 37 patients; we do not have full inhouse computer capability (this probably will be available to us in 12 to 18 months—too long to wait) and the cost factor and turn around time is reasonable and efficient. The classification sheets arrive from the units by 9:00 A.M. and within one hour information is available to us giving total census, total and average patient type, total workload and projected staffing for four shifts, all of which can be transcribed to the daily management report.

WORK WILL CONTINUE

A year has passed since we originally began our work with the Medicus Corporation and adopted the staffing with quality assurance programs. We officially completed the project in June of 1976 but we have never really "finished" our work, nor do I visualize that we will. The program is one which is ongoing within the institution with some continued limited involvement from the consultants. Our management report over the year has shown us that the acuity of our patients has increased on almost every unit bringing about the daily need to add additional staff on most shifts. Therefore, as we head into another budget year, we have again contracted with Medicus to do a detailed two week review of classification, workload and goals matrix to find where

We officially completed the project in June of 1976 but we have never really "finished" our work, nor do I visualize that we will. The program is one which is ongoing within the institution with some continued limited involvement from the consultants.

Table 1. Sample projected budgeted staff FY 1976–1977

Unit Daily Staffing

Units/Shift	Positions Per Shift							Patient Care				Administrative			
	HN	CH	TL	Staff	LPN	NA	Total	RN	LPN	NA	Total	HN	CH	TL	Total
2W D	1	0	3	0	5	1	10	1.8	5	1	7.8	1	0	1.2	2.2
E	0	1	1	1	5	1	9	2	5	1	8.0	0	0	0.4	1.0
N	0	1	0	1	4	0	6	1.4	4	0	5.4	0	0.6	0	0.6
Total	1	2	4	2	14	2	25	5.2	14	2	21.2	1	1.2	1.6	3.8
2E D	1	0	2	3	4	1	11	4.2	4	1	9.2	1	0	0.8	1.8
E	0	1	1	4	4	1	11	5	4	1	10.0	0	0.6	0.4	1.0
N	0	1	1	1	5	2	10	2	5	2	9.0	0	0.6	0.4	1.0
Total	1	2	4	9	10	4	33	11.2	10	4	29.2	1	1.2	1.6	3.8
3W D	1	0	2	0	3	1	7	1.2	3	1	5.2	1	0	0.8	1.8
E	0	1	1	2	4	1	9	3	4	1	8	0	0.6	0.4	1.0
N	0	1	0	2	3	1	7	2.4	3	1	6.4	0	0.6	0	0.6
Total	1	2	3	3	11	3	22	6.6	11	2	19.6	1	1.2	1.2	3.4
3C D	1	0	0	2	0	0	2	2.0	0	0	2	1	0	0	1.0
E	0	1	0	0	2	0	3	0.4	2	0	2.4	0	0.6	0	0.6
N	0	1	0	0	1	0	2	0.4	1	0	1.4	0	0	0	0.6
Total	1	2	0	2	4	0	7	2.8	4	0	5.8	1	1.2	0	1.2
3E D	1	0	2	2	4	0	9	3.2	4	0	7.2	1	0	0.8	1.8
E	0	1	1	1	3	1	7	2	3	1	6.2	0	0.6	0.4	1.0
N	0	1	0	1	5	0	7	1.4	5	0	6.4	0	0.6	0	0.6
Total	0	2	3	4	12	1	23	6.6	12	1	19.8	1	1.2	1.2	3.4

Table 1. Continued

Unit Daily Staffing

Units/Shift	Positions Per Shift							Patient Care					Administrative		
	HN	CH	TL	Staff	LPN	NA	Total	RN	LPN	NA	Total	HN	CH	TL	Total
4W D	1	0	2	1	3	0	7	2.2	3	0	5.2	1	0	0.8	1.8
E	0	1	1	1	3	0	6	2.0	3	0	5.0	0	0.6	0.4	1.0
N	0	1	0	2	3	0	6	2.4	3	0	5.4	0	0.6	0	0.6
Total	1	2	3	4	9	0	19	6.6	1	0	15.6	1	1.2	1.2	3.4
4C D	1	0	0	4	2	0	7	4	2	0	6.0	1	0	0	1.0
E	0	1	0	3	3	0	7	3.4	3	0	6.4	0	0.6	0	1.0
N	0	1	0	4	3	0	8	4.4	3	0	7.4	0	0.6	0	0.6
Total	1	2	0	11	8	0	22	11.8	8	0	19.8	1	1.2	0	2.2
5W D	1	0	2	2	4	0	9	3.2	4	0	7.2	1	0	0.8	1.8
E	0	1	1	1	4	0	7	2	4	0	6.0	0	0.6	0.4	1.0
N	0	1	0	1	5	0	7	1.4	5	0	6.4	0	0.6	0	0.6
Total	1	2	3	4	13	0	23	6.6	13	0	19.6	1	1.2	1.2	3.4
5C D	2*	0	0	6	1	0	9	6	1	0	7.0	2*	0	0	2.0
E	0	1	0	4	1	0	6	4.4	1	0	5.4	0	0.6	0	0.6
N	0	1	0	5	1	0	7	5.4	1	0	6.4	0	0.6	0	0.6
Total	2	2	0	15	3	0	22	15.8	3	0	18.8	2	1.2	0	3.2
all units D	10	0	13	20	26	3	71	27.8	26	3	56.8	10	0	5.2	15.2
E	0	9	6	17	29	4	64	24.2	30	4	58.2	0	5.4	2.4	7.8
N	0	9	1	17	30	3	61	21.2	30	3	54.2	0	5.4	0.4	5.8
Total	10	18	20	54	85	10	196	73.2	86	10	169.2	10	10.8	8.0	28.8

*1 Assist. Head Nurse

Unit		Unit Census	Assigned Staff			Required Staff			Float Sent to			Staff Pulled To Unit			Staff Pulled From Unit			Illness and/or Absence			Vacations			Actual Staffing			Average Patient Type				Avg. Pt. Type	Nsg. Care Hours
			RN	LPN	NA	RN	LPN	NA	RN	LPN	NA	RN	LPN	NA	RN	LPN	NA	RN	LPN	NA	RN	LPN	NA	RN	LPN	NA	I	II	III	IV		
2E	D																															
	E																															
	N																															
3E	D																															
	E																															
	N																															
3C	D																															
	E																															
	N																															
4C	D																															
	E																															
	N																															
5C	D																															
	E																															
	N																															
2W	D																															
	E																															
	N																															
3W	D																															
	E																															
	N																															

Figure 2. Sample daily administrative survey form

changes in staffing are indicated on a long-term basis.

Quality assurance reviews are done on every unit quarterly so that we are able to determine what changes, if any, are taking place. Results are reviewed by the Division of Staff Development and inservice programs are planned on the unit level in an effort to strengthen areas of weakness as well as improve in those areas where we are strong.

We have utilized a float pool very effectively allowing us to have a flexibility within our staff each shift with limited pulling from unit to unit and limited utilization of agency help. Until acuity levels became so high and the census in ICU began running more than 100 percent, we did not use agency staff for a total of six months.

We have found that there is not the need to have a professional person doing the day to day staffing; this is done by a staffing assistant who has learned to interpret the data and assign staff as needed. Staffing assistants only seek the assistance of a nursing coordinator or head nurse when they are not able to solve a staffing problem.

It has also been apparent to us that Medicus feels the program should not be stagnant. They are continuously looking for ways to improve the methodology. As they find a better way, it is shared with us so that we too may continue to advance.

Staffing for quality patient care continues to be the concern of nursing administration in our institution. We feel we have found a method which will help us reach that goal.

REFERENCE

1. Sanders, E.J., et al. Results of Nurse Utilization and Staffing Control Methodology for Children's Hospitals (New York: Western New York Association of Hospital Management Engineering Programs June 1970).

Part IV
Study and discussion questions

1. How is patient acuity defined—historically and presently?
2. What was the finding that Robert Connor reported in the early 1960s that changed the health care industry's assumptions about the nature of the nursing department's workload?
3. Please identify and describe three approaches to measuring nursing time consumption.
4. Why are patient classification systems considered to be basically imprecise?
5. Describe the two primary types of "measurement errors."
6. Describe one way to obtain "face validity" on your measurement process.
7. What prompted Children's Memorial Hospital to investigate and create a patient classification system?
8. How long did it take the organization to complete the project? What were some of the reasons for that time frame?
9. Why was it so difficult for nursing groups to come to agreement on definitions for each indicator?
10. Why was it important to establish a baseline of quality care before monitoring the program's effect on delivery of care?
11. Why does the author feel that "we have never really finished our work?" What does that say about the nature of patient classification systems?

Part V
Delivery of patient care services

June Werner, R.N., M.S.N.
Clinical Professor
College of Nursing
University of Illinois
Chicago, Illinois

The delivery of patient care services is an issue as old as nursing itself. Following World War II, as nurses became better educated and, therefore, became more leaders than just managers, the concept of the professional accountability of nurses evolved as a natural consequence. The nursing care of patients became complicated by the complex nature of diagnosable patient illnesses and related therapies. Consumerism developed over time. Patients and their families increasingly wanted to participate in the decisions related to their care and in the care itself.

When nurses explored the question, "How could we deliver care more effectively and more appropriately?" we moved from functional nursing to team nursing and in the 1970s to primary nursing. This evolution parallels the increase in more appropriately educated nurses.

Primary nursing, presented in *NAQ* (Winter, 1977), has not only increased patient satisfaction, nurse-physician collaboration, and nurse satisfaction with their practice, but it has also become the foundation upon which nursing case management has been developed in the 1990s.

Editors of *NAQ* have acknowledged the changing patterns in delivery systems in the country presenting articles that reflected these changes. Marie Manthey is cited in the *NAQ Forum* (Winter, 1977) as the author of the first presentation on primary nursing in an article in *Nursing Forum* in 1970. Luther Christman forecasted correctly that many of the opportunities for progress were inherent in the primary nursing role. He predicted that legislative and accreditation standards would increase and suggested that a major intellectual responsibility for leadership in the endeavor to establish high quality standards was an obligation of the leaders in nursing.

The role of the clinical specialist as practitioner, educator, consultant, and researcher began to emerge in the 1970s. This expanded role has been successful in supporting nurses in the development of professional practice climate. Resident clinical specialists offer access to on-site expertise on matters of complex patient care issues, enhanced collaboration, research, and mentoring.

Beth Israel's model of professional nursing practice is described by members of the staff in two articles. It was in this fertile climate of professionalism and the many characteristics of excellence in nursing practice that the Beth Israel Center of Excellence emerged.

The emphasis on clinical competence and nursing accountability was defined in the 1970s. Paula Sigmon's article on clinical ladders makes the case for the complemen-tary relationship of primary nursing and the clinical advancement system.

Evans and Brown's article cites the necessity for developing models to evaluate the structure, process, and outcome of primary nursing.

Across the last 16 years *NAQ* has traced the development of delivery systems for nursing in this country, presenting the strands in the fabric of professional nursing, weaving the fabric, and defining the environment in which delivery systems presently exist and forecast nursing's potential in the future.

The Evanston story: Primary nursing comes alive

PRIMARY NURSING: THE EVANSTON HOSPITAL MODEL

The present trend in health care is consumer oriented. The consumer has become verbal, is aware that health care is an expensive item in his family budget, and is determined to call for an effective product. Coupled with this reality is the trend in nursing education since World War II. Nursing now is seen as a clinical discipline in which students are prepared by nursing educators to practice in terms of a process related to a body of knowledge—a role parallel to that of medicine and not subordinate to it. Prior to the women's liberation movement, nurses were seeking opportunities to function as professionals accountable for the results of their practice, which they rightfully assumed should be conducted in terms of the physician's plan for any given patient. In settings where health and prevention and not illness was the focus of the practice of both nurse and physician, the role of the nurse was often perceived as dominant, relating to health maintenance and teaching rather than to therapeutics. The significant factors in the changes relate to the present day nurse's view of nursing practice, and to her concept of the meaning of professional nursing.

In 1966 the Board of Directors of Evanston Hospital, at the request of the administration, determined that nursing was indeed a clinical discipline and should have a chairman, like every other clinical department. This chairman was to be a top level decision maker, be accountable for the clinical practice of nursing in the institution, and plan and control the nursing budget, which was in excess of $6 million. For four years the groundwork was laid, first a network of new communication patterns, then the position of chairman in nursing was established at the policy making level of the institution. In 1971 a second chairman replaced the first, with the intent to build on the base constructed in the first four years.

In January 1971 nursing care at Evanston Hospital still was being delivered in functional and team nursing models. Although the department of nursing was a clinical department, the effect of the administrative change had not been felt by staff nurses rendering care. The new philosophy of the department began to focus on a plan to

Nurs Admin Q, 1977, 1(2), 9–50
©1977 Aspen Publishers, Inc.

provide quality nursing care to patients, based on the ideal that any citizen in our community requiring hospitalization is entitled to competent, humane, individualized care, including attention to the needs of their family under such circumstances.

We established certain important premises:

The department was to be administered in a facilitative model. That is, the chairman and chairman's assistant (or associate) would educate the nursing coordinator, who acted as the nursing director for a clinical service (or a part of one). Coordinators would be expected to educate head nurses who, in turn, would be expected to educate staff nurses so the ultimate objective of providing nursing care of high quality to patients would be accomplished.

Leadership staff in the department were to be selected on the basis of two primary criteria: (1) clinical excellence, which would serve as professional role models for the staff, and (2) leadership potential, including human effectiveness, personal strength, and professional commitment.

Department policy was to be developed, collaboratively, processed in staff meetings, through head nurse meetings in the clinical departments and then through the nursing executive council, which would include coordinators and consultants (clinically excellent nurses who replaced the conventional supervisors who worked evenings and nights as resource persons), and the administrative staff in nursing (chairman, assistant, and associate chairman). Action was to be taken on the basis of consensus rather than by majority rule. Action initiated in the Nursing Executive Council would be processed through head nurse meetings and staff meetings. Nurses, particularly those in leadership positions would be expected to view (1) physicians as colleagues and assume the many obligations of colleagueship, and (2) staff in other depart-

ments with respect and concern assuming their importance in the institution in whatever capacity they functioned. (See Figure 1.)

Professionalism was to be based on accountability, which infers the willingness to live with the results of one's nursing practice. An analogy we found helpful was the architectural model. The architect is not employed simply to do the tasks related to his work on a daily basis. He is employed because of the expectations of the results of his work, the edifice he has planned and developed. Similarly, nurses are not employed simply to do the tasks related to their work, but they are employed because of the expectations of the results of their work, the nursing care provided holistically for their patients. It became clear that it would be necessary to build into our delivery system continuity and accountability, based on the process inherent in nursing practice.

Under primary nursing at Evanston Hospital . . . professionalism was to be based on accountability, which infers the willingness to live with the results of one's nursing practice.

In the spring of 1971, we read with interest Marie Manthey's article on primary nursing. We were intrigued with the idea of establishing a way to deliver comprehensive nursing care to patients in "nursing service" rather than in nursing education. Although we read the article with interest, the Nursing Executive Council felt strongly that we were not ready to launch into such a project, despite the encouragement of the chairman and her associate. However, these two optimists, pioneers at heart, decided to move toward that objective with an informal look at feasibility without staff participation. A

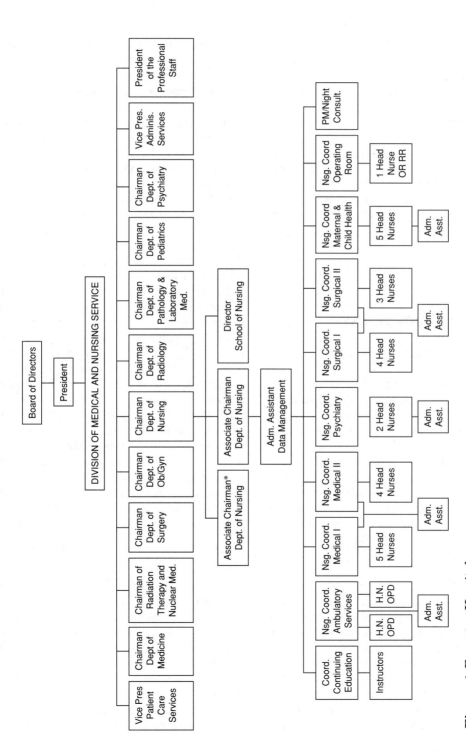

Figure 1. Evanston Hospital

primary nurse from the Minnesota program agreed to discuss her experience as a guest of the Nursing Executive Council in the late spring. This young nurse, a graduate student, engendered so much enthusiasm for the Manthey model that our staff began to feel consideration of primary nursing would be worthwhile. The seeds sown in that conference at Evanston Hospital that spring afternoon in 1971 fell on fertile ground, have been carefully cultivated, and have resulted in an ever increasing growth for the nursing service.

June Werner, R.N., M.S.N.
Chairperson
Department of Nursing
Evanston Hospital

RESTRUCTURING THE SYSTEM

Modular nursing for primary care

The alarming rate of inflation in health care costs has caused a great deal of budget curtailment in most health related institutions. These efforts pose difficult problems for all professionals in the health fields who are dedicated to improving the quality of their services. Unfortunately, improvement is usually accompanied by rising costs, and somehow these opposing factors must be reconciled if we are ever to reach our goal of quality health services for the entire population.

The work assessment project

The Department of Nursing at Evanston Hospital responded positively to the belt-tightening challenge that occurred there in the early fall months of 1971. A work assessment project to evaluate the functioning of the entire institution was recommended by the Board of Trustees at Evanston, and nursing asked that its department be evaluated first. In September 1971 a project team

was formed, consisting of three members of the planning department at Evanston Hospital, two management consultants from Arthur Anderson and Company (an outside consulting firm), and a nurse consultant from the Department of Nursing. The broad primary goal of the work assessment team was to analyze the functioning of the various departments and to recommend and implement constructive changes consistent with the efforts to reduce the budget.

Because the Department of Nursing at Evanston Hospital is committed to high quality, patient-centered nursing practice, the work assessment team decided to study intensively four representative patient care units and to base all recommended changes on the actual nursing practice observed on these units. In addition, the executive council of the Department of Nursing was consulted at least on a weekly basis, and it is from those discussions that many of the concepts for change arose. An observation tool was devised; and four trained, nonnurse observers were assigned to the four patient care units to gather data. These patient care units were utilized in both the data collection and implementation plan phases of the work assessment project. Intensive orientation sessions were held with the nursing personnel on these units during the entire project to facilitate the process of change.

Staffing and scheduling the nursing units

One major objective of the work assessment project in nursing was to formulate a staffing and scheduling system based on patients' needs. It has long been recognized that costs can be minimized when the number of personnel present equals the work load. This concept, however, is very difficult to carry out in situations such as patient care units. First, the actual patient census can fluctuate greatly from day to day (it is not always possible to predict daily admissions and discharges). Second, and more important, nursing has no system to assess objectively and accurately patient care needs. Instead, nurses have become adept at subjectively gauging their staffing needs by thinking about patients in terms such as "light" or "heavy care." It was important, then, to formulate some objective means of defining patient needs to determine precise staffing patterns for each patient care unit at Evanston Hospital.

A complex classification tool was developed for use in the data gathering phase of our study. Each patient on the four study units was to be classified once daily at the end of the first shift. The patient could receive a score from four to 12 points, based upon the extent of his needs in four categories: activities of daily living, treatment schedule, observation and assessment, and teaching and emotional support. In addition, the observers spent one week collecting data from the evening shift and sixteen hours from the night shift. Patient classification data were collected from those shifts during those periods. The classification scores of the patients were correlated with the kind and duration of nursing activities carried out for them as recorded by the observers. This produced specific data on the amount of time necessary for the care of the various classifications of patients on all three shifts. This information was turned to practical use as the basis of staffing and scheduling patterns for nursing personnel. Within six months all patient care units, except for highly specialized areas such as labor and delivery, were utilizing a simplified classification tool and establishing their data base for both daily staffing patterns and long term staffing projections.

Inefficiencies in personnel management

The second major objective of the work assessment project in nursing was to analyze the organization and functions of personnel providing patient care to determine whether inefficiency existed. The primary conclusion arising from the data analysis was that team nursing was neither efficient nor effective as an organizational approach to providing quality patient care. It was found that the nursing assistants were giving the bulk of nursing care, even to the sickest patients. The RN team leaders were working very hard, but 75 percent of their time was taken up by duties away from their patients, such as giving assignment conferences to all the team members, preparing medications, checking orders, and numerous other clerical duties. Even though nursing assistants were providing much of the direct patient care, this group of personnel had a consistently high percentage of "available" time, that is, time spent in coffee breaks, reading magazines or other such nonproductive activities. Most nursing assistants, particularly on the day shift, spent between 40 and 60 percent of their time on duty in these "available" activities. These assistants were not lazy; they were task-oriented personnel who believed that morning care consists of getting the patient bathed, his bed made, his room straight-

Most nursing assistants before primary care were providing much of the direct patient care, but they spent between 40 and 60 percent of their time on duty in "available" activities: coffee breaks, reading magazines, or other such nonproductive activities. . . . It was not economical to pay personnel for eight hours when in reality they might work only four.

ened, and performing a few specific treatments, and that's all. The nursing assistants just did not know how to care for patients except in terms of well-defined tasks. Consequently, when they had finished their tasks, they felt they had finished their care.

These findings had strong philosophical implications as well as economic ones for the Department of Nursing. It was not economical to pay personnel for eight hours when in reality they might work only four. The department showed strong interests in the model of primary nursing care in which the RN establishes a close, sustained relationship with each primary patient. The work assessment team sat down with the nursing executive council and began brainstorming about possible modifications in the patient care delivery system to meet both fiscal and philosophical objectives.

The modular nursing model

The result was the modular nursing model, in which patient care is carried out by one or two nursing personnel assigned to a relatively small group of patients. All experienced RNs function as module leaders, either working by themselves giving total care to a small group of patients, or working with a nursing assistant or LPN in caring for a larger group. In effect, modular nursing breaks the nursing team into smaller team units.

It was believed that the modular form of patient care delivery would have several advantages over the team structure. First, the RN would be giving direct, total care to certain patients. Second, the nurse working with the assistant or LPN would only have one individual for whom to be responsible, and thus it would be a realistic expectation that the RN could guide and supervise the assistant in a full eight hours of patient care activities. Third, the planning and initial implementation of the primary nursing pilot project had already begun. The modular structure seemed to be very close in form to the primary nursing model of care.

The major theoretical disadvantage of modular nursing was that it required a sufficient number of professional nurses to implement the pairing concept with nonprofessional personnel. After much consideration and some initial experience with modular nursing, the Department of Nursing decided that this was not a disadvantage. A basic premise is that each patient deserves professional care, and the decision was made to stop training nursing assistants and to use those funds and staff development efforts toward developing a team of competent RNs who can function as primary nurses.

It is relevant to share briefly some of our experiences at Evanston Hospital during and since the implementation of modular nursing. Progress in adapting to the new organizational model was uneven. Some nurses responded eagerly to the demands of change; others were reluctant to give up old work patterns. Nursing assistants initially felt very threatened by the changes, but over the years those who have retrained in the system have responded in a positive fashion. Indeed, the informal observation has been made that both modular and primary nursing enhances the feelings of self-esteem within this group of personnel. Following the model of the registered nurses, the nursing assistants have become more involved in their patients and take more pride in their efforts to provide high quality patient care. Certain LPNs certified to pass medications at Evanston Hospital also function as module leaders working alone with a small group of patients. Since LPNs do not function as primary nurses at Evanston, the modular system of organization utilizes their skills in patient care and helps maintain the LPN's status within the nursing hierarchy. Each LPN module leader is responsible to an RN who supervises his/her patient care and performs such tasks as checking orders and maintaining IV therapy. An LPN can become a permanent associate nurse for uncomplicated patients.

Modular nursing seems to be an ideal organizational structure to support primary nursing. In this system the RN not only plans and supervises patient care but also delivers nursing care. The entire experience with the work assessment project has been a fruitful one for the Department of Nursing at Evanston Hospital. The data bases for the nursing personnel budget and staffing patterns have been generated from the concepts and methods applied by the work assessment team. More important, the rationale and theory for the modular structure arose from the analysis of the work assessment data. This was accomplished by the nursing executive council in collaboration with the work assessment team.

Jo Ann Page, R.N., M.S.N.
Nurse Practitioner
North Communities Health Plan
Evanston, Illinois
(Formerly Medical Coordinator
Evanston Hospital)

The primary nursing care project

The initial effort in the restructuring of our nursing care system was called the Primary Nursing Care Project. As project director, it was a most gratifying experience. Instead of maintaining the traditional "crisis-orientation" of nursing, of always "putting out the fires," or "coping" (creatively or otherwise), we were in a position to arrange and control a system that would allow the clinically competent nurse to nurse.

We determined that in this setting the primary nurse had to be a professional registered nurse who would be responsible for the results of her implementation of the nursing process. She would be the patient's advocate from the time he entered the hospital until his discharge and, in some cases, even beyond discharge.

In 1971 primary nursing was not as commonplace as it has since become, and information or resources were limited. The proposed project was divided into three phases: (1) orientation, (2) implementation, and (3) evaluation. Briefly, the following outlines these phases of the project.

1. *Orientation.* Preliminary steps—including review of literature, field visits, introduction of goals of project to hospital community in general and project units in particular, patient care assessments through surveys and audit.

2. *Implementation.* The system of primary nursing care for patients was initiated and observed for three months.

3. *Evaluation.* Assessment of the primary nursing care system through (a) survey questionnaires involving patients, nursing personnel, and physicians; (b) general evaluation by project director and clinical coordinator with report to nursing executive council.

Orientation toward primary nursing

The project, once approved by the nursing executive council, began the first phase in earnest in September 1971. A review of the literature and plans to explore available methods and resources elsewhere were initiated. In October 1971 an exploratory visit was made to the University of Minnesota Hospitals to assess the model of primary nursing as described in the literature by Manthey. This visit was made by the project director and the clinical nursing coordinator from the project unit. Together we interviewed head nurses and staff nurses involved in primary care as well as the nurse clinician and clinical director. This exploratory visit was an enlightening experience. Not only were we able to discuss first hand the primary care project as it was done at Minnesota, but we were also able to see for ourselves how important it was that we at Evanston Hospital determine our readiness to implement a similar plan of care.

The philosophy and autonomy of the Department of Nursing at Evanston compared favorably with what we experienced and observed at Minnesota. It was determined that we were ready to begin active plans to implement our primary nursing care project.

In addition, a field visit was made to the Loeb Center for Nursing and Rehabilitation of the Montifiore Hospital and Medical Center in New York by our department chairman, where primary nursing as practiced in a rehabilitation setting was observed.

We were fortunate in having the advice and counsel of Phillip Bashook, Ed.D., a member of the Illinois Regional Medical Program, who agreed to be our consultant on the project. With his help we developed a research design and formulated several questionnaires for patients to assess the care they received. In addition to the patient questionnaires, we developed one for physicians. For nursing personnel we developed two separate but similar forms—one for the professional registered nurse and one for the nursing assistants. The categories covered in all the survey questionnaires included the following: (1) role perceptions, (2) communications, (3) family involvement, (4) continuity of care, and (5) general management of hospital care.

A brief audit was also done on a sample of patients' charts, which indicated the fragmentation of care under the prior system (i.e., notes by many different nurses attend-ing to different needs of the same patient with little prior planning).

As a next step within this phase, we set about pretesting the patient population in an effort to measure their perception of the assumed fragmentation. This pretest was completed before the implementation of the primary nursing care system, and a follow-up test would be done after the three-month trial period of the project.

Implementation

The reactions and interactions of those immediately involved—nurses, physicians, and patients and their families—with the transition from team to primary nursing on the project unit were ones of great interest and, in effect, set the pace and climate for the ultimate evolution of the project's success.

We recognized that restructuring any system within a community such as the hospital would affect all other systems in some way. We were most prudent in our deliberations and tried to include the entire hospital community in our plans (e.g., special feature articles in the hospital newspaper in which we introduced our concept and goals). By formal presentation at clinical department meetings and informal discussions with physicians and hospital administrators, we found for the most part that all who attended were receptive and supportive of our goals.

Through written memos and formal and informal exchanges we explained our project and responded to the physicians who were involved on the project units. We met with all the nursing personnel of the project unit several times, allowing ample time for questions and discussion from one meeting to the next. All nursing personnel were given a choice as to whether they wished to participate in the project. Those who did requested to participate by signing a simple statement of commitment to the concept of the primary nursing care project on the pilot unit.

This was as much a symbolic gesture as a need for us to do what we could to make this transition take place with actively involved participants who were truly conscious of what was involved in the change.

Only two staff nurses (RNs) expressed real concern about "getting involved." After further discussion, one decided to stay on the unit, and one was transferred to another unit.

Evaluating primary nursing

The resistance that surfaced first was from the house staff, who perhaps felt that it would be easier to develop a working relationship with one nurse (i.e., head nurse). Some of the secretarial staff also seemed to resist the additional chart-keeping which was necessary (i.e., posting the name of the primary nurse on each patient's chart along with the name of the patient and the physician). With experience, these concerns proved to be self-limiting and soon disappeared.

Role confusion within the ranks of the nursing personnel crystalized within the time span of the project (three months). We were to learn that the appropriate mix of nursing personnel necessary for accomplishing our goals would have to be adapted to the constraints of the particular unit. For our project, it was decided that every patient that came to the unit would have a primary nurse within twenty-four hours of his admission. Although we did succeed in this "assignment," we recognized the need for more thorough and thoughtful matching of patients' needs and nurses' skills. We arbitrarily set a target date and quite remarkably, the transition from team to primary nursing was officially begun on February 14, 1972. Needles to say, a more selective and gradual approach has been used since then.

For example, our next unit was pediatrics and staffing along with the priorities of patients' needs had to be dealt with more realistically. There was no assumption that a patient would automatically be assigned a primary nurse within twenty-four hours of admission. Indeed, many "short term" pediatric patients would have been admitted and discharged within that time frame!

It became clearer that the head nurse in her decentralized role within this system would no longer have an indepth report on all the patients of her unit all the time, though she would generally be aware of their conditions and needs. In addition, as time and experience demonstrated, she became increasingly aware of her staff's strengths and needs and was able to focus on the further development and support of her staff through conferences and resources available to her. The nurses themselves found it necessary to improve their clinical competence by reviewing disease entities and related clinical material and defining questions for conferences, both spontaneous and planned with the various health team members. All this points to the flexibility of the staff, their value systems, and willingness to learn and grow with the new system.

Multidisciplinary conferences increased along with the staff meetings, which provided the open communications so necessary on such a project. In addition, the project director met informally with all staff during daily visits to the unit. (This included some weekends and other "odd" times, as well.)

The positive relationship between the project director and the clinical nursing coordinator for the project unit was based on mutual respect and trust, which went a long way toward providing the foundation for open communications throughout the unit. Decision making involved an open, ongoing exchange between the project director and the clinical nursing coordinator with input from the head nurse and the staff.

The reality of change implies a potential threat to those who would view such a project of reconstruction as a problem, rather than as a challenge to meet and grow with. As systems change, roles change; such transitions create tensions which must be recognized and dealt with in a realistic manner. Essential, built-in support systems for all the staff undergoing the transition evolved to the extent that the project director and the clinical coordinator were always accessible and available for counsel.

We recognized that not all nurses would be comfortable with the kind of involvement implied in the primary nursing care system, nor should all nurses feel compelled to do this. We do maintain that the concepts of the primary nursing system (individualized, continuous care) provide the opportunity for the clinically competent and compassionate nurses to nurse in such a way as to rehumanize the hospital experience for patients and their families.

Olga Church, R.N., M.S.N.
Pilot Project Director
for Primary Nursing Care
Evanston Hospital

The pilot unit: an on-going challenge

In looking back over the last four years, I have found the challenge of being the head nurse on the pilot unit for primary nursing care has been the keystone of my professional growth. This was my first experience as a head nurse.

Part of my responsibility was the preparation of the staff. In staff meetings and open discussions the concept was defined, and we were able to express our feelings and apprehensions. As a new head nurse, what better way is there to acquaint myself with my staff than by creating an environment for discus-

sion? There were some apprehensions and feelings of insecurities that did surface, but I found that peer discussion groups helped in alleviating some of these fears. There were meetings with the medical staff, whose support was so vital to the success of our project.

At first, I had the responsibility of assigning primary patients to a primary nurse. The assignment of a patient to a particular primary nurse was based on the ability of the nurse to give the kind of care the patient required. The patient's needs and how they were to be met were always the focus. As time went on, I became more familiar with the strengths of each primary nurse and could identify those areas where I as a head nurse could assist in the primary nurse's development as a young professional. Needs for on-going continuing education became apparent. I had to help my staff develop the tools to care for patients not only by giving them my support but also by providing them with an avenue to increase their own competence. I set up teaching conferences with the house staff and also utilized the expertise of different members of the department of nursing. As the primary nursing model developed, the continuing education department facilitated the primary nurse in many different ways. Also, primary nurses now select their own primary patients. I can safely say there are times I wish there were more patients to benefit from the eagerness and commitment of the staff in their quest for quality care.

The development of the colleague relationship took time, but I feel it met with little resistance. There were some raised eyebrows and startled looks as questions from nurses directed to physicians regarding goals and discharge planning were posed, but our commitment was always so obvious that it was part of the growth process that took place. The recognition by the physician

---

On the Scene

TO: Our Patients and Their Families
FROM: The Department of Nursing, Evanston Hospital
SUBJECT: Your Primary Nurse

The Department of Nursing at Evanston Hospital wants to provide you and your family with competent, sensitive, individualized nursing care. We attempted to do this by providing each patient with a primary nurse soon after admission to the hospital, usually within the first twenty-four hours. Your primary nurse is accountable for a plan of care for you on a continuing basis, twenty-four hours a day.

Your primary nurse will work very closely with your physician in accord with his plans for your care. She will also work with all other Evanston Hospital personnel involved in your care in an effort to make it as effective and efficient as possible. She will be able to answer questions for you and your family to provide a clearer understanding of your care and hospital policy. She will help to prepare you to go home in terms of your physician's long range plan for you.

A primary nurse has four to six primary patients at any given time. She is an associate to other primary nurses when they are not on duty and cares for their patients too. Since a primary nurse has twenty-four-hour accountability for a plan of care of her primary patients and cannot be on duty at all times, she is assisted by associate nurses, licensed practical nurses, and nursing assistants.

We hope you will find it helpful to have a primary nurse. We will appreciate your comments about this system. Our goal is to provide excellent nursing care for every patient.

---

of the primary nurse became apparent. As in the custom today, the attending physician would seek out the primary nurse before making his rounds, and a common sight at the patient's bedside was his doctor and his primary nurse.

As I write about the colleague relationship, I can remember so vividly the young thirty-four-year old mother dying of lymphoma. She found it very difficult to ask her physician questions for she felt he was so busy. She wanted to have her husband present on one of his visits. She expressed this desire to her primary nurse. Realizing the only way to alleviate some of her fears would be by a discussion with her physician and her husband, the primary nurse approached the physician and shared with him their patient's apprehensions. The physician made it a point to visit her one evening when her husband was present and spent much time with them. As the week went on, the patient was much less anxious and appeared more comfortable. She died two weeks later. The primary nurse was truly her patient's advocate.

These last four years have been years of tremendous growth for myself personally and professionally, for my staff and for the concept of primary nursing. The development of new graduates into clinically oriented primary nurses has been particularly rewarding. The challenge and stimulation continues despite the fact the pilot project was conducted four years ago because of the constant need to orient new nurses to a holistic approach to nursing. The system provides me with considerable job satisfaction since I also care for my own caseload of primary patients. In doing so, I am able to act as a role model for my staff and to demonstrate personally the quality of care I expect for all patients.

As I reflect back, the rewards have been many: the development of clinically competent professionals, the satisfaction of seeing a patient discharged after having been individually involved at every stage of his stay; the expression of relief from a primary patient that even though the physician will be on vacation, at least you (the primary nurse) will be here; the words of gratitude from a patient's daughter who tells you you cared for her mother (your patient) as if she were your own mother. Perhaps the best way to express my deepest satisfaction, that of pro-

viding quality care to all patients, is hand carved on a wooden plaque that hangs on the unit. It was carved by a young patient with Hodgkins Disease, whom I first cared for four years ago when his diagnosis was made. He was admitted to us once a month for a year for chemotherapy. The plaque states it clearly and best of all:

"To the staff of 1-West, especially the nurses, thank you for the greatest care ever. Thanks. Feb. '75-Feb. '76."

Nancy T. Esposito, R.N.
Head Nurse
Primary Nursing Pilot Unit
Evanston Hospital

On The Scene

The concept of primary nursing as it is utilized in today's health care system has been a widely publicized and controversial issue in many journals over the past few years. It is not my purpose to debate the pros and cons of primary nursing but rather to illustrate how the Evanston Hospital model of primary nursing has facilitated my growth as an individual and as a professional.

I must begin by stating that my convictions are based on a comparison with a prior experience in a functionally organized medical unit. Low morale and an attitude of noncommitment permeated the atmosphere among the staff. I had become more disillusioned with myself and my profession. Primary care seemed a viable alternative, and I transferred to a primary care unit. I came with many expectations and hopes for a more meaningful way to practice nursing and to utilize my concept of nursing care.

Primary nursing care is based on the strong bonds of communication. I have been able to form these with each of my primary patients. Not only have I enhanced my communication skills, but I have developed many intense relationships of trust with my patients. I feel this is made possible by the day-to-day contact I maintain with them and their families. My commitment to the patient is not based on meeting only the physical needs brought on by his illness, but also to deal with the patient and his response to his illness on a holistic basis. In my contact with the patient, I strive to respond to his physical, emotional, and psychosocial needs—thereby aiding him in *his* adaptation to the experience of illness.

I have found also that the better I get to know my patient, the more pertinent information I uncover, which helps to improve care.

For example, M. K had severe arthritis and had a whirlpool bath ordered as part of his therapeutic regimen. He consistently refused it, stating that his pain was too severe to undergo the therapy and that it "was not worth it." When I explored this with him, the outcome of our conversation was actually his fear of possible financial dependence on his son for the costs of the

continued on next page

treatment. I checked into his insurance coverage, found that his policy covered the cost, and Mr. K consented to the treatment. Thus, the patient was made more comfortable, and I realized that it was only by virtue of an effective relationship that he was able to share his real reason for refusal.

Primary nursing affords an opportunity for purposeful interaction and communication among the nurse and other allied health professionals. I have found repeated satisfaction in approaching the physician (with a thorough knowledge of the status of our patient) with requests for alternate means of meeting all patient needs. I find myself analyzing which approach would accomplish my purpose best when I approach the physician with suggestions for ways to provide better care, or with the discovery of a previously unknown variable which indicates a change in care. Thus, a professional collaboration between doctor and nurse is fostered with the patient's welfare at its center.

Obviously, one cannot communicate with physicians without a working data base. Therefore, primary nursing provides me with an impetus to increase my knowledge of the patho-physiology of disease entities, diagnostic testing, and therapeutic measures. Because I have increased my knowledge I feel I am more effective in utilizing the nursing process and in patient education. I have learned to develop a data base using the nursing process to foster patient education in the following manner:

1. Data Base: What does the patient know and what are the facts involved in his disease process?
2. Assessment: What does he know and what do I feel he should learn?
3. Plans and Action: How can I best help him learn?
4. Evaluation: How much has he learned and which areas need further exploration and/or reinforcement?

Finally, primary nursing has been for me a vehicle of self-expression. I have developed pride in myself and my role as a professional nurse, and I feel I can inspire this same enthusiasm in others. I take an active role in assisting other staff members to become involved in comprehensive patient centered care. This adds up to high quality patient care as the entire staff works together toward one common goal.

I have spoken about all the things primary nursing has done for me. It has sharpened my communication abilities with both patients and other health care members. It has provided me with an environment for intellectual growth and self-actualization. But the most important aspect of primary nursing for me has been the sense of achievement that I experience each time one of my primary patients leaves the hospital. I feel that I have taken an active part in helping him deal with his disease entity and the effect it could impose on him and his family.

For example, Mr. M., 27 years old, with three children under the age of five suffered a myocardial infarction. His anger and fears caused him to alienate himself from his family and the staff and provided me with a challenge I was initially reluctant to undertake. Once I realized that this man had many misconceptions about his cardiac status, I was able to alleviate much of his anxiety and educate him with regard to his future life style, especially as sexual partner, father, and provider.

Mrs. F, 74 years old, had a massive myocardial infarction after which she suffered repeated attacks of severe congestive heart failure. She was a delightful lady, whose only desire was to return home to her daughter and her family and to enjoy the rest of her life surrounded by their love. At first glance, her physical condition seemed to necessitate an extended nursing care

continued on next page

facility. However, I provided health care teaching for the daughter, and arranged for oxygen, a hospital bed, and other equipment for the home. The Visiting Nurses Association was utilized to provide needed professional help. She was able to have her wish as a result of this help and yet was not a burden to her family.

As you can see, the demands of primary nursing are great; the emotional and physical investment at times is almost overwhelming. But how quickly these are forgotten when I hear "thanks, Linda, I could not have made it without you there with me!"

Linda Grover, R.N.,
Staff Nurse
with *Jenifer Golback, R.N.,*
Staff Nurse
Evanston Hospital

FISCAL MANAGEMENT OF PRIMARY NURSING

Competitive fiscal management

Regardless of the modality of care, competitive fiscal management has become progressively more important, especially to those who have the accountability for nursing, which represents the largest segment of manpower in health care. Legislative and regulatory pressures on hospitals impact heavily on nursing service to justify costs, maintain standards of care, and meet the appropriate and necessary needs of consumers.

Primary nursing, eight years after it was first implemented in the University of Minnesota Hospitals and later adopted by hospitals in various parts of the country, has been proven to be cost-effective. Despite such findings, too often primary nursing is fraught with resistance from both nursing and hospital administrators who assume that any system requiring more professional nurses has to be more expensive. One must not forget that productivity is closely linked with attitudes, motivation, and self-actualization of staff, which if engendered in any system, pro-

duces immeasurable results. This phenomenon in primary nursing makes it unique from other modalities of care.

Fiscal accountability begins with the head nurse and staff. It is this group of people who knows best the needs of patients. Through the leadership of the head nurse, a unit budget should be planned, implemented, controlled, and evaluated by the staff closest to the consumer. Corrective actions are more effectively dealt with at this level. The overall Department of Nursing budget is simply a conglomeration of these unit budgets.

Obviously, head nurses need to be prepared for this management expectation. When negotiating for the position, the chief nursing administrator and the candidate should carefully and totally explore the administrative and clinical requirements of such a key position. It is not unusual that a candidate might not fully realize the burden of the position. This is when a period of

Fiscal accountability begins with head nurses and their staffs. It is this group of people who know best the needs of their patients.

acting head nurse can be helpful. (Evanston Hospital has a four-month acting period for its head nurses.) During this time, an intensive orientation and development program is planned and carried out for the individual acting head nurse, whose orientation includes an understanding of this new role as outlined in an appointment letter:

- 24 hour responsibility for the provision of care for the patient on the unit.
- The setting of nursing standards on the unit which will guarantee high quality nursing care, hopefully employing the model of primary nursing.
- The selection, development, and control of a nursing staff which can maintain these standards utilizing prudent cost effectiveness measures.
- A colleague relationship with physicians to support these standards.
- A collaborative relationship with employees in all other departments in the hospital to facilitate expeditious and excellent care.
- The utilization of materials and supplies within the fiscal expectations which the head nurse helps develop.

Orientation to and development in fiscal management cover the following areas:

- Knowledge of the various forces affecting the nursing care delivery system—community environment, hospital environment, nursing administration, and the individual nursing unit.
- Agreement in the standard of care the hospital has "contracted" to deliver in that particular community.
- Applied skills in the budget process—planning, implementing, controlling, and evaluating (including corrective actions).
- Development and/or utilization of a comprehensive reporting system—position control, daily recap of nursing hours per day, acuity and census trends, and so forth.

- Personnel allocation and staffing.
- Nurse scheduling.
- Update of related studies.
- Integration of fiscal responsibilities with those of quality assurance.

The administrative demands of the head nurse role can be in conflict with the clinical aspect of the role if adequate administrative support is not provided. The department as a whole should have an effective system for providing administrative backup for the head nurse. At Evanston Hospital the presence of an assistant nursing administrator in charge of data management who works closely with the assistant chairperson and the nursing coordinators has proven most effective. Nursing coordinators have an administrative assistant who works with the head nurses in that clinical area.

Since primary nursing was initiated at Evanston Hospital costs have been carefully monitored and documented. Nursing hours per patient per day are recorded daily. During the first three years, the patient classification system, which reflected acuity levels and hours required per category of patients, indicated no significant increase in the nursing hours per patient per day. In terms of dollars, the primary nursing system did not cost any more than team nursing did. In spite of the difficulty of comparing one hospital to another because of varied accounting and reporting systems, the comparative exercise indicated less manhours and less cost for the Evanston Hospital patients.

So, after five years experience in primary nursing, it is fair to state that the patient gets the most quality of care for his dollar in this system.

Tita Corpuz, R.N., M.S.N.
Director of Nursing
American Hospital Association
Chicago, Illinois
(formerly Associate Chairperson
Department of Nursing
Evanston Hospital)

The operational level

Operational level fiscal management allows for the inputs to be determined by each institution in whatever fashion is appropriate to their management style. At Evanston Hospital, the inputs are acquired from two sources: (1) The head nurse of the patient care unit defines his/her expectation of staff ratio, patient needs, and acuity; and (2) the assistant chairperson supplies factual data of past trends in nursing hours per day per patient and percent of occupancy. The process of calculation is completed, and the output is the number of time equivalents or positions budgeted to any given unit. Because the hospital environment is ever changing and the nursing care system is affected by many forces, a responsive feedback system is necessary to maintain a viable budget. Accurate data collection with comprehensive bi-weekly interpretation and possibly corrective action must take place. The head nurse is the change agent in this system, the key to the planning, implementation, control, and evaluation of the budgeting process.

The cost effectiveness can be documented by the following data (*Source:* HAS 6-Month Report, June 1976), which is a comparison of Evanston hospital (EH), teaching hospitals with 400-599 beds (A), and hospitals of the Chicago Hospital Council (B).

	EH	A	B
Medical/Surgical			
Nursing Manhours Per Patient Day	4.96	5.71	5.51
Percent RN	52.51	37.91	37.12
Salary Expense Per Patient Day	29.53	30.91	30.93

Nursing administration is challenged by this system to facilitate the primary nursing concept in a fiscally sound structure. The Evanston Hospital Department of Nursing has been able to meet this challenge during the past four years.

At the outset, a basic fact must be established. The situation in any given hospital is not the same as Evanston Hospital. Because of this fact, adoption of this concept of budgeting and monitoring of the budget has to take place according to each institution's unique setting.

A systems approach schematic (Figure 1 on the next page), however, can synchronize the budgeting process and allows for each institution's philosophy and idiosyncracies.

Rhonda Anderson, R.N., B.S.N.
Assistant Chairperson
Department of Nursing
Evanston Hospital

PHARMACY AND PRIMARY NURSING: CAN UNIT DOSE BE UTILIZED IN A PRIMARY CARE SETTING?

Unit dose to the pharmacist is like primary care to the nurse. Both are a step in the professional growth of clinical practice.

Perhaps the biggest hurdle is in the planning stages of incorporating the two systems. The pharmacist needs to be given a good explanation of what primary care means—that it is not a foreign object but a reorganized method of providing a better quality of patient care; that to the concept of primary care nursing there are some nonnegotiable areas, but there are also some aspects of flexibility. The nurses involved must be made aware of the philosophy of unit dose as seen by the pharmacist, the givens of the system, and the negotiable areas. With both disciplines accepting and respecting each other's systems, the initial ground work is laid.

One of the nonnegotiable aspects of primary care is the continuity of patient care as it relates to the consistency of daily assign-

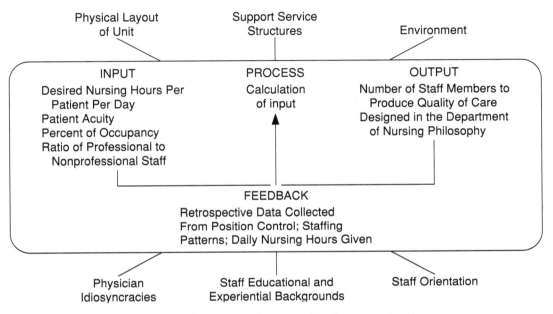

Figure 1. Schematic for cost-effective organization

ments of primary nursing case loads. There is no guarantee that the primary nurse's patients are in rooms of any close numerical order. The pharmacist would prefer that each unit dose medication cart be set up in numerical order according to patient room numbers.

As part of a solution to this dilemma we took our 47-bed unit and geographically located the primary nurses and the patients in three large modules. The primary nurses are still able to select their case loads from within the large modules, and the consistency of primary nurse and associate is built into the system. Upon readmission, every effort is made to admit the patient into the geographic area where he had been previously. His primary nurse is again caring for him. This enables the pharmacist to establish three unit dose medication carts in numerical order of sixteen patients each. This

adaptation does not alter the effectiveness of either system.

Another step in incorporating the two systems is for both the pharmacist and the nurse to look together at the "routines" that are already in practice, such as drug administration schedules, narcotics policies, necessity of drug refrigeration, and a clear definition of "stat," just to name a few. Both groups, addressing themselves to considering workable solutions to these mutual areas of concern, will make the follow-through by the primary nurse and the relationships with the pharmacist more effective.

The primary nurse should know, for resource purposes, the unit dose pharmacist assigned to the unit. A wealth of information concerning the patient and his medications can, and very often needs, to be exchanged.

It has been my experience that if the primary nursing staff and the pharmacists have mutual respect and understanding, the two systems can be effectively incorporated. Developing that kind of relationship takes effort on both parts and does not happen overnight. In my experience, the outcomes of a unit dose system in a primary care setting are beneficial to everyone—patient, pharmacist, and primary nurse.

Selma Arp, R.N.
Head Nurse
Medical Unit
Evanston Hospital

On the Scene

The quality of care the patient and family receive, assessment of nursing needs of patients, planning and implementation of care, delegation of responsibility for the nursing care of the patient, supervision and evaluation of nursing care, discharge planning, building colleague physician/nurse relationships—are these dimensions of patient care different today than they were six years ago? As one might anticipate, that answer is yes!

Six years ago, we employed the team nursing approach in caring for patients. The specific functions for the team leader were assignment conferences, patient care conferences, passing medications for a team of patients, initiating and updating care plans, checking off orders, making rounds with the physicians, giving more complex treatments, teaching patients and families, educating nursing personnel how to use a new product or render a new procedure, supervise personnel, chart, report, etc. All these functions were expected of the team leader for 17 to 20 patients.

From this briefing, one can ascertain the magnitude of the team leader's responsibilities. Her shared responsibilities with other team members made the nursing care rendered to the patient quite fragmented. By virtue of the staffing pattern, she frequently spent much of her time teaching nursing assistants and LPNs why and how to deliver the care. I usually participated as a team leader.

Our goals of assessing each patient and implementing a plan of care with the major emphasis of care upon the patient's feelings, concerns, and goals in assisting him and his family through medical therapy most often culminated with the major emphasis of care upon medications, treatments, checking off orders, and assisting the physician with technicalities. The result of our efforts achieved maintenance, but could rarely bring about change.

We talk about reality shock and role deprivation in nursing. In retrospect, I can see how unrealistic were our expectations of team leaders. The system promoted transiency of nurses due to frustration. Rarely did a nurse stay beyond a year. My role as a head nurse never ceased to be a maze. Job satisfaction for the professional nurse was difficult to achieve because she was unable to render comprehensive patient care. Three years of experience with primary nursing has helped in identifying the real problem. When a patient is the responsibility of a team of people, he is no one's responsibility except for the head nurse.

The difference primary nursing has made to my life as a clinically-oriented patient care advocate is a sense of freedom. By decentralizing the decision making, I am able to carry my own caseload of primary patients. Staff nurses have the opportunity of seeing their head nurse as a practitioner of nursing utilizing the nursing process. In essence, I am able to be their role model.

I can promote the development of new staff by evaluating the care a primary nurse renders, identifying problems, and supporting these nurses in improving their competence. Building a

continued on next page

cohesive relationship with the staff nurses allows us to solve problems together. Staff nurses' active participation in this process develops their clinical expertise, which helps them to become accountable. They are concerned with outcomes of patient care and are able to see the fruits of their effort.

Under the guidance of a designated nurse, the new nurse is able to apply his/her knowledge to clinical practice and helps to develop his/her capacity for self-direction. The freedom to care for patients in this manner develops the new nurse's self-confidence.

Constructive collaboration of staff members has provided us with the opportunity to develop our standards of nursing care. Working together, we are able to modify our nursing practice to include disease prevention and patient and family teaching.

Participation in a primary nurse system promotes creativity in nursing care. Nursing histories, patient assessment, patient problem lists, patient care plans, collaborative physician/nurse relationships, patient and family education, discharge planning, and pertinent referrals for continuity of care are the realities of nursing practice in a well-developed primary nursing model.

In the conventional setting as head nurse, I was the advocate for thirty patients. In the primary nursing model, it is the primary nurses who are the advocates for their primary patients. As head nurse, I am now the advocate for the staff on my unit, facilitating their personal and professional growth and supporting them in their pursuit of excellence in providing nursing care for patients.

Rita Garber, R.N.
Head Nurse
Surgical Unit
Evanston Hospital

DISCHARGE PLANNING AND PRIMARY CARE

Primary care is, in my opinion, the only system of nursing in which discharge planning is an integral part. With any task-oriented system of nursing care, discharge planning will have a low priority, if it is considered at all. Because the primary nurse is responsible for the total plan of nursing care and could be caring for her primary patients through more than one hospital admission, she has a vested interest in arranging for continuity of care into the community.

Primary nurses know their patients' needs emotionally as well as physically, their strengths as well as weaknesses.

Therefore, their calls to me tend to concern exactly what resources can be used in the particular community where their patient lives. Their planning for discharge also begins earlier, which means we have more time to consider alternatives and arrange for adequate care.

The Evanston VNA patient care coordinator and I promote communication between the primary nurse in the hospital and the VNA primary nurse. On the first visit, a visiting nurse fills out a card giving identifying information and the patient's current status. I pass these cards onto the primary nurse here who I encourage to keep in touch with the visiting nurse.

This plan has been enthusiastically received by our nurses. Knowing how the plan they made is really working should serve as a learning experience and increase the primary nurse's feeling of satisfaction.

Dee Smoller, R.N., M.S.N.
Home Health Care Coordinator
Evanston Hospital

Maintaining continuity of care as a person moves from one level of health care to another is paramount. Direct, effective communication among primary care providers is the preferred mechanism to accomplish this objective.

The Visiting Nurse Association has begun to designate formally a primary and associate nurse for an individual at the time of an admission team conference. The primary nurse becomes responsible for integrating the total plan of care.

Because both Evanston Hospital and the Evanston Visiting Nurse Association maintain a system of primary care, the essential communication is facilitated. Primary nurses seek and obtain important direct information integral to a total plan of patient care from each other. The continuity of care coordinators from the hospital and the VNA maintain the system of referrals and feedback mechanisms that are extremely critical during periods of readmissions and discharges from the hospital.

Carol Diemert, R.N., M.S.N.
Evanston Visiting Nurse Association

PRIMARY NURSING AND THE SPECIALTY UNIT

The clinical specialist in primary nursing

The roles of clinical specialists can be enhanced or hindered by the health care system in which they are employed. For this reason it is important that clinical special-

ists evaluate the structure and philosophy of the system in which they are employed.

In my first position as Rehabilitation Nursing Clinical Specialist I was fortunate to be employed by a health care system in which primary nursing was the mode of nursing care delivery. The key components inherent in the primary nursing role, responsibility, accountability, and development of professional collegial relationships, are also the key components seen in the role of the clinical specialist. Therefore, one role complements the other. Each primary nurse makes a commitment to the delivery of quality nursing care and a commitment to personal growth as a professional. These commitments are also evident in the role of the clinical specialist. With the advent and spread of the primary nursing delivery system and the increase in the numbers of nurses being educated and performing as clinical specialists, nursing is growing as a profession in the eyes of other health care professionals.

Rehabilitation nursing as a special case

Those of us in rehabilitation have long recognized the importance of the multidisciplinary team approach in the delivery of quality rehabilitation services. Add the primary nursing concept to the rehabilitation team, and the patient benefits from consistency in the nursing discipline. This situation enhances the quality of the rehabilitation program. Then, if you believe the success of any rehabilitation is dependent on the effectiveness of the nursing discipline, and that discipline is in need of education to develop a quality rehabilitation nursing clinical program, the clinical specialist role is recognized.

When I entered my first position as a clinical specialist, the following elements were available: the nursing service department was committed to the primary nursing concept and practice; the physician–leader of the rehabilitation team recognized the importance of the nursing discipline; and hospital administration personnel recognized the importance of and were committed to the development of an effective, quality rehabilitation program to serve the community. These given components facilitated my role.

The role of the clinical specialist can be whatever one wants it to be, if clinical specialists are given the freedom to assess the situation and develop their roles according to the needs and problems recognized by them and the nursing staff. I had that freedom as I assessed the situation and developed my job description. I began by assuming the responsibility for a small primary patient caseload as we moved to define and develop the primary nursing system and define the rehabilitation nursing areas that needed clinical education. I worked closely with the head nurse, for the relationship of the clinical specialist and the head nurse is critical to the success of the former's role. If the head nurse, who as the "manager" of the nursing personnel sets the tone and expectations for the unit, does not support the role of the clinical specialist, I imagine the clinical specialist more than likely would not be effective in his/her role.

Facilitator, clinical resource and teacher, liaison, role model, consultant, and researcher are the many hats the clinical specialist wears. As a clinical specialist I primarily concentrated on developing strong consultant relationships with primary nurses and head nurses on the rehabilitation unit and in other areas of the hospital. Also recognizing the importance of team communication, I acted as a liaison between nursing and the other rehabilitation disciplines as we worked to facilitate communication between the primary nurses and other health care professionals, including the physicians.

Primary authority as an aid to communication

In the health care system as it exists today, most physicians tend to communicate with those in nursing or in other disciplines who have administrative authority. This situation, which the nursing profession has fostered in the past, is now changing with the advent of primary nursing and the clinical specialist role. The primary nursing system and the role of the clinical specialist fosters professional growth and the recognition of the knowledge of the nurse who stays at the bedside. Because of this, professional collegial relationships are developing.

Primary nurses and clinical specialists have made a commitment to continue the learning process and have an investment in the nursing care their patients receive. They are now accountable for their actions. Clinical knowledge and expertise is developed and eventually recognized. This recognition leads to the development of professional collegial relationships, which are a prime source of personal satisfaction. Most of us need to know from those professionals with whom we work that we have knowledge that is unique to our profession and that what we contribute does make a difference. But satisfaction in nursing should also depend on the patient–nurse relationship. Primary nursing provides us with the atmosphere for the development of this relationship.

I believe that in my experience as a clinical specialist in a primary nursing setting I was able to be effective because of my commitment to the primary nursing concept and practice and each individual nurse's own commitments to patients. We recognized the need for further knowledge and skills as we developed professional collegial relationships with physicians and other professionals in this particular health care setting. At this point in my career I believe that the primary nursing system is the most ideal situation for clinical specialists to develop their roles and be effective. This is not to say that clinical specialists cannot be equally effective in a team nursing structure, just that I am unable to make a comparison at this time. I can say, though, that each nurse's individual commitment to the delivery of quality nursing care and to professional growth is the key intangible factor that must exist for the clinical specialist role to flourish.

Marge Schultz, R.N.
Clinical Specialist
Rehabilitation Unit
Evanston Hospital

The nurse clinician in primary nursing: Two views

Nurse clinicians play an important part in the development and integration of primary nursing. Since they also function as staff nurses on the unit where they are clinicians, they must fulfill those obligations; but their responsibility does not end there.

One of the objectives of a nurse clinician is that of being a role model. This applies where primary nursing is concerned. Nurse clinicians set an example by choosing a full caseload of primary patients and writing individualized plans of care, including discharge planning. Staff nurses have that same function, however, clinicians go a step further. They assist and encourage fellow staff members to select and follow through with their patients. They also assist the head nurse in promoting the primary nursing model to accommodate patients on that unit in an optimal way.

Nurse clinicians are resources for less developed staff. Each clinician has a clinical specialty area. Primary nurses consult clinicians if they need assistance with their plans of care. For example, I work on a surgical oncology unit and I am often asked to consult on other units in the care of patients with colostomies and mastectomies.

Another important area is that of orientation of nurses new to this hospital to the concept of primary nursing. Many new employees have never had any contact with primary nursing before coming to Evanston Hospital. Because of this, they need an extensive orientation of its goals and the way nurses function to reach those goals with patients and their families. Nurse clinicians participate in much of this process as they are often the new employee's designated nurse. A designated nurse is one who is responsible for the implementation of the employee's orientation plan and is his/her advocate in the system.

I am proud to be involved in such an advanced care system. I could not tolerate functional nursing after experiencing this type of responsibility and accountability. I enjoy the relationship between physicians and other members of the team and hope more hospitals will adopt this system.

Barbara Babineau, R.N.
Nurse Clinician
Surgical Unit
Evanston Hospital

The role of the nurse clinician in primary nursing is one of leading by example. Ideally, he/she should be familiar enough with all the patients on his/her unit to assist each primary nurse in the effort to identify problems and set reasonable and workable goals for patients. If the unit size makes this impractical, the nurse clinician should share these responsibilities with the head nurse.

Second, the clinician should make a personal assessment of each new patient soon after admission. With this knowledge, he/

she should try to identify patients with potentially complex needs and choose these as his/her own primary patients. In this manner it is possible not only to act as the patient advocate and avoid patient–staff conflicts, but to establish quickly a rapport with the patient and his family and perhaps relieve some of their anxieties and doubts.

Finally, clinicians must be able to recognize that some problems cannot be resolved, no matter how hard they try, and then be able to help each primary nurse on their units accept this fact.

Betty Steiner, R.N.
Nurse Clinician
Evanston Hospital

Primary nursing adapted to a renal specialty unit

Historically on our unit the team nursing concept was utilized successfully. This success was measured by the RNs' satisfaction that patient needs were being met, but as time passed it became increasingly difficult to give quality patient care consistently. It was six months ago that our unit successfully changed to primary nursing.

The unit discussed in this article is a 15-bed renal specialty unit. Peritoneal dialysis is done on our unit, but hemodialysis is done in a separate area by a separate staff.

On The Scene

Some people working on a busy hospital unit feel primary nursing is a difficult idea to grasp. I have heard staff members say, "The floor is too acute—I don't have time to take primary patients." If any of these people worked 11 P.M. to 7 A.M., they would realize primary nursing is the only type of nursing care for patients.

Primary nursing is a continuous, everyday process. Because I am one of the two nurses available at night on a busy 30-bed unit, I utilize the nursing process and am 100 percent accountable for the outcomes of nursing care for each patient for that eight-hour period, acting as associate primary nurse. Planning care for each specific patient and evaluating all their needs, both physiological and psychological, is what I do every night I work no matter how acute the unit might be.

Besides being a night associate to primary nurses, I also have the added responsibility of being a nurse clinician. As nurse clinician, it is my duty to help other staff members develop in response to the expectations of primary nursing. If these staff members worked nights, they would begin to understand about caring for each patient using the primary nursing model to plan nursing care.

My morning report conveys the idea of comprehensive nursing care: a problem oriented report is given, and I attempt to cover all aspects of care—physical and psychological. I attempt to communicate *daily* with each patient's daytime primary nurse (or associate). I do add to the Kardex on occasions and have written up care plans. I consider myself associate primary nurse for *each* patient on my unit. I am responsible for all aspects of their care. I have attempted to take certain patients as my own primary patient and hope to increase that number in the near future.

Jane Tobias, R.N.
Night Nurse
Evanston Hospital

Long term relationships

End stage renal disease with the necessary repeated hospitalizations gives the nurse an ideal opportunity in which to form a long term relationship with a certain number of patients. That number is different for every nurse, as are the characteristics of each patient chosen. In dealing with chronic illness, a long term relationship is optimal before proper assessment of needs can take place. Primary nursing on our unit allows each RN to have a caseload of patients for which he/she is accountable. The necessity to utilize primary nursing became increasingly apparent as our patient population grew. There was a time when each RN could remember enough about each patient to give quality patient care. Today our patient population has increased threefold and is still growing. There are now three satellite dialysis centers that admit only to our hospital, and we are the center for transfers from local hospitals in which there are no dialysis centers.

Within his/her caseload of patients, the RN now has the capability to form long term relationships with each primary patient beginning with their first admission. Because of the longevity of the formed relationships, modifications to primary nursing were deemed mandatory. Our experience has been that it is not necessary for each primary nurse to do the day-to-day care for each primary patient. The reason for this is that the dependency on one nurse that can follow is far from beneficial. The primary nurses are responsible for assisting the patient and his family in the initial acceptance of his disease, for the tremendous teaching needs of a new renal patient, for the ongoing support necessary during any chronic illness, and for the critical care knowledge and ability necessary during the acute episode for which the patient is hospitalized. The primary nurse and the attending physician are responsible for coordinating the day-to-day and long term goals to meet best the needs of each primary patient.

Associate nurse system

Consistent with the long term relationships formed with chronically ill patients is the associate nurse system we have developed. Our associate nurses are the nurses working in the hemodialysis unit, and we are theirs. There are needs that can best be met during hemodialysis, and our associates help us to meet those needs. Each primary nurse has one hemodialysis nurse with whom he or she consistently works. We have informal meetings to discuss short and long term goals and the best way to reach them. The hemodialysis nurse can also be the primary nurse, and we work as their associate. The same system works both ways. The theory behind having a primary-associate team of the same two nurses is simple: teams have been formed in which the strengths and weaknesses are complimented in their partner. A collegial relationship is formed on the patient's behalf, which enables maximum utilization of professional strength in contributing to patient care.

The day to day patient care load by an RN on our unit consists of a module of three to five patients. If the RN has an assistant he/she might have six to eight patients. One or two may be primary patients. RNs give direct, individualized patient care for their modules. They assist other primary nurses with follow-up care on their primary patients; i.e., return demonstrations of shunt care or peritoneal catheter care. Most importantly, they coordinate and take full accountability for assessing and meeting the needs of each of their primary patients. The satisfaction gained from meeting these needs is the most rewarding aspect of primary nursing.

Sandy Dixon, R.N., B.S.N.
Head Nurse
Renal Unit
Evanston Hospital

Primary nursing in psychiatry

As we considered the implementation of primary nursing on our psychiatric unit, we assumed the transition would be made easily and without much effort. The one-to-one nurse-patient relationship was already a model we practiced, and it seemed that just a semantic change would be required. Not so.

Now, several months later, we have succeeded in implementing primary nursing, and in the process have introduced a new word into our vocabulary: accountability. Not only nursing, but also all the other disciplines which impact on patient care in psychiatry have more clearly defined their role on the treatment team in planning and implementing patient care.

In the past, a patient would be assigned to a staff member each shift with no guarantee he would have the same nurse on tomorrow's day shift as he did today. If a relationship developed between the nurse and the patient, it was a tool for delivering

As we considered the implementation of primary nursing on our psychiatric unit, we assumed the transition would be made easily and without much effort. The one-to-one nurse–patient relationship was already a model we practiced, and it seemed that just a semantic change would be required. Not so.

nursing care, and the patient benefited. However, these relationships just grew, often more by accident than design. The scope of the relationship and of the nurse's role was narrow, directed toward the "here and now" as it related to life in the milieu. From time to time a nurse would become involved in discharge planning and make a home visit or accompany a patient to a placement facility upon discharge, but that was not formally part of the nurse's role. The patient who was seen as "interesting" by the staff received much attention; those other not-so-interesting patients were treated routinely.

Today, every patient on both our twenty-five bed and eleven-bed units has a primary nurse, and we have a much more effective interdisciplinary care team as well. Unlike most other units which have a high complement of professional nurses, we staff with almost equal numbers of RNs and psychiatric technicians. Our "PTs" are almost all college graduates, many with a major in psychology. Some of them have come to us with experience working in other psychiatric settings; some are in graduate school. They are a highly motivated and bright young group of people who represent a variety of backgrounds and, with the nurses, provide a staff group that complements the patient group. We devote a great deal of time and energy in educating them so that they are able to function and utilize the nursing process in the care of patients. If we were able to draw a number of male nurses to join our staff, we would consider converting to all RN positions, but that is not an option at present.

Incorporating the psychiatric technician

We needed to modify the primary nursing concept to incorporate the role of the PT who was already sharing accountability for individual patient care. We determined that PTs could function as "primaries" for patients if an RN shared that accountability with him. We then assigned the staff to permanent day and evening modules, led by an RN, to guarantee continuity of care—this structure provides for both primary and associate primaries and identifies each staff member with permanent resources in their module to assist in problem solving.

For some time, we had struggled with the considerable task of managing twenty-five patients in the milieu on our open unit. Primary nursing has made it possible to respond more effectively. With two day and two evening modules, we set up relationships between days and evenings and formed two "teams." The patient group was then divided in half and assigned to one of the teams. Now the team has only twelve or thirteen patients for whom to plan care.

At this point, we had only a nursing structure and needed to incorporate social service, occupational therapy, psychology, special education teacher, and psychiatric residents into the team. This was accomplished by making permanent team assignments of these fellow professionals with a resident as the designated leader. The role of the primary nurse was widely discussed and was seen as pivotal. The primary nurse would admit the patient, collect the information for the data base from both the patient and the family, and with the team formulate an initial treatment plan. The therapeutic nurse-patient relationship would begin on admission and as the nurses learned more about the patient through that relationship, and by observing the patient in the milieu, he/she would alert the social workers or the occupational therapist to the patient's or family's need for their increased involvement and continue to develop, coordinate, and implement the care plan.

Primary nursing has been accepted enthusiastically by patients who have a con-sistent nurse-advocate in the milieu from admission through discharge. Some of our patients have been readmitted and have been reassured to have their primary nurse again. The nursing staff initially felt stressed by their increased accountability, but they now have become comfortable with it and enthusiastic to see the quality of care increase. The other disciplines of the psychiatric team have been most supportive of this change and work closely with each patient's primary. While initially concerned by what the change would mean, most of our attending psychiatrists have come to see primary nursing as a positive stride forward on the unit.

Suzanne Durburg, R.N., M.Ed.
Associate Chairperson
Department of Nursing, and
Nursing Coordinator
Psychiatry
Evanston Hospital

PRIMARY NURSING AND THE STUDENT

Providing learning experience

A frequently voiced concern of nursing educators and nursing service administrators is the adaptation of the new graduate nurse from the role of student to the role of a staff nurse. Many new situations confront new staff nurses. They must adjust to longer hours, different shifts, new relationships with others on the health team, and greater responsibilities, particularly larger patient loads.

As educators and administrators we believe in total patient care, identifying and meeting the patient's and his family's needs during hospitalization including teaching, counseling, and discharge planning. We teach these principles to students, and the expectation is that they will develop and

On the Scene

In my two and a half years as a staff nurse at Evanston Hospital I have been a primary nurse for a number of patients. As an evening nurse, I found it exceptionally rewarding to admit the patient, meet the family, establish a trusting relationship that is sometimes unique to the admitting nurse and maintain this relationship throughout the patient's hospitalization. This shift provided an excellent opportunity for teaching, interactions with the family during visiting hours and support for the patient after he has had an exhausting day. I firmly believe that primary nursing is as beneficial to the family as it is to the patient and the nurse.

I can illustrate this with an example of a primary patient who helped me grow as a professional nurse. Mrs. E. was transferred to us from the intensive care unit. At 56, she had metastatic cancer and a serious cellulitis of her left arm. She was experiencing much discomfort most of the time and needed gentle care as well as heavy sedation. Her family was very attentive, spent every evening visiting her and became active in her care. Mrs. E. said very little but would smile appreciatively whenever I cared for her. At times we would need to put some restrictions on her family visits, especially when Mrs. E. would become tired. After approximately a month-and-a-half of pain and hospitalization, Mrs. E. died. Soon after this I received a copy of a letter Mrs. E's daughter had written to the chairperson of the Department of Nursing. In her letter she explained how difficult her mother's hospitalization had been for everyone and how grateful they were for the support they had received from the primary nurse. She commented on how her mother had referred to me as her "guardian angel." In this mobile society, families are too often separated in times of crisis. An identifiable professional who has a sustained relationship with the patient can reduce the anxiety of significant family members who cannot be present continuously during the time the patient is on the threshold of death.

Being a primary nurse was not always smooth sailing. On a few occasions I had become "too involved" and had to remove myself from the patient's care for a few days. Sometimes I felt inadequate and unreliable. I thought I needed to be there whenever my primary patient needed someone. It took time and lots of growing to learn to trust the rest of the staff and delegate to the associate primary nurses. This is not always an easy thing to do, especially when you become so committed and involved. It is essential to develop a sense of balance. I needed to develop a trusting relationship with the other staff members and to be willing to be a good team member. One way I accomplished this was to become an associate nurse whenever possible and develop that role. Another way is to hold care conferences routinely and share ideas with other staff members.

Working on the evening shift I found myself in the role of the patient advocate; a liaison between the patient, his physician, and other hospital disciplines; as well as the coordinator of his total care. Good communications are essential. There is often so much activity going on through the day that the patient needs his primary nurse to help him to endure diagnostic procedures and therapeutics while conserving his energy and his equilibrium. Discharge planning also is usually accomplished during the day because of the availability of the physicians and other hospital services. However, an evening associate nurse is extremely helpful in working with the family, expanding the data base, and implementing the teaching program.

A day associate for an evening primary nurse is useful for coordinating the care with the physician, who might only be present during the day. If the primary nurse and his/her associate

continued on next page

have fulfilled the expectations of the primary nursing model in terms of a well developed care plan, the night nurse can maintain continuity for the patient and become a significant contribution to the plan and to the patient's well-being.

In September 1974, I accepted a position as head nurse on an acute care, infectious disease unit. The staff on this particular unit was attempting to work within the modular nursing assignment plan, but this was still in its initial phase. I felt it was important for the staff to understand the structure of modular nursing with the concept of primary nursing. We first worked with the modular leader and modular mate delivery of care and the necessity for good teamwork. This is easier said than done, and it took us almost a year of hard work before we were fairly certain of where each of us was coming from. We worked as a group and also on a one-to-one basis with the focus being quality patient care and job satisfaction. I have to say that it took much support from my former head nurse, my coordinator, the nursing consultants, and the chairperson of the Department of Nursing for me to get through this experience. They served in the role of counselors, teachers, and at times, a friend. At one point, the chairperson of the Department met with my entire staff to clarify her support of our goal of quality patient care for every patient in this unit. The entire department of nursing was available to serve as resources and support.

Finally, primary nursing was slowly introduced on our unit. I started by taking one or two primary patients and serving as a role model. Then I observed the staff, identified a patient that one of them became involved with and suggested that they take the patient as a primary patient. As part of the orientation for new nurses, the orientee will choose or be assigned two or three patients from a module and care for these patients only, but still have the support of the module leader. The orientee would be responsible for the total care of these patients and also have the support of their designated nurse. (Each new orientee has a designated nurse as an advocate during orientation.) These patients would be their primary patients.

The growth of primary nursing on our unit has been slow but steady. Due to the variety of patients and the nature of their illnesses, we became frustrated with our inability to provide quality, total patient care at all times. With the assistance of the entire Department of Nursing we have developed a practice of primary nursing that works for us. Because of the specialty of our unit, we often transfer patients to different parts of the hospital to accommodate a more infectious patient. We have made a special effort to maintain a complete and current care plan, problem list, and to start early discharge plans. When possible, we have a primary nurse come from the unit to which the patient is being transferred to meet the patient and discuss his care. We often do this with the rehabilitation unit and with the surgical units because those are circumstances allowing us to plan ahead. Due to the variety of patients we accommodate, we have utilized psychiatric nurses, rehabilitation specialists, and the renal nurses to assure competent, comprehensive nursing care, as well as other various hospital resources.

Our nursing consultants and coordinators are extremely helpful when exploring hospital resources and units for transfer of our patients. I have consulted them as professional colleagues by explaining the situation, possible solutions to my particular problem, and requesting feedback. In every case, they have responded to me or to the primary nurse involved and relayed helpful suggestions and information.

It has taken almost two years to develop and facilitate primary nursing on our unit. As the head nurse, it has been a frustrating but rewarding experience. I have interviewed nurses who are frustrated and unhappy with their profession and want so much to be a "real nurse." In my

continued on next page

opinion, primary nursing is the only way to be a "real nurse." Many of my staff members have been content in their role as primary nurses and have been rewarded with the kinds of experiences and professional growth that I have experienced. My favorite hours are spent talking with these nurses about their patients, the goals they have set, and accomplishments they have achieved. I have stacks of thank you notes from grateful patients with a special note to their primary nurse. We also have recently been receiving positive feedback from the attending physicians—instead of asking for the "charge nurse" they ask for the primary nurse.

I have been able to delegate some of my administrative duties to two nurse clinicians, allowing me the luxury of being a primary nurse again. I have found myself envying my staff nurses and longing for the past when I was a primary nurse all the time. Now I must limit myself to two to three primary patients, and I do mean limit myself. This is not always an easy thing to do. Last weekend, I worked the evening shift and by Monday morning I found myself with five primary patients. So you see, I tend to get carried away at times. This is unfair to my patients, my staff, and myself. I am learning to divide my time appropriately among all three interests. For me to enjoy job satisfaction as a head nurse, I must have the opportunity to be a primary nurse. At times, this means working the evening shift or delegating another staff nurse to be the resource person on the unit. This provides times for me to concentrate on direct patient care. For me primary nursing is the only way to be a nurse!

Sue Guilianelli, R.N.
Head Nurse
Evanston Hospital

demonstrate this philosophy through their care to patients. All too often, however, the new graduate finds it impossible to continue to practice in this fashion in the real life work situation. The new graduate becomes frustrated and disillusioned, as has been extensively documented by Marlene Kramer in her book *Reality Shock* (C.V. Mosby Company 1974).

From student nurse to primary nurse

All these concerns and more were particularly of interest to me as the management instructor for senior students at Evanston Hospital.

How could I as an instructor facilitate the role change from student nurse to young professional nurse during the short seven weeks in which senior students were in the management module?

Students entering the course had cared for one to two patients during morning clinical experiences. The transition to six to ten patients for eight hour periods was overwhelming to most. The transition to larger patient loads and increased responsibility must be gradual. Students must feel guided and supported during the experience, with frequent opportunities to share experiences and feelings with their peer group. The primary nursing philosophy of Evanston Hospital, implemented through the modular system, provided an excellent clinical setting in which to provide these opportunities to students.

Students could begin as module assistants with RNs who were primary nurses. This provided students the opportunity to participate in the delivery of care to larger groups of patients without the responsibility for total care. They observed the primary nurse delivering care as they, the students, had been taught—it really was possible! When students felt comfortable as module assistants (after approximately two weeks), they then would "buddy" with an RN for several days and ultimately become the module leader with the RN as module assistant. The student acted in the capacity of Module Leader for a minimum of four weeks. Toward the end of this period the student became module leader with an LPN or nursing assistant as module assistant. In this role, students assess, plan, implement, and evaluate with the primary nurse the care plans for their individual modules of six to ten patients. The effectiveness of this progression of responsibility is enhanced by conferences with the student, the primary nurse, and the instructor to evaluate the student's level of mastery. Of equal or greater importance are weekly scheduled meetings with the student nurse, his/her instructor, and the head nurse. In these meetings students discuss their responses, feelings, or problems, ask questions, and receive feedback on individual performance. The meetings are considered high priority by all, and all involved participate actively. Once weekly, at the end of the three-day clinical experience, all management students gather for an evaluation and problem solving conference. The instructor is present, but in the role as a resource person for the students.

Rewards of clinical experience

The clinical experience provides the students a number of rewards. Nursing knowledge and skills are increased as students actively participate in the care of patients. Management theory is directly applied in the clinical setting and developed as the student interacts with all members of the health team. Students observe excellent role models of professional nursing as they work with primary nurses and head nurses. From an educator's viewpoint, it is an ideal clinical environment in which to teach management. On the one hand, students are able to

practice nursing in the manner in which they have been educated; on the other hand, it is a real-life situation which potentially will decrease the role conflicts of a new graduate.

To evaluate the effectiveness of the program, one must look at the performance of the new graduates. Graduates from the program are well received throughout the country. Graduates who remain at Evanston Hospital following their education become excellent primary nurses themselves. A number of graduates who leave the institution for other employment options return. Their response when questioned is rewarding: "I wanted to come back to Evanston and be a primary nurse as we were taught."

Janet Scherubel, R.N., M.S.N.
Medical Nursing Coordinator
Evanston Hospital
(formerly Instructor
Evanston School of Nursing)

The role of head nurse in developing young professionals

My career at Evanston Hospital started four and a half years ago. The birth of the primary nursing pilot project and my first day were almost simultaneous. As primary nursing grew and flourished, so did my professionalism and competence as a primary nurse. So when offered, I felt ready to assume a head nurse position. I would be working on a general medical floor, which was to become a cardiac teaching unit. The professional nursing staff consisted of one RN with three years' experience on the unit, and 12 RNs who had been employed at Evanston less than one year—many of the 12 were new graduates. We also had LPNs and nursing assistants with experience and they were a great stabilizing force with a new staff.

Armed with enthusiasm, many new ideas, and a positive attitude that my new staff had great potential, I started my new job. The concept of primary nursing was something new and strange for my staff—they had heard the term frequently and knew it worked well in other areas of the hospital, but they were reluctant to try it. Since I had been actively involved in primary nursing since my first day at Evanston Hospital, I decided the best way to show my new staff was to be a model primary nurse by: (1) choosing primary patients, (2) writing and updating care plans, and (3) initiating discharge planning. We also had a staff meeting for the registered nurses and discussed their concept of primary nursing. They certainly had the right ideas: (1) being responsible for planning a patient's twenty-four-hour care and sharing this plan with coworkers by writing care plans, (2) informing the patient and his family that you are his nurse, and that he can feel free to ask you any questions, (3) informing the physicians you are the primary nurse and communicating daily with them, and (4) assuming responsibility for patient and family teaching and necessary discharge planning. Though the staff certainly seemed able to identify how they perceived primary nursing on our unit, implementation was another matter.

I had some ideas about implementing primary nursing, but I first checked them with my coordinator and former head nurse. They agreed with my ideas and offered some other good suggestions, which I tried. I spoke with two members of my staff who were respected by their coworkers for many reasons. These two nurses had been consistently choosing primary patients and writing care plans. I asked them to help me by continuing to be role models for their peers and encouraging the other nurses to begin choosing primary patients. My next step was to schedule another staff meeting. I told

the nurses I thought they were all practicing primary nursing and they just needed to give it that name by telling the patients and physicians and signing their names on our primary nursing board. The staff agreed and set a projected date one week later for every nurse to have a caseload of two primary patients. They met this goal successfully. We now meet weekly and continue to discuss primary nursing process and to set goals for ourselves and the unit.

We still encounter some "bumpy roads" on our unit, but I think that is due to a new staff and new head nurse. Overall, we have come a long way in a short time. The nurses are choosing primary patients, writing care plans, and getting involved in patient teaching and discharge planning. We are all learning, showing, and growing together; and I think that is part of what being a professional is all about!

Wendy Law, R.N.
Head Nurse
Medical Unit
Evanston Hospital

Primary nursing and the student nurse

I consider myself fortunate in that I was taught my nursing skills with primary nursing as a conceptual framework in which to operate. Fortunate, too, because I never practiced under another type of nursing structure so I had no old habits or beliefs about nursing to dispel to let myself accept primary nursing.

I started in Evanston Hospital's School of Nursing in September 1973. I had worked as an aide in other hospitals in other areas all through college. I always wondered how the nurses ever get enough data together to be able to give reports to the doctors every morning. As a nurse's aide, I was the one who was with the patient all morning giving him his bath and talking. All the RN had done was pass him two pills and give him a shot. I knew, innately, the patient was being lost in the shuffle but had no idea there was anything better "out there" to rectify the situation.

When I started hearing about primary nursing as a freshman in nursing school, something clicked. I began to see this as the only solution to the problems I saw patients having in other hospitals. It came as no big change in my care-giving because as an aide, I was enjoying the nurse-patient relationship that an RN is allowed to develop *only* under primary nursing. But I had the least amount of educational preparation to handle the relationship. Is this not just what primary nursing does? It turns things upside-down, so those with the most knowledge are the ones most intimately involved in patient care.

Becoming a primary nurse

By the time I was a senior in nursing school, I felt confident that I had enough physiology and basic nursing skills to care for patients using primary care, but I still had never handled more than two patients a day and never for more than three days in a row. That is where management had its impact on my career. We were on the floor four days a week for six to eight weeks. I remember being astounded to walk on to the floor and find every Kardex filled with up-to-date and well organized care plans—just like we had done for two years in school! But the reason why, of course, was primary nursing. How nice to work under these circumstances. To look up a new patient, I would only flip to the Kardex and have all the pertinent information I needed.

After the first two weeks on the management team, we could act as a module leader with other RNs or LPNs as module assistants. By the fourth week, I began to realize

that this would be a golden opportunity to try my hand at a primary nurse relationship while I still had an instructor to lend support and guidance.

I chose my primary patient to be someone with whom I already had built good rapport. I decided to be a primary associate instead of a primary nurse for the patient because I knew I would be leaving the floor at the end of the course and did not want the patient's care to suffer for my learning experience. The minute I took on this added responsibility, I began to feel the extra pressure of that task. I was accountable for that patient's plan of care and the outcome of it for the whole time he was there. I began to work harder and to carry that by now well-known "baggage" of nursing accountability home with me. But, at the same time, it was the most rewarding patient care experience I had in school. I had a say in the care of the patient. The physicians would seek me out to catch up on the patient's daily progress. The entire weight of whether that patient had a positive, mediocre, or negative response to his experience (clinically and psychosocially) was on my shoulders. I began to think, act, and feel more like a professional health care giver. It was energizing.

Comforts of primary nursing

I have now graduated and have been working at Evanston Hospital in the coronary care unit for three months. As a new graduate in a critical care area, I have had much to learn and am slowly becoming familiar with the details of cardiology and arrhythmias. The one big strength I knew I could rely on was that comfortable feeling I had developed in management with primary nursing. Although I am having to learn many new medical concepts, I am accustomed to the 24-hour accountability and feel confident living with it. It is one of the important ways I have maintained my own sense of equilibrium. I am still feeling the rewards of primary nursing. Without it, the past three months would have been even harder.

We at Evanston Hospital are fortunate to have primary nursing. Fortunate that the Department of Nursing had the courage and pluck to develop it. It bands all of the nurses who work here into a professional, thinking, acting colleagueship. We are all proud of what we do here for our patients, and I will have that feeling to carry with me wherever my career takes me. I know one thing for sure; if and when I do leave Evanston Hospital to seek employment elsewhere, my first question will be, "Do you have primary nursing?"

Pam Segan, R.N.
Staff Nurse
CCU
Evanston Hospital

EVANSTON REFLECTS ON PRIMARY NURSING

The evolving role of the Department of Nursing in the hospitals of this country continues the search for professional peer recognition and organizational visibility and structure. The particular approach that the primary nursing model is pointing toward reflects a major change of direction in the quest for achievement of the above mentioned goals.

For the past two decades nursing has been divesting itself of many of the important routine and relatively mundane duties that were directly related to the care of the patient. The professional nurse, either by intent or because of necessity resulting from a shortage of nurses and the need for nonprofessional assistance, found less and less occasion to be with the patient to not only provide direct clinical care but also to observe the need for and the results of this care

application. The significant need of the patient for support in other areas was not possible with the staffing availability or the plan itself for staffing.

The usefulness of the primary nursing model seems to be in the commitment by the Department of Nursing to the concept that the professional nurse is in charge of and will be an active participant in seeing to it that the care plan of each patient is accomplished. It directly reaches the disturbing problem in many hospitals where there is no one in charge of each individual patient's regimen of care. It finds the professional nurse giving clinical care and other social support to the patient and his family.

I have found this concept an important element in the development of highly successful *esprit de corps* in the nursing department, enthusiastically accepted by members of the professional medical staff and enjoyed immensely by the patients and their families. From my vantage point, it is encouraging to observe the above reactions to this concept and to have the opportunity to support the significant role and responsibility that the professional nurse and the department of nursing carries in our hospital.

Bernard J. Lachner
President, Chief Executive Officer
Evanston Hospital

Upon beginning at Evanston Hospital as a new graduate in 1975, my knowledge of primary care was little more than a short paragraph I had seen in a book somewhere. All I knew was that the team approach lacked what I was looking for in the nursing field.

At Evanston Hospital, I found the standards, beliefs, and priorities in nursing care to be more like my own. I was finally at the bedside giving total patient care. Working with my primary patients has shown me that the patient can truly learn, grow, and have positive feelings about his hospital stay. I, as a primary nurse, learn a great deal from my patients. I can admit to having personal and job satisfaction through this type of management.

Not only have I found better patient care given through primary nursing, but I find a better rapport and working relationship with the physician. The attending physician, the house staff, and the primary nurse work together as a team to keep each other aware of the patient's progress and decide what approach would be best suited for the patient. On the whole, I have seen this work quite well with most doctors.

I do not believe primary care is flawless, but I do think we have come a long way for the patient as well as the nurse. It is the only kind of nursing I will ever be a part of!

Anonymous Staff Nurse
Evanston Hospital

The concept of primary nursing care was born of a concern to put the nurse into a more dynamic role in the care of the hospitalized patient. This goal has been achieved at the Evanston Hospital. As a result of the primary nursing program a colleague relationship has been established between physician and nurse; and a warm, trusting, and workable relationship has been established between patient and nurse.

My personal observation is that the primary nurse has filled the communication gap between the patient and the physician. In this system the nurse cannot hide professionalism behind the patient, nor abdicate to the physician the need to understand thoroughly the complexities of medical problems. These nurses can fulfill their role only by involvement with the patient, the physi-

cian, and the illness. The scope of this involvement is only limited by the dedication, intelligence, and energy of the nurse. I am proud to say that these qualities are highly developed at the Evanston Hospital.

Harry J. Miller, M.D.
Chairman of the Medical Executive
    Committee 1975-1976
President of the Professional Staff
1974-1975
Evanston Hospital

In my care corps work, I have encountered numerous comments from patients regarding primary nursing as it is now practiced at Evanston Hospital. The greater majority of the patients who comment on this service find it a real plus: "It's really nice to know there will be one special person in charge of you the whole time you're in the hospital. That way you can really get to know them. It's friendlier, you know? And then to have the same one if you have to come back in— that's really great!" That, in essence, is the enthusiasm espoused by the happy recipients of primary nursing.

It is my feeling that the preponderance of the patients I see who talk about the high level of nursing care at Evanston Hospital feel that it adds a "special dimension" to their total care in that they have one particular person—their primary nurse—who will serve as their special line of communication during their hospitalization. Because of this increased interaction between the primary nurse and the patient, I feel that the hospital contributes greatly toward the alleviation of the stigma of "institutional impersonalization."

Marcine Reed
Evanston Volunteer Corps

Clinical nurse specialist role creation: An achievable goal

Kathleen Hanson Morris, B.S.N., R.N.
Coordinator, Staff Development
Nursing Administrative Supervisor
Critical Care Department
Milwaukee County Medical Complex

Janice A. Schweiger, M.S.N., R.N.
Cardiovascular Clinical Nurse Specialist
Milwaukee County Medical Complex
Milwaukee, Wisconsin

CLINICAL NURSING specialty, a reality in the community, seemed an unreachable goal at the Milwaukee County Medical Complex. The organizational chart (Appendix A) is rigidly structured to exclude any position that does not fit into either a staff or management nursing framework. (see Figure 1.) There is no civil service classification for specialists (see Table 1), there is no salary budget flexibility for creation of new positions, and requests for additional numbers of existing positions or for any new positions require volumes of paperwork for justification, approvals by committees concerned with multiple county issues and one to two years lost in the process.

This was the situation encountered one year ago by nursing administrative personnel in the Critical Care Department when they identified the need for a clinical nurse specialist.

IDENTIFICATION OF NEED

Historically, specialization in nursing can be traced back to the early 1900s.[1] Over the years the definition of a specialist as well as the educational and clinical requirements for the position have varied. The common agreement, however, has been that the specialist is a person who could function as an "expert practitioner and role model."[2] The presence of a clinical specialist within a setting conveys the implications that change or improvement is needed.[3] At the Milwaukee County Medical Complex, the need for change and improvement had been identified prior to the appearance of the

Nurs Admin Q, 1979, 4(1), 67–79
©1979 Aspen Publishers, Inc.

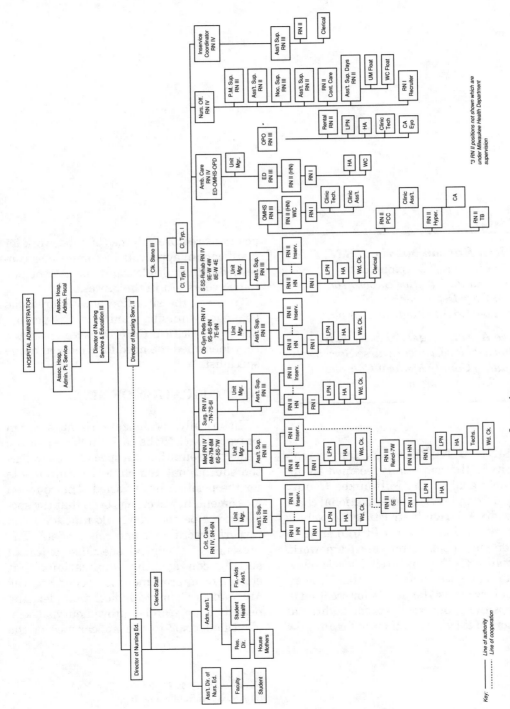

Key: ——— Line of authority
     ·········· Line of cooperation

Figure 1. Organizational chart, department of nursing

Table 1. Civil service classifications for RNs at the Milwaukee County Medical Complex

Classifications	Positions	Civil Service Allocations (Maximum allowable)
RN I	Staff nurses	Allocated per unit
RN II	Head nurses	One per clinical unit
	Staff development educators	One to three per department
RN III	Department assistant supervisor	One per department
RN IV	Department administrative supervisor	One per department
Director of nursing service		One
Director of nursing service and education		One

specialist. This need in the Critical Care Department arose from expansion of bed capacity and an increase in the number of diagnostic cardiac procedures, open-heart surgeries and complex nursing procedures. With the expansion and diversification of knowledge inherent in nursing today, complex patient and family problems were being identified by the staff nurses. Owing to time constraints and lack of higher educational preparation, the staff nurses were becoming increasingly frustrated over their inability to meet those needs.

The nursing administrative personnel in the Critical Care Department initiated problem-solving sessions in an attempt to investigate and outline potential methods of gaining support and obtaining a position for a clinical nurse specialist. Those persons within the institution from whom support would be necessary were identified as the director of nursing service and education, hospital administration and the cardiology and cardiothoracic medical staff.

CREATING A SPECIALIST POSITION: THE BACKDOOR METHOD

During this time, the staff development educator position for the surgical/medical intensive care unit was vacant. To the surprise and delight of the interview team, a cardiovascular clinical nurse specialist sought to be interviewed. Recognizing this as an opportunity to capitalize on the goal of hiring a specialist, the critical care nursing administrative personnel began the implementation process.

After receiving approval from the director of nursing service and education, the administrative staff initiated negotiations with the specialist. The nursing supervisor and the applicant discussed the philosophy of the clinical specialty role, specific responsibilities and accountabilities, hours, and salary. They reached agreement, and the specialist was hired into a staff nurse position, at the top of the pay scale. From the specialist's point of view, the challenge of being part of a role-creation and -development process and the flexibility of hours were primary incentives for accepting the position. She did not view salary as a priority item. Hiring a specialist prior to inclusion of this role in the organizational chart would allow for justification for the role through visible and documented achievements.

Role of the administrative supervisor

The administrative supervisor's role relative to this challenge included obtaining support from the director, facilitating the hiring procedure, and approving the job description.

Role of the assistant supervisor

The critical care assistant supervisor, whose responsibility is coordination of staff development for the area, was identified as the most appropriate person to work with the specialist on role implementation. This decision was based on her greater availability than the administrative supervisor and her strong personal dedication to clinical specialty.

The assistant supervisor's responsibilities for this new role included orientation for the clinical specialist, introduction to the nursing staff, medical staff, and other key personnel, and collaboration on writing the job description.

Job description

A complete job description was essential to successful implementation of the role. The initial prospect of preparing one seemed exciting and challenging. No civil service or institutional guidelines existed that would limit creativity. Area hospital job descriptions for clinical specialists were carefully

From the specialist's point of view, the challenge of being part of a role-creation and -development process, and the flexibility of hours, were primary incentives for accepting the position.

reviewed, current literature relative to roles and responsibilities of clinical specialists was consulted, and the American Nurses' Association[4] and Wisconsin Nurses' Association position papers were obtained. Eventually the specialist and the assistant supervisor adapted a job description from these sources and from the Position Statement on the Clinical Nurse Specialist in the State of Wisconsin,[5] which delineates responsibilities and functions into four major categories: practitioner, educator, consultant and researcher. Role responsibilities are in conformity with Milwaukee community standards (see Appendix).

Acceptance: Initial effort

Successful introduction of any new role within an established organization involves planning and continual evaluation. Oda describes three phases of role development as essential components of the process of role implementation: role identification, role transition and role confirmation.[6] The process of acceptance for the new role at the Milwaukee County Medical Complex was similar to Oda's first and second phases in that activities were directed toward clarification, interaction, obtaining feedback and utilization of this information to fit the role into this institution.[7] The basis for these activities was the job description and the mutual philosophy of the clinical nurse specialist and the department assistant supervisor.

Evolution of a Role: Clinical Nurse Specialist

Increased technological advances, development of consumer advocates and social protest movements are factors responsible for some of the changes in health care today. Scientific advances, federal health legislation, a more enlightened public and inherent characteristics of nurses are additional factors effecting change in nursing practice.

In conjunction with changing concepts of health care delivery and general standards for care, there has to be a shift in emphasis on clinical nursing practice.

Quality patient care is dependent on qualified nurses. Increased emphasis on improved nursing care has resulted in a move toward more individualized comprehensive care for the patient and more interest in the clinical aspects of nursing care.

Historically we have labeled our nurses as general-duty staff nurses. They diligently cleaned, washed, organized, trained, supervised, managed and operated the patient care services. We must recognize and provide for nursing practice to have priority over nonpatient care-related activities. There is a need for nurses possessing advanced knowledge in nursing and clinical expertise—knowledge of greater depth and scope than that of the nursing generalist.

Mrs. Bucilla Petross, M.S., R.N.
Director of Nursing Service
Milwaukee County Medical Complex
Milwaukee, Wisconsin

A welcoming party was given to introduce the clinical specialist to personnel from all nursing departments, nursing administration, hospital administration, and critical care staff physicians. This provided the framework for future formal interactions.

The clinical specialist sent the job description to Critical Care Department head nurses and staff nurses, cardiology and cardiothoracic staff physicians and hospital administration prior to the initiation of formal meetings. Clarification to, interaction with and feedback from these individuals were considered essential during the acceptance process.

The head nurses proved to be enthusiastic and supportive. Philosophically, they agreed with the clinical specialist, and their perception of the role was consistent with the job description.

Staff meetings were held with each nursing unit within the Critical Care Department. The objective was to provide the opportunity for communication regarding the clinical specialist's role, philosophy and job description. The staff were encouraged to ask questions and offer suggestions. Emphasis was placed on feedback from the staff as being important for development and evaluation of the role.

Cardiology staff physicians' responses to the new role varied from total agreement to questioning the need for clinical nursing specialty. The majority of the physicians supported the concept.

Discussions with the cardiothoracic staff surgeons indicated that they believed the quality of patient care could be improved through the educator component of the clinical nurse specialist role. The other components—practitioner, consultant and researcher—were considered to be less significant in reaching their objectives.

The director of nursing service and education met with the hospital administrator to present the job description and introduce this new role. His response was positive.

One common denominator—continual clarification and communication, essential for effective implementation of the role—was evident as a result of the formal and informal meetings. Oda emphasizes these as crucial components of all three phases of role development.[8] The most difficult task for the clinical specialist was the necessity to clearly articulate a role that was not fully developed. She expected that as the role evolved, and as experience in the implementation process grew, role articulation would be facilitated. During this initial period, the department assistant supervisor served as mentor for the clinical specialist, a function that proved to be essential.

Communication with nursing administration

Lines of communication, authority and accountability are usually delineated on institutional organizational charts. This position, not fitting into the structure of the existing organization chart, lacked visible lines of communication with nursing service administration. Establishment of a communication network with the nursing department was deemed essential to retaining support for the role and for accomplishing implementation. Monthly meetings between the clinical specialist and the director of nursing service were initiated. These meetings started with discussion of the mutual philosophy of clinical specialty and progressed to the design and evaluation of goals, problem solving and role clarification within the institution.

Continual role evaluation

Further exposure to the nursing and medical staff and unit policies, procedures and routines was accomplished by allowing the clinical specialist to work as a staff member in each of the clinical units within the Critical Care Department. This experience facilitated colleague relationships and provided visibility to the nature and scope of the job description.

The first patient/family referral, initiated by the department assistant supervisor, came at the end of the first three months. Subsequent referrals came from head nurses, then staff nurses and finally physicians, both resident and staff. In addition to receiving referrals, the clinical specialist was consulted about nursing care standards and identification of nursing needs, participation in patient and family teaching and staff development programs.

Initially, the specialist wrote weekly goals and discussed them with the department assistant supervisor. Because of the diverse responsibilities and necessary flexibility of the role, these goals proved to be ineffective for long-term planning and evaluating. As a result, yearly goals with target achievement dates were developed. These reflected all four components of the job description and provided direction for the job. In addition, the clinical specialist has kept a log for documentation of activities and for use as a role evaluation tool. Presently the clinical specialist consults with the department assistant supervisor as needed for clarification of civil service statutes, for assistance with implementation of components of the job description and for introduction to new staff members.

PROGRESS TOWARD CIVIL SERVICE RECOGNITION

Two factors have contributed to the progress toward establishment of the position within the civil service structure. First, positive feedback attributed to accomplishments of the clinical specialist was received from nursing and medical staff, as well as from patients and families. The resultant feelings of encouragement provided motivation for continuing efforts toward creation of an authorized position. This factor, along with a community trend toward utilization of clinical specialists, led to the second factor, the formation of an executive nursing supervisory subcommittee. Its mission was to investigate the role of the clinical specialist within the county institution and the feasibility of adding the position to the organizational chart.

The subcommittee held its first meeting in June of this year. This group is composed of executive nursing supervisors from the specialty departments and the clinical specialist. Areas for consideration charged to this subcommittee are identification of the role within this institution, educational requirements for the position, clinical specialty versus nurse clinician positions, organizational structure changes including line versus staff placement, hiring process, salary and accountabilities.

Developing a philosophy

A philosophy of clinical specialty needed to be developed in conjunction with definition of the role. The subcommittee reached agreement on components of the role to be consistent with the existing clinical specialist's job description: practitioner, educator, consultant and researcher. The basic belief is that through these four components, a clinical specialist will enhance the quality of nursing care.

Setting standards and salary

Educational preparation is required at the master's level, in accordance with recommendations from the American Nurses' Association and the Wisconsin Nurses' Association position papers. For salary to be competitive with the community and to provide adequate compensation for higher educational preparation and clinical expertise, the specialists would be placed in RN III positions. The number of clinical specialists needed for the hospital has been established as 12, one for each specialty unit plus two medical-surgical specialists.

Discussions within this committee continue to progress. Location on the organizational chart will be determined, as well as line-versus-staff accountability. Justification for creation of the positions, based largely on documented accomplishments of the specialist, will be written and submitted to the appropriate committees and finally to the county board.

REASONS FOR SUCCESS

Once support for the project was received from the director of nursing service and education and the director of nursing service, nursing administrative staff members felt confident that eventually they would reach their goal. Circumstances facilitated movement in that direction earlier than planned. Progress is presently being made, through the clinical specialist subcommittee, toward acceptance by the county board.

Many factors influence successful achievement of a goal. In our particular situation, three factors stand out as most

The basic belief is that through the four components of practitioner, educator, consultant and researcher, a clinical specialist will enhance the quality of nursing care.

influential. One is a strong commitment and a willingness to demonstrate that throughout the goal-directed process. Another factor is the establishment of an effective communication system that serves to describe, reinforce and clarify the goal-directed process. The third involves active, strong administrative support, which not only serves to facilitate achievement of the goal, but also provides increased role satisfaction for the clinical specialist.[9]

The most important lesson learned from this is that nothing is impossible, even in the county and civil service system. The visual and documented achievements of an individual already functioning within the system can be utilized to overcome seemingly insurmountable obstacles inherent in existing hiring practices. This backdoor method of introducing a new role into a system provided a basis for justification of position creation in this one instance.

REFERENCES

1. Smoyak, S.A. "Specialization in Nursing: From Then to Now." *Nursing Outlook* 24:11 (November 1976) p. 676-681.
2. Baker, C. and Kramer, A. "To Define or Not to Define: The Role of the Clinical Specialist." *Nursing Forum* 9:1 (1970) p. 46.
3. Smoyak. "Specialization in Nursing," p. 676-681.
4. American Nurses' Association. *Resolutions on Role Titles* (Kansas City: ANA October 1976).
5. Wisconsin Nurses' Association. *Position Statement on the Clinical Nurse Specialist in the State of Wisconsin* (Madison: WNA October 1972).
6. Oda, D. "Specialized Role Development: A Three-Phase Process." *Nursing Outlook* 25:6 (June 1977) p. 374-377.
7. Ibid.
8. Ibid.
9. Schaefer, J.A. "The Satisfied Clinician: Administrative Support Makes the Difference." *Journal of Nursing Administration* 3:4 (July-August 1973) p. 18-21.

Appendix
Milwaukee County Medical Complex
Department of Nursing

Critical Care Department

Civil Service Title:

Title: Cardiovascular Clinical Nurse Specialist

Definition: A registered professional nurse who possesses a master's degree with emphasis in clinical nursing and who is responsible for the management and innovative improvement of nursing care for selected patients with cardiovascular alterations.

Personal Attributes: Candidate must demonstrate:

1. clinical expertise in cardiovascular nursing;
2. leadership ability;
3. knowledge and effective application of teaching–learning principles and methods as they relate to patient teaching and staff development;
4. a concept of nursing utilized in professional practice.

Accountabilities: The cardiovascular clinical nurse specialist is directly responsible to the Critical Care Department inservice coordinator. His/her primary accountability is to the consumer.

Nature and Scope: PRACTITIONER
1. develops and utilizes a concept of nursing practice;
2. participates in organizations which facilitate the practice of professional nursing;
3. assists cardiovascular patients with identification of nursing needs, and assists patient and/or nursing staff to satisfy identified needs through individual plan of patient care;
4. communicates with the patient, significant others, nursing staff, medical staff and related disciplines to:
   a. define health in light of the individual's illness state;
   b. define goals of hospitalization and/or home care;
   c. facilitate discharge planning from the hospital and/or from close clinic follow-up to occasional medical check-up;

     d. facilitate attitudes of choice and self-direction within the patient, through awareness of the services available to him/her and through awareness of the potential course of his/her illness;

5. evaluates the effectiveness of this nursing care;
6. identifies need for departmental and/or institutional change relating to the cardiovascular patients;
7. assists the critical care departmental nursing supervisor, head nurses and nursing inservice staff to define, implement and evaluate nursing care standards for the Critical Care Department.

EDUCATOR

1. designs, implements and evaluates health teaching within a nursing framework for the cardiovascular patients and their significant others;
2. assists nursing staff in the development of their teaching skills;
3. assists with planning, implementation and evaluation of the Critical Care Department orientation program for RNs;
4. assists with planning, implementation and evaluation of the advanced critical care class for RNs;
5. plans, implements and evaluates the staff development program in cardiovascular nursing.

CONSULTANT

1. maintains a level of clinical and theoretical expertise in cardiovascular nursing in order to provide consultation to colleagues, allied personnel, physicians and consumers of health care within the institution and/or community;
2. plans for own personal growth and professional development;
3. assists Critical Care Department nursing inservice with evaluation of systems by which care is delivered.

RESEARCHER

1. identifies clinical nursing problems and pursues their systematic investigation;
2. utilizes appropriate research findings to define nursing practice.

Clinical ladders and primary nursing: The wedding of the two

Paula M. Sigmon, R.N., M.S.N.
(Former) Director
Continuing Education Department
Methodist Hospitals of Dallas
Dallas, Texas

MANY HOSPITALS are considering or implementing either clinical ladders for nursing or primary nursing. Many are implementing one of the two while developing the other. Clinical ladders and primary nursing are a well-matched pair, each complementing the other; together, the two concepts define a solid mode of nursing care delivery and nursing care appraisal.

The time is long past for sitting by and waiting for positive change to occur within the nursing profession. For today, "change is an inevitable and continuous process within the hospital, with the specific professional services within its bounds having an obligation to make every effort to constructively channel this process to meet the needs of the patient, the staff, the hospital, and the community."[1]

With the steadily increasing influence of government on all aspects of health care, temporary placement agencies breathing down the back of nursing, and rising costs in health care, it is *not* enough that nursing *must* validate what it is about, what it does and for what part of the cost picture it is responsible. Nursing must also make it advantageous to and satisfying for its key people—clinical staff nurses—to want to stay in nursing, increasingly involve themselves with patient care, and experience personal and professional growth and movement within the organization employing them.

In other words, just believing that one's nursing care makes a difference is not enough. Criteria must be developed to justify both the need for and the effectiveness of one's nursing actions.

THE CLINICAL LADDERS CONCEPT

Development of clinical ladders for clinical progression is not only the method by which such criteria can be developed, but is also the approach most suitable to interface

Nurs Admin Q, 1981, 5(3), 63–67
©1981 Aspen Publishers, Inc.

with primary nursing. Essential to the wedding of these two key concepts must be nursing's contention that clinical ability and subsequent progression be measured not by educational preparation and/or experience but by the professional, expert, quality behaviors that are observable, cumulative, and descriptive of what nurses do indeed accomplish in their day-to-day delivery of nursing care.

In the clinical ladders concept, the measurable, progressive behaviors that are consistently employed and documented by nurses can be identified, collected, tallied, and used for promotion; the essence is progression by peer review, the true reason for the initiation of clinical ladders and a method by which quality nursing can indeed be documented.

The clinical ladders concept describes a system of promotion, then, that recognizes the professional nurse's clinical knowledge, competence, and performance. Levels for advancement in the clinical ladders concept provide a clinical nursing organizational line complementary to the administrative one. Nurses are therefore able to choose their own area of career advancement as their interests, motivation, and competence evolve.

Drawbacks of the traditional approach

The traditional system, on the other hand, usually rewards clinical competence by moving the nurse away from direct patient care into a management role. Professional nurses across the country have recognized two constraints to this traditional approach. First, highly competent professional nurses are not necessarily qualified for or interested in roles oriented to "nursing the system"; often the management role interferes with the nurse's retention of those clinical skills that led to that position. Second, the available management posts in most organizations are few in number; opportunity for upward mobility is therefore restricted.

Advantages of clinical ladders

Under the clinical ladders system, staff nurses can advance professionally, be rewarded according to their professional accomplishments as "practicing nurses" and be instrumental in the evaluation of their accomplishments; these are the *direct outcomes* of the clinical ladders concept.

Indirect or secondary gains/outcomes include improved personal and professional satisfaction; increased motivation to continue or improve upon the job being done; decreased staff turnover; increased positive attitudes toward self, role, and organization; and documented quality care for patients. Interestingly, these secondary gains (outcomes) are the same as those described for primary nursing.

THE PRIMARY NURSING CONCEPT

Primary nursing is a mode of nursing care delivery. Its purpose is both to maximize the benefits of care to patients and to assure maximum utilization and development of nursing staff.

For many patients primary nursing is the way nursing "used to be" or "ought to be." Patients remember when they had the same nurse taking care of them and that those nurses "cared" for them.

Indirect outcomes of the clinical ladders concept include improved personal and professional satisfaction; increased motivation; decreased staff turnover; and increased positive attitudes toward self, role, and organization.

Although the theme of primary nursing is not new, it was put aside as the delivery of nursing care evolved over the years into a team modality requiring that the total care of any one patient be shared by several nurses during a single shift. What may have been the best utilization of staff during those years has resulted in highly fragmented patient care and deterioration of the professional nurse's personal and job satisfaction.

Patient satisfaction is expected to be the major outcome from the primary nursing approach. With an increase in both direct nurse-patient contact and nursing acceptance of responsibility and accountability for the direct nursing care given, fewer errors, less fragmentation and more multidisciplinary communication should follow. As an indirect result, work satisfaction for the staff should increase and nursing recruitment results subsequently improve.

THE INTERFACE OF TWO CONCEPTS

Primary nursing interfaces easily with the clinical ladders concept in several other ways than having the same expected outcomes. First, when these two approaches are jointly implemented in the acute care setting, the goal of care is not only individualized nursing care but patient-centered care, which includes consideration of physical, mental, spiritual, psychosocial and cultural/environmental concerns for patient well-being. This care involves patient and primary nurse input along with the contributions of various other levels of nursing and the significant others in the patient's "world."

Second, the capabilities of the nurse, the needs of the patient and family, and the actual work to be done are considered in accepting and assigning responsibility and accountability for nursing care of patients; with "total" responsibility for quality nursing care of designated patients, the primary nurse becomes an autonomous nursing practitioner with the right to make joint decisions with the patient regarding nursing care.

Third, continuity of care is provided by assigning one patient to one nurse so that the coordination of patient care is the best possible; in other words, the primary nurse communicates patient status with other health care professionals for collaboration.

Fourth, clinical nurses are responsible and accountable for initiating the nursing process (assessing needs, planning, implementing and evaluating the nursing care of patients) and following standards set for patient categories by need; they therefore ensure the delivery of comprehensive, quality nursing care. Quality nursing care is defined as nursing care based upon sound biological, physical and psychosocial principles, which is adaptable to the needs of the individual, family and community during health and illness, and which is free from the unnecessary burden of nonnursing functions that are the responsibility of unit management.

Fifth, meeting the nursing health needs of patients requires highly skilled and knowledgeable nurses willing to be accountable for their actions, care and judgments; continuous staff development, through inservice activities or other means, will prepare the clinical nurse not only for patient care at present but also for the increased demands of the future and the promotion and maintenance of health in the community.

Primary nursing is an expression of a patient-centered philosophy of care; the patient and the nurse are envisioned in the center with all systems extending out from them as quality nursing care is pursued. The primary nurse becomes the "patient-advocate" who utilizes "principles of rehabilitation and patient teaching extensively to assist the patient in achieving goals that he participates in making."[2]

Primary nursing not only interfaces with but is essential to the successful implementation of the clinical ladders concept. In combination, the two concepts make it advantageous to and satisfying for the key people—clinical staff nurses—to want to stay with nursing, constantly improve the quality of their nursing care, increasingly involve themselves with patients and significant others, work cooperatively with various levels within nursing and with other disciplines to ensure quality patient care, and to experience personal and professional growth and movement within the employing organization.

The wedding of these two produces criteria that can both define professional nursing and justify the need for and effectiveness of one's nursing actions, based upon the nursing process. In other words, the various clinical levels denote behaviorally specified differences based upon the nursing process.

IMPLEMENTATION OF TWO CONCEPTS

To implement a philosophy that weds the concepts of clinical ladders and primary nursing, specific questions must be addressed by the individual facility considering adoption of the two. The questions are centered around the identified need for such a "marriage," the definition, the "interface" and the potentials for conflict.

Does a need exist within the nursing department of the institution for the development of *both* primary nursing and clinical ladders? If yes, why? If no, why not? What factors make it "ripe" or "unrealistic" for development and implementation of such approaches at this point in time?

What are clinical ladders and what is primary nursing? What restrictions (if any) are needed to define clinical ladders and primary nursing for the specific institution? What is feasible (and not feasible) within the system? One must consider budget, staffing needs, staffing availability, and staffing possibilities among others.

How do the concepts of clinical ladders and primary nursing "fit" with the concepts of peer review, nursing process, competence, performance, and management and head nurse positions? Do clinical ladders clearly interface with primary nursing? Or are the two in any way in opposition or in conflict (either philosophically or as they are being developed by the specific facility)? Is there overlap evident? Where? Why? And is such overlap needed? Wanted? Confusing?

Once these questions are satisfactorily addressed and answered by the nursing department, the wedding of the concepts of primary nursing with clinical ladders can be implemented. By identifying the need, defining the specifics of the concepts, noting the constraints inherent to the system that will affect the implementation of primary nursing and clinical ladders, anticipating the possible areas of conflict and dealing with organizational fit prior to implementing clinical ladders and primary nursing, the institution takes the initial first step toward successfully wedding the two.

REFERENCES

1. Smith C. "Primary Nursing Care." *Nursing Administration Quarterly* 1:2 (Winter 1977) p. 3.

2. Ibid. p. 5-6.

A model for evaluating primary nursing

Roger W. Evans, Ph.D.
Research Scientist
Health and Population Study Center
Battelle Human Affairs Research Centers
Seattle, Washington

**Barbara J. Brown, R.N., Ed.D.,
   F.A.A.N.**
Assistant Administrator
Nursing Services
Virginia Mason Hospital
Seattle, Washington

ALTHOUGH primary nursing is increasingly being presented as a viable alternative to team nursing, few attempts have been made to develop models for evaluating this type of nursing care.[1,2] This is indeed a shortcoming since thorough evaluations require models from which study hypotheses can be formulated and study results interpreted. Such models can be either descriptive or explanatory, and their utility depends on the extent to which they accurately represent the phenomenon they allegedly depict.

Traditionally, the role of models in science is best described as tenuous.[3,4] For example, Duhem argues that models serve only a psychological function and are mental crutches for feeble minds.[5] On the other hand, Hesse argues that a model provides "the context of natural expectations in terms of which a theory can be tested."[6]

Regardless of one's philosophical position, models do serve a useful function: forcing researchers to state testable hypotheses. They are a cornerstone in the conduct of science. Most models represent a movement from induction to deduction with further reformulation based on induction.[7] Often, this iterative process is ignored and models are presented as deductive facts rather than collective statements of hypothesized interrelationships to be subjected to empirical tests, and then reformulated.

As noted by Starfield, research in health services often takes on the character of policy research when it is performed in response to stated or perceived needs for information to guide sociomedical action.[8] This is

Nurs Admin Q, 1981, 9(3), 93–100
©1981 Aspen Publishers, Inc.

particularly true of many studies of primary nursing wherein attempts are made to evaluate a new method of delivering nursing services. Thus it is not surprising that concepts often used to evaluate health services can serve as the framework for a model to be used in collecting and analyzing data required to assess primary nursing.

The concepts most appropriate to this task were originally introduced by Donabedian.[9] They are structure, process and outcome. They provide the basis for the model in Figure 1, which identifies and categorizes the main components of health services and illustrates the importance of nursing services within the context of the system. The model is a variation of a model of health services delivery presented by Starfield. Moreover, the same concepts that serve as the basis for this model have recently been used in a comprehensive study by Wandelt and associates of conditions associated with RN employment in Texas.[10]

THE MODEL

Outcomes in nursing care and medical practice have attracted considerable attention.[11-17] Outcomes in this context refer to more than simply the result of nursing care provided to patients. They have been expanded to include the assessment of outcomes of primary nursing by others (for example, patients, physicians, administrators and the patient's family or significant others). As conceptualized here, outcomes (whether they be nursing outcomes, patient outcomes or assessments of primary nursing made by others) are dependent on structure and process variables. Unfortunately, researchers studying primary nursing have failed to recognize these interrelationships.[18,19]

The model in Figure 1 makes the interrelationships among structure, process and outcome explicit. A comprehensive evaluation of nursing outcomes must include each of these components. Failure to do so will tend to overemphasize the impact of various aspects of the nursing care process.

Structure of nursing care

Structure delineates the context within which nursing care is administered, and includes the instrumentalities that produce it.[20,21] Representative elements include a variety of job-related elements, including personnel (e.g., number, type, training); physical facilities (e.g., number, type, accreditation, standards); administrative policies, staffing patterns, equipment, organization (e.g., coordination, accessibility, appropriateness); information systems and records; other logistic elements needed to perform the task of patient care; and financing (e.g., payment by patients, reimbursement of providers). As noted by Starfield, all structural elements involve both capital and operating expenses, as well as what it costs the patient for the use of the nursing care system. Other structural factors that affect the cost of providing care are the volume of patients seen in a health care facility and the average amount of time that nurses spend with patients for whom they are responsible.

In the model two separate structures are recognized, although in reality they could be combined: (1) the hospital structure and (2) the nursing service structure. The following

---

As conceptualized here, outcomes are dependent on structure and process variables. Unfortunately, researchers studying primary nursing have failed to recognize these interrelationships.

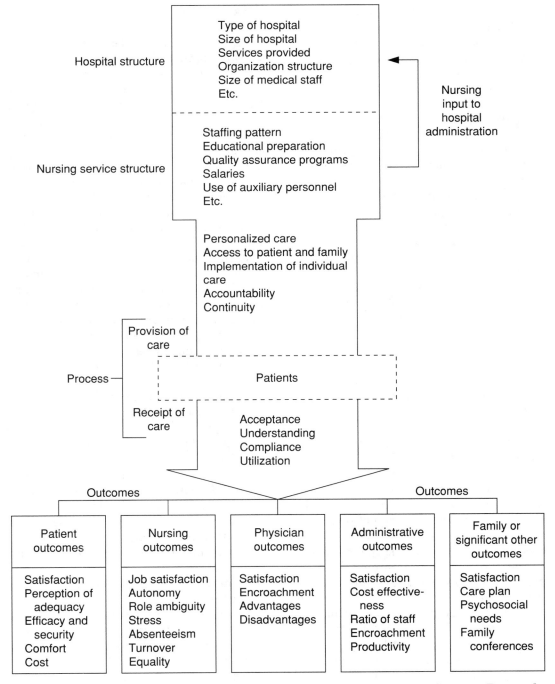

Figure 1. A model of nursing care. Adapted from Starfield, B. "Health Services Research: A Working Model." *New England Journal of Medicine* 289:3 (1973).

variables are considered to be indicators of the hospital structure:

- type of hospital;
- size of hospital;
- organizational structure;
- services provided;
- size and composition of medical staff;
- accreditation standards;
- total number of personnel;
- interdepartmental relationships;
- nurse relationships with structure;
- nurse/physician committees;
- educational programs;
- rate of occupancy;
- average length of stay;
- number of outpatient visits

Nursing service structure variables include:

- organizational structure (i.e., centralized, hierarchical versus decentralized);
- staffing pattern;
- educational preparation of personnel;
- quality assurance programs;
- budget (planning and coordination);
- educational programs;
- salaries;
- use of auxiliary personnel.

Frequently, structural indicators are used to establish standards of care. A problem arises, however, when there is little objective support for their validity, as is often the case. Starfield has argued, for example, that with regard to the provision of health services provider-patient ratios, continuity and record keeping are necessary for adequate medical care. Similarly, in nursing, assertions are often made that a nurse-patient ratio of 1 to 5 is required for "good" nursing care, that continuity is necessary for "optimal" nursing care and that "sound" record keeping is essential to excellence in nursing care. More properly, in making evaluations, these structural indicators should be considered in relation with the process and outcome components.

Process of nursing care

Process of nursing is less commonly used to evaluate the efficacy of nursing practice. Process elements or variables, as noted by Wandelt and associates, "are those that define the role of the nurse as a professional and include autonomy, accountability, inclusion in policy and decision-making, opportunity to practice professional nursing care, recognition and respect as a professional person, responsibility for nursing practice, authority provided by administrators to carry out nursing, and other conditions needed to allow nurses to practice their profession."[22]

In the model, nursing process measures include organizational features of primary nursing—the manner in which primary nurses care for their patients. The following are examples of primary nursing process measures and have been described at length by Marram and her associates[23]:

- nurse's opportunity to deliver personalized care;
- nurse's accessibility to the patient and family (through nursing history taking);
- nurse's implementation of individualized care;
- patient participation in planning and implementing the nursing care plan (evolves from nursing history taking);
- nurse's accountability for patient care (documentation system, 24-hour charting, progress note recording by primary nurse);
- nurse's continuity and coordination of care;
- nurse's discharge summary.

Although it is often questionable at precisely what point effective care has been delivered, theoretically, it can be argued that when the manner in which nurses care for their patients and patient behavior (e.g., acceptance, understanding, compliance)

converge to deal appropriately with episodes of acute need, effective care has resulted.

Outcome of nursing care

The outcome of nursing care is, of course,
the ultimate test of its effectiveness. Patient
outcomes are indicators of nursing care outcomes, and patient satisfaction attests to the
efficacy of the nursing care received. The
figure makes this relationship explicit. Many
studies of outcome have primarily focused
on how the structure and process of care
influence outcomes.[24,25] Several of these studies share the common assumption that adequate resources and technology (structure)
contribute to adequate nursing care process,
which in turn results in favorable patient
outcomes. The model takes into account the
complex interrelationships of all three.

The patient outcomes, or obversely, the
nursing care outcomes, with which the
model is most concerned include: patient
satisfaction with nursing care, patient perception of adequacy of nursing care, patient
sense of efficacy and security, patient perception of the primary nurse role and patient comfort.

As indicated above, the model used to
explain patient outcomes is also used to
explain how other medical personnel and
the patient's family (or significant others)
assess the outcomes of primary nursing. The
outcomes, however, may vary according to
who is making the assessment. For example, a hospital administrator, nursing
supervisor, physician and primary nurse
are all concerned with different aspects of
primary nursing. In making assessments,
the nurse may be most concerned with job
satisfaction; the physicians, with the threat
of encroachment; the administrator, with
cost effectiveness; the nursing supervisor,
with equality among nursing staff; and the
family, with the management of the patient.

Much like the model of patient outcomes, all
these outcomes are also influenced by the
nursing and hospital structure as well as the
nursing care process.

For example, the nursing care process
(e.g., accountability, ability to deliver personalized care) can have a significant impact on primary nurse satisfaction. Similarly, the organizational structure of the
hospital may affect the nursing care process
which may affect, for example, the physician's
satisfaction with primary nursing.

Outcomes appropriate to the needs of
nurses, administrators, physicians and patients' families can also be measured during
any data collection effort. *Nursing* outcomes
include:

- job satisfaction;
- autonomy in delivery of care;
- role ambiguity;
- stress level;
- motivation to work;
- perceived equality among nursing
  staff;
- professional orientation among nursing staff;
- absenteeism;
- turnover;
- clinical ladder;
- peer review;
- shared management with staff;
- decentralized decision making.

Outcomes most pertinent to *physicians*
include:

- satisfaction with nursing care (generally);
- concern with perceived encroachment;
- satisfaction with various aspects of
  patient care;
- advantages of primary nursing;
- disadvantages of primary nursing.

Outcomes most relevant to *administrators* include:

- cost effectiveness;
- concerns about assignment and organization of staff;

- level of threat (encroachment) of primary nurses, as indicated by physicians;
- productivity;
- relationships with other departments (e.g., dietary, pharmacy, social services).

Finally, there are several outcomes with which the *patient's family* (or significant others) is most concerned:

- satisfaction with the management of the patient;
- length of stay;
- understanding of the care plan for the patient at discharge;
- nurse support for the psychosocial needs of the family;
- evaluation of how well the patient understands his/her illness;
- satisfaction with family conferences.

Again, it should be emphasized that all the outcomes identified here are intricately related to the nursing care structure and nursing care process. Little is learned about the delivery of nursing care if attention is limited to the end results. The end results are, in effect, determined by structure and process measures. Omitting the most important independent variables in the study of primary nursing can hardly qualify as an adequate research design.

LIMITATIONS OF THE MODEL

All models are abstractions, and the model presented here contains a very large number of variables. However, no model is completely able to explain all of the variance in the event or phenomenon under study. Furthermore, in other published studies, many of the variables in the model (e.g., accountability, job satisfaction, stress, nursing care outcomes) are measured by a vari-

> *The amount of data required to complete a comprehensive evaluation multiplies rapidly, depending on the number of complex constructs that are measured. Nevertheless, this should not deter interest in the evaluation of primary nursing.*

ety of scales and indices.[26-33] Consequently, the amount of data required to complete a comprehensive evaluation multiplies rapidly, depending on the number of complex constructs that are measured. Nevertheless, this should not deter interest in the evaluation of primary nursing. In light of budget limitations and time constraints, as well as the difficulty of measuring some variables as discrete constructs (e.g., organizational relationships), it is possible to test less complex versions of the model.

In operationalizing those variables included in any variant of the model, however, it is recommended that standard measures, where they exist, be used. Among the standard measures, those with demonstrated reliability and validity in other similar studies should be given priority for inclusion. In other instances, it may be necessary to develop new measures or to derive single item indicators (e.g., equality among staff) which meet the objectives of the study. Although there are often many constraints placed on the magnitude of the data-collection effort, every attempt should be made to include multiple indicators of those constructs that are most ambiguous or defy simple operationalization (e.g., accountability, patient satisfaction, nurse satisfaction, and stress level).

REFERENCES

1. Marram, G. et al. *Cost-Effectiveness of Primary and Team Nursing* (Wakefield, Mass.: Contemporary Publishing 1976).
2. Marram, G., Barnett, M. and Bevis, E. *Primary Nursing: A Model for Individualized Care* (St. Louis, Mo.: C.V. Mosby 1979).
3. Shapere, D. *Philosophical Problems of Natural Science* (Chicago: University of Chicago Press 1965).
4. Kuhn, T. *The Structure of Scientific Revolutions* (Chicago: University of Chicago Press 1963).
5. Duhem, P. *The Aim and Structure of Physical Theory,* trans. P. Wiener (Princeton, N.J.: Princeton University Press 1954).
6. Hesse, M. *Forces and Fields: The Concepts of Actions at a Distance in History* (Edinburgh and London: Thomas Nelson and Sons, Ltd. 1961) p. 21.
7. Zellner, A. "Statistical Analysis of Econometric Models" *Journal of the American Statistical Association* 74:367 (1979) p. 628-643.
8. Starfield, B. "Health Services Research: A Working Model." *New England Journal of Medicine* 289:3 (1973) p. 132-136.
9. Donabedian, A. "Evaluating the Quality of Medical Care." *Milbank Memorial Fund Quarterly* 44 (suppl) (July 1966) p. 166-206.
10. Wandelt, M. et al. *Conditions Associated with Registered Nurse Employment in Texas* (Austin, Tex.: Center for Research, School of Nursing, University of Texas 1980).
11. Marram et al. *Cost Effectiveness of Primary and Team Nursing.*
12. Marram, Barnett and Bevis. *Primary Nursing: A Model for Individualized Care.*
13. Starfield. "Health Services Research: A Working Model."
14. Brown, B.J. (ed.) "Primary Nursing." *Nursing Administration Quarterly* 1:2 (1977) p. 1-119.
15. Ciske, K. "Primary Nursing: Evaluation." *American Journal of Nursing* 74:8 (1974) p. 1436-1438.
16. Starfield, B. "Measurement of Outcome: A Proposed Scheme." *Milbank Memorial Fund Quarterly* 52:1 (1974) p. 39-50.
17. Brook, R. et al. *Quality of Medical Care Assessment Using Outcome Measures: An Overview of Method.* Pub. No. R-2021/1-HEW (Santa Monica, Calif.: Rand Corporation 1976).
18. Marram et al. *Cost-Effectiveness of Primary and Team Nursing.*
19. Marram, Barnett and Bevis, *Primary Nursing: A Model for Individualized Care.*
20. Starfield. "Health Services Research: A Working Model."
21. Wandelt et al. *Conditions Associated with Registered Nurse Employment in Texas.*
22. Ibid. p. 4.
23. Marram, Barnett and Bevis, *Primary Nursing: A Model for Individualized Care.*
24. Brook, R. *Quality of Care Assessment: A Comparison of Five Methods of Peer Review.* Publication No. (HRA) 74-3100 (Hyattsville, Md.: Health Resources Administration 1973).
25. DeGeyndt, W. and Ross, K. *Evaluation of Health Programs: An Annotated Bibliography.* (New York: Health and Planning Council of Southern New York 1969).
26. Marram, Barnett and Bevis. *Primary Nursing: A Model for Individualized Care.*
27. Brown. "Primary Nursing."
28. Daeffler, R. "Patient's Perception of Care under Team and Primary Nursing." *Journal of Nursing Administration* 5:1 (1975) p. 23.
29. Manthey, M. "Primary Nursing Is Alive and Well in the Hospital." *American Journal of Nursing* 73:1 (1973) p. 83-87.
30. Baider, L. and Sarell, M. "Evaluation of the Role of Primary Nurse in an Oncology Department." *Mental Health and Society* 2:1 9 (1974) p. 110-117.
31. Ciske, K. "Accountability: The Essence of Primary Nursing." *American Journal of Nursing* 79:5 (1979) p. 891-894.
32. Nehls, D. et al. "Planned Change: A Quest for Nursing Autonomy." *Journal of Nursing Administration* 4:1 (1974) p. 23-27.
33. Felton, G. "Increasing the Quality of Nursing Care by Introducing the Concept of Primary Nursing: A Model Project." *Nursing Research* 24:1 (1975) p. 27-32.

Primary nursing revisited

Barbara J. Brown, R.N., Ed.D.,
F.A.A.N., C.N.A.A.
Editor, Nursing Administration Quarterly

"Primary Nursing Revisited" reveals a significant change in the organization of nursing care delivery systems since "Primary Nursing" (*Nursing Administration Quarterly* 1:2, Winter 1977). In the earlier issue readers were cautioned that primary nursing could be "here today and gone tomorrow"—just as team nursing had become a fad, had been tried out in a multiplicity of ways and had never been fully implemented in a way its designers intended. Similarly, although primary nursing was organized to maximize registered nurse professional accountability in hospital-based nursing practice, it has taken on many shapes and forms since 1976. The study of those shapes and forms has brought *NAQ* full circle, to reexamine primary nursing today. It is an editorial privilege to register excitement about this delivery system which espouses the ideals of nursing practice in all corners of the country and indeed has affected nursing care delivery in other countries.

What makes primary nursing so exciting, from the point of view of the nursing service administrator as well as that of the staff nurse? We often speak of creating an environment conducive to the professional practice of nursing—creation of this environment is at least begun by the primary nursing organizational patterns, which represent individual and unique nursing administrative directions.

The single most unique characteristic of primary nursing is primary nurse accountability. Where possible the nurse assigned to the particular patient and family assumes professional accountability for that case, as does the primary physician, throughout the length of hospital stay. No physician practices without partners or associates. In the primary nurse partnership, an associate nurse takes care of the patient when the primary nurse is not available.

Communications about the patient are made by the nurse who is the direct care giver to the next care giver. This allows a face-to-face continuity of patient care re-

Nurs Admin Q, 1981, 5(3), viii–x
©1981 Aspen Publishers, Inc.

porting not previously possible in the team method of assignment. The primary nurse becomes the one to make the nursing decisions and carry out the communications of other members of the health care team. This provides a new sense of autonomy to the direct care giver and creates a decentralization of authority.

Management positions change, and nurses begin to be rewarded for competence through shared management positions in peer review, consultation, teaching, practice, research and other administrative aspects. Regardless of the system of primary nursing, there are certain constants. In the true primary nursing setting each nurse who is called a primary nurse has 24-hour accountability. This requires that the nurse assume assignment for the patient and family, in the case system nurses learn as students.

The primary nursing system requires direct communications between the primary nurse and the associate nurse, the physicians and other members of the hospital team. This significant aspect of communication becomes more visible when a primary nursing message board is used, because the fact that the primary nurse is accountable along with the physician is there for other care givers to visualize. In a teaching hospital the name of the lead resident or intern may also be affixed to the communication board, in clear recognition of the status of primary resident physicians assigned to that patient.

In broadening the base of communications for improvement in patient care, the partnership relationship between physician and nurse is also shown in more conspicuous ways. It is not uncommon, for instance, to see a physician approach a primary nursing unit and quickly see which nurse is responsible for a particular patient and then seek that nurse out.

While decentralized decision making and accountability, patient care advocacy, and enhanced communication between professionals are positive results of primary nursing, there are many unanswered questions relating to cost and quality of care that require continuing study and research. Some of the factors that must be looked at are related to the nursing service department itself.

What philosophy and what goals and objectives give direction to primary nursing? Does the organizational structure change? It has been my experience that primary nursing flourishes within a decentralized organizational structure that includes a high level of clinical accountability, focusing on clinical competency and standards of patient care. The staffing pattern is also different, and there is a significant increase in the number of registered nurses in comparison with team nursing.

In most settings the staffing pattern changes from one of 35 to 45 percent registered nurses to approximately 65 to 70 percent registered nurses, and in some instances 90 to 100 percent registered nurses. The educational preparation of personnel can significantly enhance the growth of the professional environment, in that the more rapidly the professional environment changes, the more rapidly the better prepared nurse is led toward professional achievement.

Significant budgetary effects are confronted in planning and developing primary nursing. A common fallacy is that because the salary level of the registered nurse is higher than that of the nonregistered nurse, the same quality of care by the primary system is proportionately more expensive. However, factors such as staff retention, job satisfaction and recruitment should be analyzed along with salaries. In most instances in which such an analysis has taken place, primary nursing has proved to be more cost effective in the long range.

For ultimate success, primary nursing requires substantive quality assurance and peer-review programs. Evaluating standards of practice in relation to both patient care and the competency level of the nurse is the only way in which a qualitative analysis can be made of the differences between primary nursing and other organizational modalities.

It has also been found that most nurses are not quite ready for the degree of professional accountability that primary nursing requires. Substantial changes and improvements in educational programs are necessary.

In most settings a staff nurse needs to learn basic history and physical assessment in order to develop a comprehensive patient care plan. In addition, specific areas of clinical competency such as oncology nursing or cardiovascular nursing or maternal-child nursing need to be strengthened by increased continuing education. Nurses cannot use knowledge they do not have. Increased knowledge leads to increased authority and respect in collegial relationships, based on knowledge rather than on position and assertion of person.

Staffing policies should be reviewed so that there is a sense of 24-hour commitment, with some fair-shared responsibilities by all nurses for 24-hour, 7-day-a-week hospital-based nursing practice. Primary nursing will have a difficult time flourishing in a system that rewards people for "hanging in" and promotes them to "days only," using evenings and nights as a punitive system of "putting in time" at entry level until the reward, "allowed to be on days," is earned. Under such a system, the least experienced and least qualified nurses will often be left alone evenings and nights. This practice certainly does not create an environment conducive to the professional practice of nursing.

Concerns about collective bargaining and staffing and scheduling should be addressed when implementing primary nursing. It would be poor management for a nursing administrator to move fool-hardily into an all-registered nurse staff in a community that has had a history of strike. Primary nursing leaders must look at such professional accountability collectively and be able to assure the organization that nurses will truly be professional and not "walk off the job."

Because of the depth and breadth of the changes made in introducing primary nursing, in operationalizing it and in exploring the roles of the primary nurse, leadership positions and changes in organizational structures, *NAQ* is dedicating issues 5:3 and 5:4 to "Primary Nursing Revisited."

We are most fortunate in being able to present to our readers an outstanding two-part "On-the-Scene" from Beth Israel Hospital in Boston. It is hoped that these two issues, as well as past issues, will help nursing services look at the future and develop significant changes in environment through primary nursing. This would allow each nurse to practice with a high level of accountability and to be responsible for improvements in patient care. This would increase the level of satisfaction for every nurse practicing in hospital-based nursing.

Part V
Study and discussion questions

1. What characteristics of the Primary Nursing model have been translated into present practice?
2. Given the many changes in health care from the late 70s to the early 90s what contribution has the development of contemporary nursing delivery systems made to the continuous quality improvement model (TQI)?
3. What impact has primary nursing made on role development and expanded practice?
4. What obligations of a professional practice environment are imposed by (a) a Primary Nursing model, and (b) a Clinical Advancement model?
5. Discuss the component of accountability in professional nursing as it relates to contemporary nursing care delivery systems.
6. What impact has developing models of delivery systems for nursing had on (a) collaboration with physicians, (b) with other disciplines, and/or (c) curricula in nursing education.
7. Given nursing's history in developing systems for care, what projections would you forecast for nursing's role in the changing health care climate?

Index